The Problem of Difference
Phenomenology and Poststructuralism

D1155510

Beginning with Plato and Aristotle, philosophers throughout history have built their theories around the problem of reconciling a fundamental distinction, as for example, Plato's distinction between knowledge (reality) and opinion (appearance), Descartes's mind/body distinction, and Kant's *a priori/a posterior* distinction. This 'problem of difference' is a classic theme in philosophy, and one that has taken especially intriguing turns in recent decades. Jeffrey A. Bell here presents a finely constructed survey of the contemporary Continental philosophers, focusing on how they have dealt with the problem of difference.

Bell's work centres around three key figures – Husserl, Merleau-Ponty, and Deleuze. He also considers the positions of such thinkers as Foucault, Derrida, and Rorty, who have called for an end to the traditional response to the problem of difference – an end to the search for any ultimate foundations on which our varied experiences of the world might be based – and thus, in effect, an end to traditional philosophy.

In clarifying the relationship between phenomenology and poststructuralism, Bell analyses the role of paradox in both traditions, in particular the role it plays in accounting for difference. Not only philosophers but also teachers and students in the area of comparative literary theory will benefit from this book.

JEFFREY A. BELL is Assistant Professor of Philosophy at Southeastern Louisiana University.

The Problem of Difference

Phenomenology and Poststructuralism

Jeffrey A. Bell

UNIVERSITY OF TORONTO PRESS
Toronto   Buffalo   London

ISBN 0-8020-4253-8 (cloth)
ISBN 0-8020-8095-2 (paper)

Printed on acid-free paper

Toronto Studies in Philosophy
Editors: James R. Brown and Calvin Normore

Canadian Cataloguing in Publication Data

Bell, Jeffrey A.
The problem of difference : phenomenology and poststructuralism

(Toronto studies in philosophy)
Includes bibliographical references and index.
ISBN 0-8020-4253-8 (bound)   ISBN 0-8020-8095-2 (pbk.)

1. Difference (Philosophy) – History – 20th century.   I. Title.   II.Series.

B809.9.B44 1998   110   C97-932000-3

University of Toronto Press acknowledges the financial assistance to its
publishing program of the Canada Council for the Arts and the Ontario Arts
Council.

The author and publisher are grateful to Southeastern Louisiana University,
and in particular Roman Heleniak and the Department of History and
Government, for financial support in publishing this book.

For Elizabeth, with love

Contents

Acknowledgments

This book would not have become a reality without the help of so many. I would like to thank John Glenn, Jr, and Michael Zimmerman of Tulane University for their support in this and many other of my projects. Their feedback has been invaluable. The comments of the anonymous readers for the University of Toronto Press were also of great assistance in cleaning up some of the repetition and ambiguity in this text. Ron Schoeffel, Editor-in-Chief, in particular, was especially helpful and supportive throughout the process of this book's publication. I would also like to thank the copy-editor, Beverley Beetham Endersby, for her efforts. And I would be remiss if I did not acknowledge Professor William Neblett of Occidental College for introducing me to the work of Husserl.

Finally, I owe a special thanks to my wife, Elizabeth. Without her support, and, at times, patience, this book would not have been completed as quickly as it was.

Problem of Difference

Phenomenology and Poststructuralism

Introduction:
The Problem of Difference

In the history of philosophy, one finds many examples of a fundamental distinction forming the cornerstone of a philosophical theory. There is Plato's distinction between knowledge (reality) and opinion (appearance); Aristotle's form/matter distinction; Descartes's mind/body distinction; and Kant's *a priori*/*a posteriori* distinction. But the challenge of these theories, the problem that calls for the creativity and intellectual inventiveness of these thinkers, is to show how the two sides of the distinction are nevertheless related to and dependent upon each other. This is what I call the 'problem of difference,' and it is this problem which accounts for the most interesting and important aspects of the above-mentioned theories. It is the basis for Plato's theory of *mimesis*; Aristotle's theory of *ousia*; Descartes's argument for the existence of God as well as his more problematic notion of the pineal gland; and Kant's theory of the schematism. In all these cases, the theory attempts to account for the relationship between the two sides of a fundamental difference: opinion (appearance) is related to knowledge (reality) through resemblance (i.e., *mimesis*); form and matter are two aspects of *ousia*; God is the creative force behind mind and the validation for the transcendence of objects, that is, the body; and the schematism is that which relates the *a priori* categories of understanding to the *a posteriori* experiences of sensibility. In other words, each of these is a way of responding to the problem of difference.

A variation of this problem, known as the 'problem of transcendence,' aptly describes the central concern of phenomenology: that is, how the immanence of subjectivity and consciousness, an immanence that is fundamentally different from the transcendence of ideal truths, is nevertheless related to this transcendence. The phenomenological theory of 'intentionality' is a response to precisely this problem: all consciousness is intentional, meaning it is always a consciousness of something, always an immanent consciousness that is transcending itself towards something. The two sides of a fundamental distinction, immanence and transcendence, are thus related on the basis of the 'intentionality' of consciousness. Phenomenology is therefore solidly within the tradition of formulating theories in light of the problem of difference.

In the last few decades, however, this tradition has come under increasing criticism. In both the United States and Europe, a growing number of philosophers, following the lead of Heidegger,[1] have called for a 'critique of metaphysics.' One of the premises of this critique is that the tradition of philosophy has come to an end, and, with it, perforce must end the traditional way of responding to the problem of difference. Foucault, for example, claims that an 'essential task' of his 'was to free the history of thought from its subjection to transcendence,' and the attempt to reveal 'the lost origin ... the transcendental moment.'[2] That is, his essential task was to free the history of thought from its traditional response to the problem of difference – in other words, revealing that 'lost origin' which accounts for the relationship between two sides of a fundamental difference. Foucault therefore criticizes the attempt to deduce the 'transcendental moment' which accounts for the relationship between subject and object, and claims that, despite Husserl's effort to find this moment in mathematical idealities (i.e., ideal objects as that which accounts for the relationship between the immanence of consciousness and the transcendence of objects), and Merleau-Ponty's attempt to find it in the perceived world (i.e., the always-already-given world as that which accounts for the relationship between subjects and objects), this moment has never been found.[3] Foucault's most famous contemporary, Jacques Derrida, offers a similar criticism. In setting forth his understanding of the notion différance, he claims that différance 'must be conceived without nostalgia; that is, it must be conceived outside the myth of the purely maternal or paternal language belonging to the lost fatherland of thought.'[4] In other words, he is critical of the philosophical effort to reveal the 'lost origin,' the 'lost fatherland of thought,' and his 'deconstruction' will subvert this traditional response to the problem of difference. This deconstruction will not reveal a 'transcendental moment' that will account for the relationship between the two sides of a fundamental difference, but will show that this moment itself entails a fundamental difference which forever defers any attempt to reveal a lost identifiable origin. To describe this difference that defers, that is always different, Derrida uses the word *différance*.[5] And, finally, Rorty represents a movement in the United States which has been inspired by the work of Derrida. In particular, Rorty calls for the end of the traditional effort of philosophy to discover the ultimate foundations and Truths upon which our varied and different experiences of the world are based. What he calls for instead is a never-ending conversation, a conversation that discovers ever new and different ways of describing things. This conversation will not reveal a lost identifiable origin that accounts for difference, but, rather, will entail a proliferation of difference itself, a proliferation that will not allow for such an identification. In short, Rorty, as do Derrida and Foucault, calls for the end of the traditional response to the problem of difference.

There is a distinction to be made, however, between this traditional response and the problem itself. The critique of the traditional response to the problem of difference need not, nor does it, invalidate the problem. The problem of difference is to be understood as that which motivates traditional philosophical theories, theories which answer the call of this problem but are not to be confused with it. Criticism of the traditional response to the problem of difference, therefore, need not entail a call for the end of philosophy, especially if philosophy is understood to be the endless reckoning of this problem. This is precisely how we understand and intend to interpret philosophy; consequently, Foucault's, Derrida's, and Rorty's critiques of metaphysics are not to be seen as a complete break with the tradition of philosophy. They are to be interpreted, rather, as the emergence of the problem of difference as an explicit theme, one that had already been implicitly at work throughout the history of philosophy. Put another way, the critique of metaphysics is to be seen only as a break with the traditional *response* to the problem of difference; and what this break consists of is their claim that, whereas the traditional response had attempted to *identify* the lost origin, the primal source, or that transcendental moment which accounts for difference, difference cannot be reduced to, or be accounted for in terms of, identity. The problem of difference cannot be resolved by revealing a fundamental identity; subsequently, Foucault's and Derrida's response is to show how it is a fundamental difference that is the condition which accounts for identity, or motivates the responses to the problem of difference, and how it is not a fundamental identity which is the 'fatherland' and condition for all difference. In short, the problem of difference is explicitly recognized as the problem with no *identifiable* solution.

Where does this leave us? For some, such as Habermas, this leaves us with philosophical anarchy,[6] with an 'anything goes' relativism and irrationalism. In addition, Habermas claims that this anarchy is a consequence of a critique which, despite its avowed break with metaphysics, is nevertheless fully entrenched within it. The critique of metaphysics is therefore susceptible to the same critique which Heidegger made of Nietzsche, and, in fact, Habermas cites Derrida's recognition of this criticism and claims it is equally valid when applied to both Derrida's and Foucault's work: 'The Nietzschean demolition remains dogmatic and, like all reversals, a captive of that metaphysical edifice which it professes to overthrow.'[7] For example, Habermas argues that Foucault's critique of and break with metaphysics are accomplished because 'the synthetic power of transcendental consciousness' is replaced and 'degraded into the subjectless will of a power.'[8] However, this subjectless will of a power, irrespective of its apparent break with the philosophy and metaphysics of the subject (i.e., modern philosophy), continues to presuppose and employ concepts and premises from this tradition. In particular, Habermas claims that Foucault understands modernity, the modernity he hopes to go beyond, to be 'characterized by the self-contradictory and anthropocentric form of knowledge proper to a structurally overloaded subject (a finite subject transcending itself into the infinite) ... that stretches from Kant to Fichte to Husserl and Heidegger.'[9] The critique of modernity, or the critique of metaphysics, is thus an attempt to free the history of thought from its 'subjection to transcendence,' and from its subjection to a transcendence that entails, as Habermas reads Foucault, a 'self-contradictory' ground, a paradoxical 'lost origin' – that is, the subject. Kant's subject, for example, is both transcendental and empirical; Marx's subject of history is both creative and alienated from this creativity; and Husserl's absolute consciousness is self-positing, or simultaneously positing and posited. And Kant's transcendental deduction, Marx's proletarian revolution, and Husserl's phenomenological reduction are ways of restoring this lost origin, of awakening the subject from its 'dogmatic slumber.' However, Habermas believes that Foucault himself understands power to be just this type of 'self-contradictory' ground. The subjectless will of a power is that which constitutes and makes possible the various independent discourses and discursive practices. Power is that which makes various 'regimes of truth' possible. On the other hand, this power is not to be abstracted from its historical manifestations. Power is a historical and empirical phenomenon. In short, power, as Habermas interprets Foucault, is that which brings 'synthetic performances *a priori* back into the realm of historical events.'[10] Power thus has what Habermas calls an 'irritating double role': it is both empirical and transcendental. But this is precisely the role the subject played in the philosophies of the subject, and thus Habermas concludes that Foucault's approach 'cannot lead to a way out of the philosophy of the subject, because the concept of power that is supposed to provide a common denominator for the contrary semantic components has been taken from the repertoire of the philosophy of the subject itself.'[11]

Habermas takes this same line of criticism with respect to Derrida. At first, Habermas cites with approval Derrida's critique of Husserl's position in *Logical Investigations*, most especially the First Investigation, 'Expression and Meaning.' In particular, he accepts Derrida's criticism of the view that meaning is ideal, that it is irreducibly different from and independent of both its empirical manifestations in speech and the subjects who think or express these meanings. A problem for Husserl, and a problem which we will look at in much detail in this work, is to account for the relationship between the subject who intends and expresses this meaning, and this meaning itself as an ideal objectivity. In short, Husserl is confronted with the problem of difference. Husserl's solution, as we will see, emerges in *The Phenomenology of Internal Time-Consciousness*, where he begins to argue for an absolute transcendental consciousness. The self-constituting nature of this consciousness – that is, simultaneously constituting and constituted – is that which makes possible the distinction and the relation between a constituting and intending consciousness (e.g., expressing) and an always-already-constituted objectivity (e.g., meaning as ideal). But it is precisely at this point that Derrida's criticism begins. Derrida claims that Husserl's notion of a self-constituting consciousness presupposes a temporal difference, a difference that forever subverts and defers the coincidence and identity of constituting and constituted, a coincidence Husserl claimed characterizes the absolute consciousness. It is this temporal difference which allows for the possibility of differentiating between the constituting and the constituted sides of an absolute consciousness, but it is also this difference which continually defers their coming into coincidence and identity.

It is on the basis of these arguments that Derrida will set forth his notion of *différance*, a difference that continually defers. It is also at this point that Habermas claims that, despite Derrida's apparent break with the philosophy of consciousness, he is nevertheless unable to 'extricate himself from the constraints of the paradigm of the philosophy of the subject.'[12] Just as the absolute self-constituting consciousness was that which was to be identified neither with the psychological states of an expressing subject, nor with the ideal objectivities expressed and intuited by these subjects, but as the condition which makes these distinctions possible, so, too, is *différance* that which is to be identified with neither the subject nor the object, the author nor the text, culture nor nature, and so on, but is the condition which makes these distinctions possible. Thus, although *différance* may be a fundamental condition that is not a subject, it is nevertheless functionally equivalent to the role played by the subject in the traditional philosophies of the subject (e.g., Husserl). It is for this reason that Habermas believes Derrida is still within 'the constraints of the paradigm of the philosophy of the subject.'

We could further elaborate these arguments, and, given time, we would, but at this point I want to respond to Habermas's criticisms by discussing two points that will be of central concern in this work. First, Habermas is correct to claim that Derrida and Foucault remain within the tradition of which they are critical. This is so, as we have asserted and will further argue in this work, because they are continuing to respond to the problem of difference. Second, Habermas is not, however, correct to say that the work of the poststructuralists is simply the negation of the modern tradition in philosophy. It was this assumption that led Habermas to accuse Derrida and Foucault of philosophical anarchy, irrationalism, and relativism – that is, as the result of negating order, rationalism, and absolute truth – and it was also the reason Habermas turned Heidegger's critique of Nietzsche against Heidegger and the critique of metaphysics itself (i.e., as a reversal and negation, it remains committed to that which is negated, much as an atheist is committed to the concept of the God he denies, etc.). But the critique of metaphysics is not to be understood in this way, because it is not a reversal at all. Derrida and Foucault continue to be responding to the problem of difference, and they are simply making explicit what had already been implicitly at work within the tradition. This is far from reversing or negating the tradition. Their response to the problem of difference, however – their making difference an explicit theme – does break with the traditional *response* to this problem. They thus refuse to account for difference on the basis of identity, but attempt to account for difference in itself – that is, without reducing it to identity, as the difference *between* already-*identified* things.

Is this response to be seen, as Habermas claims, as a reductionism that is at best equivalent to the reductionism of which Derrida and Foucault are critical? If so, then perhaps Habermas is correct to see their positions as ineffectual and atavistic – for example, he characterizes Derrida's philosophy as a 'Jewish mysticism,' as 'pagan,' and Foucault's as 'anti-scientific' and 'relativistic.' But Foucault's and Derrida's critique of metaphysics should not be understood as continuing within the tradition of reducing difference to the identity of the subject, where, in this instance, it would be the identity of *différance* or power. Rather, by not reducing difference to identity, they recognize the fundamentally non-identifiable nature of that which accounts for the relationship between two sides of a fundamental distinction. In other words, they recognize the intractability of the problem of difference, and their response is neither an attempt to solve it nor a fatalistic resignation in the face of the unknown. On the contrary, they look to see how this fundamental difference is always played out in the history of philosophy, as well as in the history of culture. They seek to understand how, in philosophy and culture, certain identities, norms, and values are made possible by a fundamental difference, a fundamental problematic (i.e., the problem of difference). Their task is thus primarily to reveal that which is creative, not that which negates and says 'No.' Hence, their critique should be interpreted as a creative enterprise, as a working with and against the tradition – that is, they are always motivated by the problem of difference, for example, the problem of how their critique of metaphysics is always different from, but nevertheless related to and a continuation of, the tradition of metaphysics – and not as a solely critical and negating enterprise. Their relation to the tradition of metaphysics is not as simple as Habermas characterizes it to be, and thus to claim, as Habermas does, that Foucault and Derrida negate or reject the tradition implies a commitment to identity – namely, the identity of the tradition being negated – but it is precisely this commitment the poststructuralists refuse to take. In the end, Habermas has failed to see how the poststructuralists are continuing to work within the tradition of philosophy – that is, motivated by the problem of difference – and how their work nevertheless differs from this tradition – that is, they offer a different response.

In this work we will explore more fully this relationship between current Continental thought (i.e., poststructuralism/postmodernism) and the tradition of modern philosophy which it criticizes. There is already an extensive amount of literature in this area, much of it focusing upon what philosophy's proper task should be in the wake of the critique and end of the tradition of metaphysics and modern philosophy – that is, much of this recent work has been a delimitation and validation of *post*-modernism. A great variety of perspectives are presented in these writings, but they almost universally agree upon the need to criticize metaphysics and modern philosophy. Unfortunately, this critique, as many in the Anglo-American tradition have complained, is plagued by an unclear use of terminology and neologisms, thus masking the sense of arguments that might otherwise be easily understood. One of the results of this tendency is that it is often not made very clear why the tradition of modern philosophy needs to be criticized, or whether the criticism offered is even appropriate. The result is that these critiques are rightly perceived as largely negative and critical, and as failing to appreciate their continued relationship and dependency upon the very tradition they are criticizing. Habermas's criticisms are thus not without their proper justification.

What we hope to do in this work is to shed some light on the relationship between current Continental thought and the tradition of metaphysics. We will show that poststructuralism is continuing to develop its theories and concepts as a response to the problem of difference. To this extent, therefore, there is a continuity between what the poststructuralists are doing and what has been done throughout the history of philosophy. On the other hand, we will show that there is, nevertheless, a break with the tradition in terms of the poststructuralist response to this fundamental problem. To demonstrate the latter, we will not first set forth how the entire history of philosophy is the history of responding to the problem of difference, and then show how the many varied writers in current Continental thought mark a break with the traditional response. Although we believe this could be done, it is beyond the scope of this work. What we will do instead is to begin by discussing the work of Husserl. Husserl is the most appropriate starting-point because many of the writers in the poststructuralist tradition (e.g., Derrida, Foucault, Levinas) were originally trained in and inspired by his work. However, these same writers, as we saw with Derrida, ultimately criticized Husserl as a stalwart of traditional metaphysics, and thus their critique of metaphysics often begins with a critique of Husserl. Husserl, furthermore, is also clearly developing his theories as a response to the problem of difference. In particular, Husserl wants to show how ideal timeless truths are irreducibly different from the subjects who intuit them, while nevertheless being dependent upon and related to these subjects. That is, to avoid Platonic realism, Husserl does not accept the claim that these ideal truths pre-exist their being intuited and known – they are irreducibly different; none the less, they are dependent upon being intuited by a subject. In short, Husserl is confronted with the problem of difference.

We will then discuss certain difficulties with Husserl's position as set forth in *Logical Investigations,* difficulties that Husserl himself later recognized. The result of these developments will be the emergence of an absolute consciousness which, as discussed above, is a further response to the problem of difference. This latter position, however, is itself susceptible to certain difficulties. By arguing for the fundamental unity and self-identity of absolute consciousness as the condition which accounts for the irreducible difference between a positing subject and an ideal already-posited object, Husserl is left unable to account for another absolute consciousness. That is, he is unable to show how it is possible that there is another absolute consciousness which is fundamentally related to one's self – namely, another self – but is nevertheless irreducibly different from this self – in other words, cannot be reduced to the self. Thus, Husserl is unable to resolve the problem of difference, and, ultimately, as Merleau-Ponty argues, he reduces the other (i.e., difference) to the self (i.e., identity).

We will then turn to Merleau-Ponty's solution to Husserl's problem of accounting for the other. In short, Merleau-Ponty, at the time of *The Phenomenology of Perception,* argues that the lived body, the perceiving body, experiences itself as simultaneously constituting and constituted, perceiving and perceived, self and other. It is this paradoxical experience and coincidence which is the condition for later differentiating between perceiver and perceived, self and other. The body is thus the differentiating condition, or what we will call 'paradoxa,' which accounts for the relationship between the two sides of a fundamental distinction (e.g., self/other). Put another way, the theory of the body as paradoxa exemplifies Merleau-Ponty's response to the problem of difference. It is, however, the experience of the same identifiable body-subject which accounts for the two sides of a fundamental distinction; consequently, Merleau-Ponty ends up reducing the other to the identity of this body-subject. The 'other's body,' Merleau-Ponty claims, is 'a kind of replica of myself, a wandering double.'[13] Thus Merleau-Ponty, as did Husserl, will be seen to reduce the other (i.e., difference) to the self (i.e., identity).

Merleau-Ponty will also recognize these difficulties, and the change in his position by the time of *The Visible and the Invisible* reflects this recognition. In this later work, Merleau-Ponty will claim that there is a fundamental difference or separation (*écart*) at the heart of Being, what he calls 'wild Being,' and that this difference is the condition for differentiating between consciousness and object, perceiver and perceived, self and other. Within this context, Merleau-Ponty's notion of the flesh will be seen to be the differentiating condition for these irreducible differences – that is, flesh as paradoxa. In other words, the notion of the flesh emerges as a response to the problem of difference. But, even in this late work, we will see that Merleau-Ponty still understands difference in terms of identity. In this instance, difference is at the heart of the 'one sole Being.' This will leave Merleau-Ponty, as Claude Lefort argues, unable to account adequately for the other – that is, difference (the other) continues to be reduced to identity (self, or Being as immanent flesh, on Lefort's interpretation). The problem of difference thus remains unresolved.

In addition to our claim that Husserl's and Merleau-Ponty's work can be understood as a continuing and developing response to the problem of difference, we will discuss some interpretations of Husserl's and Merleau-Ponty's work that demonstrate a failure to understand their thought in this way. For example, Husserl's theory of the noema, and, in particular, the perceptual noema, is interpreted by us to be the differentiating condition which accounts for the difference between the sense of a perceiving act and the object that is perceived by this act; however, by not recognizing this, Dagfinn Føllesdal, among others, identifies the perceptual noema with the conceptual sense of a perceiving act, and Aron Gurwitsch identifies it with the object perceived by this act. There are thus two fundamentally different interpretations of the perceptual noema, a difference which reflects the two sides of a fundamental distinction (i.e., concept/object) made possible and accounted for by the perceptual noema understood as paradoxa. The same is true of the interpretations of Merleau-Ponty's notion of the flesh. Understood as paradoxa, the flesh is that which accounts for the irreducible difference between immanence and transcendence, perceiver and perceived, and so on, but it is not to be identified with either side. In not recognizing this, however, Lefort identifies the flesh as immanence, and M.C. Dillon identifies it as transcendence. They thus do not see that the notion of the flesh was intended to account for this difference itself, and that it is also a way of showing how immanence and transcendence are nevertheless related. In short, these interpretations have not recognized the effort on the part of Husserl and Merleau-Ponty to resolve the problem of difference.

Finally, in the last part of this work we will discuss some of the reasons why Husserl and Merleau-Ponty were unable to resolve or account for the problem of difference. In essence, their difficulty is a consequence of reducing difference to identity. Difference is understood on the basis of identity, or, for example, the other is understood on the basis of the self, and, as such, difference (the other) is never accounted for adequately. It is for this reason that the poststructuralists will not attempt to account for difference in terms of identity, and will, rather, claim that there is a fundamental difference which is the condition for the various irreducible differences that have been the concern of philosophy (e.g., self/other, mind/body).

At this point we could continue with our discussion of Foucault and Derrida, and we could also respond to Habermas's criticisms; however, we will turn instead to the work of Gilles Deleuze. The reason for this shift in focus is that, although Foucault and Derrida, by our interpretation, criticize Husserl and Merleau-Ponty for reducing difference to identity, Deleuze is more explicit than either of them on this matter. In Deleuze's book *Différence et répétition*, for example, his stated objective is to set forth a 'philosophy of difference,' a philosophy that refuses to reduce difference to identity. Deleuze has also directed much of his philosophical labours towards analysing various important figures in the history of philosophy. He has written books on Hume, Spinoza, Leibniz, Kant, and Nietzsche, and *Différence et répétition* is itself a text in the history of philosophy. As a result, we believe an analysis of Deleuze's work will aid us in explicating poststructuralism's place within the history of philosophy. This in turn will help us to respond to Habermas's criticisms, for, as we will see, Deleuze's reversal of the tradition is not a negation or a rejection of this tradition, and is therefore not susceptible to Habermas's critique, which assumes it is. In the end, an analysis of Deleuze's work should further clarify our claim that the problem of difference is a fundamental motivating factor for philosophy – the 'passion and pathos of philosophy.'[14]

To keep these discussions within the scope of this analysis, however, we will focus upon Deleuze's critique of phenomenology, a critique that mirrors his more general critique of metaphysics. This critique is most clearly presented in Deleuze's writings on cinema. In these writings he puts forth a poststructuralist theory of perception – that is, the differences of perception (e.g., perspectival variation) are not to be understood on the basis of a fundamental identity (e.g., the body-subject), but perception itself is to be understood in terms of a fundamental difference, a difference which makes possible the distinction between perceiver and perceived. In other words, we will see how Deleuze responds to the problem of difference, not by arguing for a fundamental identity, but by analysing identity in terms of difference. This analysis, however, will remain necessarily incomplete as, to be complete, it would presuppose a fundamental identity and unity with which the analysis comes into coincidence (e.g., Husserl's hoped-for completion). But neither is this analysis an irrational and relativistic one. Deleuze grants that there is truth and knowledge, but he claims that this truth and knowledge is only partial. To deny absolute truth and knowledge, and to accept a Nietzschean version of perspectivism, does not entail endorsing irrationalism and total relativism. Deleuze denies this either/or: *either* there is an absolute truth and standard, a total rationality, *or* there is only complete relativism and the irrational battle of wills. This either/or, we will argue, is itself a fundamental distinction which needs to be accounted for, a difference which nevertheless entails a fundamental relationship, and Deleuze's 'philosophy of difference' is precisely an attempt to give such an account of this fundamental difference and relationship. With this account, we will see that Deleuze's philosophy, as was the case with Husserl's and Merleau-Ponty's, can be understood as a continuing response to the problem of difference. And this, ultimately, places the work of Deleuze solidly within the history of philosophy.

PART ONE

Husserl

I. The Linguistic and Perceptual Models

1. Truth and Object-ivity

Husserl's theory of truth is simultaneously a theory of objectivity – the theories are mutually interdependent. In this respect Husserl falls within the tradition of the natural sciences: truth is not relative to what each person might take it to be in a given circumstance, but is conditioned by the possibility that, given the *same* circumstances, it will be taken as the *same* truth. It is this condition, that truth be grasped as the same by a multiplicity of scientists, which justifies both a scientific truth and its objectivity – they are mutually interdependent. Husserl, however, goes to great lengths to separate his own theory of truth and objectivity from a natural-scientific theory, and it is this effort which characterizes Husserl's idealism.

Husserl agrees that for something to be true it must be objectively true, but he does not take the object which is regarded as true to be a 'natural' object; that is, objectivity is not conditioned by the 'physically' real world, and thus truth is not, on Husserl's view, in the world. Truth has an objectivity, but it is not a real objectivity (in the sense of physically real); it is, rather, an ideal objectivity. It is this idealism, as most clearly set out in the first volume of *Logical Investigations*, which is largely responsible for the interpretation of Husserl as a Platonic idealist. This view is not without its justification. Husserl's understanding of an ideal objectivity entails a timeless realm of ideas in the classically Platonic sense: 'Each truth ... remains in itself what it is, it retains its ideal being: it does not hang somewhere in the timeless void, but is a case of validity in the timeless realm of ideas.'[1] Furthermore, this timeless realm of ideas, this ideal objectivity, also demonstrates the absolute nature of truth itself and, as in Plato, it shows that a relative truth would be self-contradictory. With Plato, for example, if truth is relative, then the reality which it is relative to either *is* (in the case of truth) or *is not* (in the case of falsity); however, for reality to be and not be would be self-contradictory, and thus Plato concludes, *à la* Parmenides, that the realm of truth must be the realm of ideal *changeless* being. Husserl argues much along these same lines in claiming that a relativization of truth would imply an absolute as the condition for their relativity: that is, a relative truth implies the objectivity (or being) it denies.[2] It is precisely the timeless realm of ideas, or ideal objectivity, which Husserl claims is the absolute that is presupposed by relativity, or the 'real'[3] condition for the relativity of the changing flux of the natural world. Despite these similarities, however, important differences from Platonism emerge as Husserl explicates the manner in which these ideal truths can be given to one's understanding.

Husserl's discussion of the manner in which an ideal truth comes to be grasped is very forthright: one grasps such a truth in an immediate intuition. By 'an immediate intuition,' Husserl means the intuitive grasp of truth itself, the immediate self-givenness and presence of truth itself: 'The most perfect "mark" of correctness is inward evidence, it counts as an immediate intimation of truth itself.'[4] It is nevertheless not very clear what the immediate intuition of truth might mean. How, for instance, is it to be distinguished from immediate sensuous intuition? In answering this question, Husserl will, in the tradition of negative theology, spend much of the first volume of the *Investigations* telling us what immediate intuition is not. For example, immediate intuition is *not* to be confused with mediate intuition, with the intuition which arises from experience. Immediate intuition is thus distinguished from the concepts and intuitions which are generalizations about experience, or with intuitions which depend for their truth upon that which is mediated – that is, the immediate sense data of experience. In short, mediate intuitions are never unconditional. Furthermore, Husserl claims that the propositions of natural science are a paradigmatic example in that they are founded upon mediate intuitions. The natural sciences acquire their truths mediately, through an approximation and generalization of that which is given immediately to the perception of the scientist (i.e., the concrete experimental results). These truths, consequently, are conditional because of their dependence upon experience, and probable because, in the tradition of Descartes, there is always room for doubt with regard to what we perceive of the natural world.

Husserl then claims further that the inner evidence of immediate intuition is *not* to be confused with psychological states – that is, with the observable facts of consciousness. In other words, psychological facts, if understood as scientifically observable and external facts of consciousness, are no more adequate than any other external fact for grounding an indubitable truth. That this has not been clearly seen has given rise to what Husserl will criticize as psychologism – in other words, a theory which explains a set of laws, in particular, logical laws, on the basis of the psychological functioning of the individuals: that is, logical laws are reduced to psychological laws. It is through Husserl's critique of this position that we begin to see more clearly what he ultimately means when he speaks of the inner evidence of immediate intuition.

Husserl's critique of psychologism follows immediately from his claim that any truth founded upon mediate intuition (e.g., scientific truth) will at best be only an approximate truth. The same claim can be made for psychological truths: 'It is universally agreed that psychology is a factual science and therefore an empirical science ... they [propositions of science] are statements about approximate regularities of coexistence and succession.'[5] As a result, he claims that the statements regarding psychological facts, the expression of psychological truths, are only 'vague' and 'probable' truths, and this will be the case for any theory that takes psychic phenomena as an objective fact which can be perceived. This is precisely the move Husserl claims Brentano made: 'When he [Brentano] consequently gives the name of "physical phenomena," not merely to outer objects, but also to these contents [presenting contents], these latter seem infected with the fallibility of outer perception.'[6] Husserl is therefore interested in these 'presenting contents' as the presence of objects, *not* in the manner of external objects of perception, but as an immediate presence of truth itself; and it is this immediate presence of truth itself which characterizes immediate intuition (or insight): 'Insight justifies no mere probabilities of their[7] holding, but their holding or truth itself.'[8] Yet, even though these objects of immediate intuition are not presented in the manner of external perception,[9] they are nevertheless legitimate objects of *subjective* experience, and their presence in immediate intuition serves to ground a legitimate, ideal truth and objectivity for this subject. In order to clarify this, it is necessary to understand the manner in which this ideal objectivity is given to intuition. In other words, we still have to explicate the way in which ideal timeless truths can be presented to the immediate intuition of an individual *subject* in time.

Husserl's strategy in approaching this problem will entail an elaboration of a distinction that is implicit in what we have said so far: that is,
the distinction between an experienced object (e.g., the truth itself as
intuited object) and the manner in which this object is given (e.g.,
whether it is given through mediate or immediate intuition). To account,
therefore, for the way in which an ideal timeless truth can be presented
to a subject in time, Husserl will attempt to explicate the correlation
between ideal timeless truths as ideal objects and the way these objects
are given to an intuiting subject through immediate intuition. Furthermore, just as scientific investigations attempt to explicate the correlation
between real objects and the manner in which these objects are given to
perception, so, too, will Husserl's 'logical investigations' attempt to
explicate the correlation between ideal objects and the manner in which
these objects are given to intuition. The result, in the first case, is real
laws which express the correlation between our perception of regularities in the world and the regularities which actually are in the world; in
the second case, the result is, for Husserl, ideal laws of pure logic (hence
the above reference) which will express the correlation between an
immediate intuition of truth and the *a priori* law which is the condition
of possibility for intuiting this truth. Husserl has therefore broadened
his distinction between ideal and real objectivity to include the ideal and
real laws of these objectivities; and, as one might suspect, Husserl goes
on to claim that psychologism has failed to grasp this distinction as well:
'The psychologistic logicians ignore the fundamental, essential, never-
to-be-bridged gulf between ideal and real laws, between normative and
causal regulation, between logical and real necessity, between logical
and real grounds.'[10]
  The ideal laws which correlate ideal objects and immediate intuition,
laws the *Investigations* will seek to explicate, helps now to clarify Husserl's position regarding the status of the ideal objects or truths. For
example, we can see that Husserl is not taking the objects of the timeless
realm in the same way that Plato did. That is, the ideal objects do not
pre-exist their actual intuition; they do not exist in this timeless realm
prior to their being experienced within immediate intuition. Rather,
these ideal objects express the *a priori* possibilities of our experience, not
as truths which exist independently of and prior to our intuition, but as
truths of our intuition itself. For this reason, Husserl criticizes Plato for
his 'realism,'[11] for granting a 'real' objectivity to ideal laws. But is this
criticism valid? How can these ideal laws and truths be independent of
subjects and yet be related to these subjects?[12] In other words, how can

an independent ideal law be in some sense dependent on an intuiting subject in time?[13] Can Husserl's criticism of Plato hold as long as these questions remain unanswered? Perhaps, but Husserl, as he turns from prefatory comments to the text of *Logical Investigations* itself, does intend to explicate the correlation between experienced ideal objects and the manner in which these objects are given to intuiting subjects. In fact, Husserl claims in the *Crisis* that his life's-work has been dominated by an attempt to explicate this correlation.[14] In other words, his life's-work was largely a response to our questions, and this response was to take many forms. However, one analogy Husserl used to help in explicating the correlation between experienced objects and the manner in which these objects are given, an analogy which has resulted in ambiguities within Husserl's own work and, subsequently, within Husserl interpretation, was developed in *Logical Investigations* and was to dominate Husserl's philosophy thereafter: that is, he uses the generalization of linguistic meaning to clarify, by analogy, the correlation of an experienced object with its manners of givenness. The analogy is thus the correlation of an experienced linguistic object (i.e., an understood 'sense') and the way in which this linguistic object is given to us (i.e., 'sense' as given through an expression, through an intending of this 'sense').

2. The Linguistic Model

Early in the introduction to the second volume of *Logical Investigations*, Husserl claims that 'all theoretical research, though by no means solely conducted in acts of verbal expression or complete statement, none the less terminates in such statement.'[13] The implications of this claim are of the utmost importance for Husserl's project. If all theoretical investigations terminate in verbal expression, the possibility for verbal expression must therefore be intrinsic to the theoretical investigation itself. The 'sense' of what is expressed at the termination of a theoretical investigation, however, is independent of its being expressed. For example, the state of affairs in the world being denoted by an expression is independent of this expression. The expression is only the means through which something about the world comes to be expressed, but this something remains independent throughout. The same is also true of expressions themselves generally. In expressing something, our concern is not with expressing in and of itself, with the physical sounds, but with the sense of what is being expressed, a sense given through an expression, yet independent of it. Husserl thus claims that 'when we normally express something we do not, qua expressing it, live in the acts constituting the expression as a physical object – we are not interested in this object – but we live in the acts which give it sense.'[14] The possibility for verbal expression is therefore conditioned by something which is independent of this expression, either by an independent object or a state of affairs, or by an independent sense which is intended through an expression. We need to point out, however, that Husserl focuses his attention upon the independence of sense as an ideal object, and not upon the objects or state of affairs which are the concern of the natural sciences. To do the latter would be to fall back into a concern for approximate truths (e.g., psychologism); therefore, our task will be simply to clarify how an independent sense can actually be expressed, or how the physical speech itself is able to deliver this independent sense.

This possibility of an independent sense being expressed through physical manifestations (speech, writing, gesture, etc.) is not a problem for Husserl. It happens all the time in everyday speech. When one is speaking to another, one is not attending to the physical utterances, to the act of expression itself, but to the meanings which are being expressed through these utterances. We therefore need to make a distinction, as Husserl does,[15] between the physical phenomenon and the acts which animate this phenomenon and give it a sense. The act which animates the physical phenomena Husserl calls a 'meaning-intention,' and thus a meaning-intention intends a sense through a physical expression, and, if the sense is successfully expressed, it is the fulfilment of this intention, or what Husserl calls 'meaning-fulfilment.' For example, in speaking I am intending the sense of what I say to be understood, either to a hearer or to myself,[16] and it is through the use of physical speech that this intention is carried out.[17] To do phenomenology, therefore, is not to be concerned with actual presentations (e.g., the spoken expression, or what Husserl calls the 'mere expression'), but is to be concerned with what lies behind the mere expression, with 'experiences which perform roles either of meaning-intention or meaning-fulfillment.'[18] This example of speech will continue to serve as the model Husserl uses for the rest of the *Investigations*, and throughout his writings, in analysing the various modes of consciousness as a correlation between meaning-intentions and meaning-fulfilments; that is, it will serve as the model for the main tenet of phenomenology itself: the intentionality of consciousness.

This linguistic model, however, has not answered our earlier questions regarding how ideal objects can actually be understood or intuited.

The question now is how a meaning-intention of a subject can actually be fulfilled by an independent ideal sense. On what basis, and with what right, can we claim that a meaning-intention is adequately fulfilled, and fulfilled in just the manner that it was intended?

The answer Husserl will ultimately give is that the meaning-intention comes into coincidence with its meaning-fulfilment. Put another way, the content of an act of meaning-fulfilment will be the same as the content of the meaning-intending act. But this content must not be thought of as what Husserl calls 'descriptive content.' Descriptive content is that which is attributable to things of the natural world, and, as such, it can be broken down and described (e.g., the syllables, sounds, and words themselves as 'mere expression' are part of the descriptive content); it is something real (Husserl uses the German word *real* in this case to characterize thing-like transcendence, and opposes to this the word *reell*, which characterizes events in the immanent stream of consciousness).[19] The 'sense' of an act, as with the sense of an expression, cannot be described in this manner. In other words, the sense of an act, an act's immanent content, is what is intended through the animation of the descriptive content, but cannot be reduced to this content. Husserl calls this content the 'intentional content,' for it is what is really being expressed (here 'real' is understood as the immanent conditions in the stream of consciousness, as *reell*) – that is, what is *really* being intended. It is this content, then, which comes into coincidence with its fulfilment, and consequently Husserl claims 'the essence of the meaning-fulfilment is the fulfilling sense of the expression, or, as one may also call it, the sense expressed by the expression.'[20] That is, if an act of meaning-fulfilment has the same sense as the act of meaning-intention, then this intention is fulfilled. However, problems arise when one considers what this sense which is the same is, and how it refers to another sense. For example, it seems that two different senses can refer to (or intend) the same object (e.g., the famous 'Clark Kent' and 'Superman' example), and it seems the same sense can also refer to different objects (e.g., Husserl gives an example of 'a horse' which has the same sense in the propositions 'Bucephalus is a horse' and 'A cart-horse is a horse,' but refer to two different objects). Therefore, if it is unclear how a sense refers, it is equally unclear how a sense can refer to another sense, and thus how the fulfilment of an intention could be possible.

In order to resolve these difficulties, Husserl clarifies the relationship between the sense of an act and the reference of an act, and he distinguishes within the intentional content itself between the 'matter' of an act, *that* which is presented, and the quality of an act which determines the manner of its presentation. For example, I can assert '2 + 2 = 4' and 'Pope John Paul II is Polish,' and, although that which is asserted in each case is different, these acts share the same quality (or act-character): they are assertive acts. Other act-characters include presentative (i.e., perception), judgmental, questioning, and wishing. The 'matter' of an act determines its referent, or that which it is directed upon: that is, it makes of an act an objectifying act.[21] The matter of an act is thus 'that element in an act which first gives it reference to an object, and reference so wholly definite that it not merely fixes the object meant in a general way, but also the precise way in which it is meant.'[22] In other words, the matter determines precisely that which is presented and which can be presented with different act-characters. For example, Husserl argues that, although the judgment 'It will rain today,' the question 'Will it rain today?,' and the wish 'I wish it would rain today' have different act-characters, they are nevertheless different ways of presenting the same matter or content: 'rain today.'

This distinction between the matter and quality of an act is not, however, equivalent to that made between an experienced object and its manners of givenness. We must not confuse the matter with an experienced object. An experienced object, what Husserl calls in this context the 'intentional object,' is that which consciousness is always transcending itself towards; it is that which consciousness is consciousness *of*. Husserl emphasizes that we are, after all, conscious of objects and not of our intending these objects. The matter of an act, on the other hand, is immanently real (*reell* as opposed to *real*) in that it determines the directedness of consciousness itself. The distinction between the matter and the quality of an act must therefore be seen as a further distinction in the manners of givenness; that is, the matter and quality together (what Husserl calls the 'intentional essence') comprise the manner in which an act is directed to an object. The intentional object therefore corresponds to the experienced object, and this object is something which has no reality in the act itself (i.e., no immanent reality), yet is that which this act is directed towards. The question now, therefore, is how the intentional object comes to be given through these acts, especially if the intentional object is not something in these acts. In other words, Husserl is led to state a form of the question we have continued to ask: how can an ideal object be related to a real subject? It now surfaces as the question of 'how something non-existent or transcendent can be the intentional object in an act in which it has no being.' In other words, how can an object transcendent to an act be related to this act? The answer Husserl gives, which he claims is a 'wholly sufficient one,' is that 'the object is an intentional object: this means there is an act having a determinate intention, and determinate in a way which makes it an intention towards this object.'[23]

We can begin to see how Husserl will answer the question regarding the way in which a meaning-intention comes to be fulfilled. If the matter of an act determines the reference of an act to be a particular object, and if 'identical matters never yield distinct objective references,'[24] then this reference itself will be the same whenever the matters of a meaning-intention act and a meaning-fulfilling act are identical. However, a difficulty arises here in that there emerge two senses in which the matter of an act can be understood: on the one hand, the matter determines *that* an act is directed to an object, that there is a fixed reference for this act; and, on the other hand, the matter determines *what* this object is fixed as, with 'the properties, relations, categorial forms that it itself [the matter] attributed to it.'[25] It is this which Husserl calls this the 'interpretative sense,' or the sense which 'makes its object count as this object and no other.'[26] The difficulty here is in explaining how the matter of an act, the interpretative sense, can determine both *that* an object be referred to and *what* it is referred to as. The difficulty arises when we attempt to account for how two different interpretative senses can determine the same referent, the same object. On the one hand, the intentional object which is immanently determined does seem to be that which fulfils an interpretative sense, for the intentional object as immanently determined by the matter of an act is also that which transcends these acts; consequently, this objective reference comes to fulfil the conditions set forth within the immanence of the acts.[27] On the other hand, since this object itself is determined by the matter of an act, by the interpretative sense, it is unclear how an intentional object could continue to be determined as the same object by different interpretative senses, by different matters, but it seems clear that this does happen. For example, we can see that, although the phrases 'the victor at Jena' and 'the vanquished at Waterloo' (to use an example of Husserl's [p. 287]) have two different interpretative senses (i.e., the relations, properties, etc. are different in each case), they nevertheless refer to the same object: Napoleon. The question which this prompts is how a reference can be fixed as the same when the 'interpretative senses,' the ways of grasping this referent, are different? How can we grasp an object as the same if the conditions which determine *what* we grasp an object as (i.e., the matter as the properties, relations, and attributes of this object) are different? Can we truly separate the object *that* we grasp from *what* we grasp it as?

In response to these questions, Husserl would point out that the meaning which is being attributed to the referent is not the same as the interpretative sense. In other words, the interpretative sense is the matter of an act which uniquely determines the directedness of this act. The meaning itself, however, and further developing the linguistic model, is independent of the acts themselves; it is that which is expressed through the acts. In fact, Husserl claims that 'meaning is related to varied acts of meaning ... just as Redness *in specie* is to the slips of paper which lie here, and which all "have" the same redness ... Meanings constitute, we may say further, a class of concepts in the sense of "universal objects."'[28] In other words, meaning as an ideal 'universal object' conditions the possibility of the same meaning being given in a multiplicity of meaning-giving acts, and thus the conditions which determine what we grasp an object as (i.e., interpretative sense) are themselves conditioned by an ideal meaning which allows for different interpretative senses to have the same ideal meaning. The question for Husserl is therefore not how a multiplicity of acts is able to refer to the same object, but how, on the basis of an ideal object in general, this object comes to fulfil a multiplicity of acts. In other words, it is not a question of how an ideal objective reference is to be fixed, but rather how a number of meaning-intentions can be fulfilled by this reference. Our question concerning the fulfilment of meaning-intentions now looms as a question of central importance to phenomenology, and, in Husserl's efforts to answer this question, to explicate how a number of meaning-intentions can be fulfilled by the same object, he returns again, as was his motivation in turning to the linguistic model, to an example where this seems to happen as a matter of course. He turns to perception. In our perceptual life we are constantly perceiving objects, yet these objects are perceived only from a particular perspective; however, an object is perceived as the same despite a multiplicity of perspectives. The same object fulfils a multiplicity of different perceptual acts; therefore, it appears that perception might hold the key to how any possible object in general could fulfil a multiplicity of acts, and, consequently, how any possible meaning-intention might be fulfilled.

3. The Perceptual Model

Perception holds a privileged position in Husserl's phenomenology for it is the clearest case of the presentation of an object itself. Husserl argues that an object is presented in an act of perception without the need for any mediating acts to found this perception, and thus that it is an act which presents an object straightforwardly: 'In sense-perception, the "external" thing appears "in one blow," as soon as our glance falls upon it. The manner in which it makes the thing appear present is straightforward: it requires no apparatus of founding or founded acts.'[29] Yet, despite the fact that perception gives us an object in a straightforward manner, and 'in one blow,' this object is nevertheless presented as a unity of parts, as a unity of the possible acts which could perceive this same object, and it is this unity which Husserl claims is presented in a straightforward manner: 'The unity of perception comes into being as a *straightforward* unity, *as an immediate fusion of part-intentions, without the addition of new act-intentions.*'[30] In other words, the question concerning how an object could fulfil a multiplicity of different acts, the question with which we closed the previous section, is answered every time we perceive an object: a perceived object is itself the unity of the different ways in which it can be perceived. This is merely another way of saying that, despite the fact that an external object is perceived only from a given aspect, from a certain perspective, we nevertheless perceive the object itself, and an object which transcends this perspective, as a straightforward unity of possible perspectives.

This discussion of the perceived object which transcends individual perspectives returns us to the issue of the intentional object. The intentional object, as we saw, was that which transcended the individual acts as that towards which these acts were directed; furthermore, we saw that the sense to be attributed to the intentional object was that of a 'universal object,' as the unity of possible meaning-intentions such that they all mean the same object. Similarly with perception, the object is 'the immediate fusion of part-intentions' which is the transcendent unity for all possible perspectives (part-intentions) of the same object. The object is therefore that which is meant in the perception, the object intended (intentional object) by an *act* of perception. Now to clarify how an object can be meant or intended in an act of perception, to understand why Husserl claims 'an object ... *is* what we mean – whether we signify, represent or perceive it,'[31] we need to understand this in relation to what Husserl calls the 'appearing content, which is *not* what we mean.'[31] In other words, we need to clarify the distinction Husserl makes between sensations and percepts.

The distinction between sensations and percepts is an example of the linguistic model as applied to perception: that is, just as meaning-intentions animate speech sounds when something is said, so, too, do percepts animate sensations when something is seen. Therefore, just as speech is simply sound-patterns (mere expression) until one is able to *interpret* the meaning intended through this sound, so, too, are objects merely sensations until one is able to *interpret* them *object*-ively. In an important sense, then, we learn to see objects;[33] consequently, we see Husserl claiming that a perception prior to experience would not see anything, it would not have had the experience (i.e., learning) necessary to see objects: 'If we imagine a consciousness prior to all experience, it may very well have the same sensations as we have. But it will intuit no things, and no events pertaining to things ... its sensations mean nothing ... they are merely lived through without an objectifying interpretation.'[34]

Sensations are therefore not what is meant in an act of perception ('I do not see color-sensations but colored things'),[35] but are nevertheless the necessary pre-givens which are interpreted by an objectifying act of perception. This aspect of Husserl's theory of perception also has its analogy in the linguistic model: 'Meaning, the characteristic function of the expressive sign, presupposes the sign whose function it is.'[36] Similarly, for perception Husserl claims that 'sense-contents provide, as it were, the analogical building-stuff for the content of the object presented by their means.'[37] In other words, in both cases there is a pre-given content taken up by an apprehending, interpreting, meaning-giving act.

This relationship between experienced contents of apprehension (e.g., the sensations and signs as the pre-givens) and this apprehension itself forms the basis of what has been called Husserl's 'schematic theory.' This schematic theory is what we have called the 'linguistic model' (i.e., language as the model for explicating the correlation of experienced object and manners of givenness), and it is an example of Husserl applying the linguistic model to all acts (e.g., perception). Husserl, however, will eventually turn away from the schematic variation of the linguistic model when he develops his theory of a *non-apprehending* absolute consciousness,[38] but he will not turn away from the linguistic model itself.

To bring these issues into fuller relief, we must emphasize that perception is an act, and, as such, it can be discussed in light of the distinctions made in the previous section. For example, perception will have its immanent contents (i.e., sensations) which constitute and determine the intentionality of perception without themselves being intended or perceived. The contents which are 'truly immanent contents, which belong to the real make-up of the intentional experiences, are not intentional: they constitute the act, provide necessary *points d'appui* which render possible an intention, but are not themselves intended.'[39] We also saw that the immanent content of an act was, in turn, divided into act-character (quality) and matter. In perception, the act-character is presentative: it posits that which is presented *as presented*. The matter of perception, however, is somewhat ambiguous. On the one hand, it seems clear that the matter is the sensuous material which is taken up in the act and objectified through the interpretation (the interpretative sense) of this material. That Husserl uses sensations as an example of the immanent content of perception (e.g., 'I do not see color-sensations but colored things'), and that perception seems to be discussed by way of the linguistic model, seems to validate the view that the matter of the act is the sensations. On the other hand, Husserl has also argued that the matter of the act is to be understood as the 'interpretative sense,' as the immanent content which determines the intentionality of an act, and he expressly distinguishes this view of matter, as we have pointed out, from matter as sensuous stuff. How are we to reconcile this apparent ambiguity?

The ambiguity seems to stem from an equivocation in the use of the term 'matter.' Husserl uses 'matter' at times to denote the form of the immanent content, the form (i.e., interpretative sense) a content (i.e., sensations) is given in an act, or *what* a content is perceived as; and he uses 'matter' as these contents themselves, as *that* (i.e., sensations) which is taken up in an act. For example, Husserl discusses the 'matter' or immanent content of perceiving 'white' as that which 'only partially coincides with the color-aspect of the apparent object,'[40] or the form or sense that can be abstracted from an actual perception; and he also discusses 'matter' in terms of 'an experienced complex of sensations [which] gets informed by a certain act-character ... [and, to] the extent that this happens, the perceived object appears.'[41] That is, the matter as the content taken up by an act, and not the matter as the form of this act which only partially coincides with this content. Husserl, however, despite this ambiguity, clearly stresses the view of matter as interpretative sense, as the form which can be abstracted from a presented content. That he does this follows the claim that an act is possible only on the basis of some presentative material (e.g., no desire unless something is desired, no act unless something is acted upon), but this presentative material is possible only as the result of an act of presentation. In other words, Husserl is claiming that sensations do not pre-exist their being taken up by an act of presentation (i.e., perception). To say this would be to commit the psychologistic error of asserting existence to mental phenomenon. Rather, sensations are, from the start, taken up in an originary act of presentation which intends these contents as interpreted, as form-al contents. It is, then, on this basis that Husserl agrees with Brentano's claim that every intentional experience is either a presentation or based on a presentation; however, his break with Brentano, as we saw, occurs with Brentano's claim that these originally presented contents are real (*real*) contents, whereas Husserl claims that they are immanently real (*reellen*) contents.

Another reason Husserl emphasizes the formal aspect of the content is to account for the fulfilment of a meaning-intention, and to account especially for the fulfilment of a linguistic intention. If there could not be a formal content abstracted from the material sensations, then it appears problematic that a perception could ever be adequately expressed, if expressed at all. But Husserl clearly states that the content of perception can be expressed and understood, and understood by someone who had not perceived that which was being expressed. Thus Husserl claims 'that a statement of perception expresses a perception, but also that it expresses the *content* of a perception ... by the "content" we understand the self-identical meaning that the hearer can grasp even if he is not a percipient.'[42] This content, furthermore, is not a content which functions as an image by presenting an object through a similarity between a given material (sensations) and the object perceived. In other words, the content of a perception is not an image which represents an object through resemblance. To claim this would result in an infinite regress, for, if an object can be presented only through an image, then there must be something present such that we know what the image is an image of, and this something must in turn be presented through an image, and so on. Consequently, Husserl claims that an act of presentation either directly presents its object or is founded upon such a presentation,[43] and a content of perception is thus *adequately* presented if the object itself is actually present, if it is presented just as it is intended in this act, and presented directly, not indirectly through an image or representation. This adequately presented content is therefore not to be understood as two objects coming into coincidence (i.e., an image and an object), but as one object whose presence *wholly* coincides with its presentation. That is, it is this completely self-given object, or what Husserl will later call an 'object in general,' which is the condition for the fulfilment of a meaning-intention.

It is this form of adequate presentation which Husserl claims is the foundation of every intentional experience: it is the self-identical kernel which founds all other acts; however, this presentation is not to be confused with the presentation of objects in external perception. An object of external perception presents itself only from one aspect, from a single perspective, and this presentation does not wholly coincide with the object in its self-identity: that is, the object as a unity of all possible aspects. For this reason Husserl marks a fundamental distinction between external and inner perception, and claims the latter to be the basis for an *adequate* theory of perception: 'in the interest of perceptual theory, we must therefore enter more exactly into the essence of inner, as opposed to outer perception.'[44] We can thus see that perception is the model for explaining the manner of fulfilment, the manner in which an object can be presented *in propria persona*. This does not, however, hold with respect to external perception, for it does not present objects adequately; consequently, Husserl's theory will turn to an analysis of inner perception, of direct intuition, to explain fulfilment.

Before we investigate the moves Husserl makes in this direction, we need to discuss the advantages and difficulties for Husserl in adopting the perceptual model to explain fulfilment. An advantage of discussing the issues here on the basis of perception is that perception seems to show that the same object can fulfil a number of different acts (the problem with which we ended the previous section), and perception also seems to present the object in a straightforward and immediate way; thus perception appears as an example of what Husserl calls 'immediate intuition' (therefore helping in the explanation of what an immediate intuition of an ideal truth would entail). The difficulty, however, is that it is still unclear how Husserl has resolved the ambiguity concerning the role of sensations. How is it possible to abstract a form (interpretative sense) from material sensations unless the sensations themselves are in some way structured? It seems clear that sensations do limit the extent to which an act of presentation can interpret them. For example, an objectifying interpretation of one sensation as pain or of another as a red-coloured object seems to entail certain conditions within the sensations themselves such that the one sensation (pain) is not interpreted as the other (red).[45] It also seems clear that Husserl cannot claim that this form *exists* independently of an act of presentation. To do this would be to fall into Platonic Realism. It is therefore difficult to see how Husserl can reconcile these two positions. In other words, it is difficult to see how the sensuous content of a perception contributes, if at all, to the meaning of any act founded upon this perception. Or, put another way, the problem is in explaining how linguistic meaning can be founded upon, and express, the contents of perception. Perhaps in recognition of this difficulty, and in an attempt to resolve it, Husserl turns to a brief discussion of demonstratives (or what Husserl calls 'occasional expressions').

Husserl's discussion of demonstratives is illuminating with respect to the relationship between sensuous intuition and a perceptual statement founded upon this intuition. For example, when I say '*This* is the man I was telling you about' or '*There* is an alligator' in the presence of that which I am speaking about, it appears the demonstratives, 'this,' 'there,' 'now,' and so on, acquire an immediate and direct fulfilment of their meaning-intentions. The intended object of a demonstrative such as 'this' is intuitively present and given to perception as exactly that which was intended, yet Husserl claims that, in the case of demonstratives, perception supplies the direction of the meaning-intention, and fulfils this intention, but is not itself constitutive of the meaning: 'Perception is responsible for the relation of my word to *this* object, but my meaning does not lie in perception.'[46] In other words, the sensuous intuition of perception supplies the content which fulfils the meaning-intention of a demonstrative, but is in itself meaningless. A demonstrative is thus an act built upon perception (Husserl calls it 'an act of this-meaning'), which is simply a generalized act of pointing realized in perception. One can therefore separate the act of this-meaning from the perceptual fulfilment such that, upon hearing a demonstrative, one can have the general thought of something being pointed out; yet Husserl claims 'the speaker has no need of the indefinitely referential ideal which functions as "index" for the hearer.'[47] In other words, one need not abstract the idea of something being pointed out, and then try to find this something. In the case of demonstratives an 'intention [is] immediately oriented to intuition,' and we have the 'conceptual thought playing the part of an intuition.'[48]

There is an analogy between demonstratives and perception. Like perception, demonstratives are immediately oriented to an intuition of the objects they intend. Demonstratives also, as in perception, 'present the objects directly, without "conceptual" mediation' (p. 684). There is a fundamental difference, however, between the two. A demonstrative is an act which intends meaning (this-meaning), whereas perception, although an act, is not a meaning-giving act. Perception is purely presentative: it presents the objects which fulfil a meaning-intention, but is not itself a meaning-intention. When we mentioned earlier that the object of perception is what is meant in perception, we were not saying that perception was a meaning-giving act; rather, we were saying that perception presents objects, and it is always an object which is meant whenever something is meant (this includes mathematical, imaginative objects, etc.). We must not confuse the givenness of an object in an act of perception with an object as taken up and intended in a meaning-giving act. As a result, it is apparent that perception, as an act of presentation which presents its object immediately and straightforwardly, is both the act that founds all other acts – that is, the presentation 'every intentional experience is based on' – and the act which fulfils meaning-intentions – 'On the side of fulfilment ... (as in the case of perception) we have components which cannot be called intentions, since they only fulfil but require no fulfillment.'[49] It is therefore on the basis of perception (what I have called the 'perceptual model') that a meaning-intention can both *mean something* and, in turn, *be fulfilled*. But at this point the distinction made earlier between inner and external perception returns. We saw that in external perception the object is not presented adequately, and that, as a result, it would be on the basis of inner perception that an adequate theory of perception could be built. It is also clear that external perception is not what Husserl has in mind when he seeks to explain the fulfilment of a meaning-intention; nevertheless, our discussion to this point has explained Husserl's attempts to explicate the correlation of meaning-intention and meaning-fulfilment (using both the linguistic and perceptual models), but this explication will remain lacking as long as the distinction between external and inner perception is itself not explained. It is in the Sixth Logical Investigation that Husserl takes up this explanation, and, considering that the Sixth Investigation is in its own way the fulfilment of Husserl's intention to explicate the correlation between meaning-intentions and meaning-fulfilments, it is not surprising that it has received the most attention from scholars attempting to come to an interpretative understanding of his thought.

4. The Paradox of Fulfilment

In the Sixth Investigation, Husserl continues to use the linguistic and perceptual models to account for the relationship between an independent sense or ideal object and the subject that intends or intuits these objects. In short, Husserl further elaborates the relationship between ideal truths that are both independent of subjects, yet, contrary to 'Platonic Realism,' nevertheless dependent upon these subjects. In our discussion of the linguistic model, we have examined the use of this model to explain how an ideal truth or meaning could be accessible to the understanding and intuition of a real subject. Its usefulness followed from the observation that, in language, one is not attending to the real sound-patterns themselves, but to the ideal meanings being expressed. The sound-pattern as a 'mere expression' is merely an act of presentation (i.e., a vocalic presentation of sound-patterns) through which what is really presented, a meaning, is expressed. As Husserl concludes the Fifth Investigation, he notes the advantage gained by using linguistic meaning in order to clarify the meaningful nature of acts generally: 'an act of presentation is directly intuited precisely where this distinction between a presentation and a presentation of this presentation is phenomenologically drawn,' and this distinction was made clear in 'becoming clear as to the difference between a *mere* sound-pattern and the same pattern understood as a name.'[50] In other words, Husserl's claim, following Brentano, that all intentional experiences '"are either presentations or founded upon presentations"'[51] is clarified when seen in the light of a vocalic presentation (act of presentation) and the meaning expressed thereby (the presentation founded upon this presentation).

Upon clarifying this distinction, however, the question arose regarding how an act of presentation is able to found other presentative acts, and how this latter act is able to fulfil the conditions set forth in the founding act. How is a meaning given on the basis of an act of presentation, and, furthermore, how is this meaning understood and intuited as given? Husserl's discussion turns here on an explanation of the founding act of presentation, and on the direct intuition of that which is presented. We then saw that, with the perceptual model, these explanations found an enlightening analogy: that is, perception is an example of direct intuition itself, of the immediate and straightforward presentation (founding act of presentation) of an object ('object' understood here in its most general sense). There was an ambiguity in this model, however, that Husserl never resolved in *Logical Investigations*. This ambiguity surrounds Husserl's discussion of sensations. On the one hand, sensations appear to be the founding 'act of presentation,' the 'matter' which is taken up by interpretative acts and is the building-blocks of these acts. On the other hand, sensations also appear to be the 'presentation of this presentation,' the form or interpretative sense of an act which allows for the possibility of an expression based upon this perception. John Brough has correctly recognized this ambiguity in Husserl when he claims that, in *Logical Investigations*, 'he did not distinguish between the experiencing or "sensing" of immanent contents and the contents themselves, e.g., between the sensed "red" content and the sensing of it.'[52] The source of this ambiguity seems to stem from the minor role the perceptual model plays with respect to the linguistic model in terms of clarifying phenomenological distinctions. Consequently, Husserl tends to understand sensations as 'interpretative sense,' as the form which is paralleled in perceptual statements, and he failed to account for the sensations themselves as the content which is taken up in an act of presentation.

This interpretation we have been following through, and the ambiguities in Husserl's thought that we have seen along the way, did not go unrecognized by Husserl. Husserl recognized his early emphasis in *Logical Investigations* upon the linguistic model as a means of becoming clear about phenomenological distinctions. For example, when stating in *Ideas* that the meaning of every act is in principle expressible, and thus that expression itself is a valid means of understanding the meaning-giving nature of acts in general, he then adds in a footnote: 'In point of fact, this was the way along which the *Logical Investigations* endeavored to penetrate into Phenomenology. A second way, starting from the opposite side, from the side, namely, of experience and the data of sense which the author has also followed since the beginning of the 'nineties, did not find full expression in that work.'[53]

It is this second way which we have called 'the perceptual model,' and here we see Husserl recognizing the minor place of that model in the *Investigations*. It should not be surprising, therefore, that Husserl also recognized some of the difficulties within his initial approach to phenomenology. It will be the task of this section to explore these difficulties in greater detail, and to map out the course Husserl's thought took in attempting to overcome them, a map we will cover more fully in the next chapter.

I

An important aspect of Husserl's theory of perception as it is stated in *Logical Investigations* is that all perception entails an objectifying interpretation. That is, we do not perceive sensations (e.g., colour-sensations); rather, we perceive *objects* as that which is interpreted on the basis of sensations (e.g., coloured things). Perception is thus an interpretative act, and as such entails an 'interpretative sense' which determines and directs this objectifying interpretation. Perception is not, however, a meaningful act. Husserl is clear on this point. A meaningful act entails a meaning-intention which seeks its corresponding intuitive fulfilment. Perception, however, is an act which only fulfils meaning-intentions without, in turn, requiring fulfilment.[54] The interpretative sense of perception is thus to be understood as the form of objectifying interpretation itself, the form of any act of presentation, and it is because of this that something can be meant at all (i.e., it is always an object that is meant). Furthermore, it is the interpretative sense of perception which is the form mirrored in all meaning-intentions, in particular, linguistic intentions: 'if presentations, expressible thoughts of any sort whatever, are to have their faithful reflections in the sphere of meaning-intentions, then there must be *a semantic form which corresponds to each presentational form.*'[55] That is, the form of the presentations themselves allow for the possibility of linguistic expression;[56] consequently, it is the interpretative sense of perception which justifies the linguistic model itself.

This last claim appears to be circular, for Husserl justifies the linguistic model (i.e., his entry into phenomenology via linguistic expressions) on the basis of a theory of perception which presupposes this model. Husserl might not consider this circle to be a vicious one. Perhaps it is simply the case, as with Heidegger's hermeneutic circle, that the investigations seek merely to determine more precisely what is already pre-given. In this case, owing to the fact that, as Husserl claims, we 'live entirely in the consciousness of meaning, of understanding, which does not lapse when accompanying imagery does so,'[57] it should not be surprising that, wherever our investigations might begin in clarifying the nature of meaningful acts, they, in the end, return to meaningful acts. We always return to examples from the sphere of meaning (e.g., language) because we are always situated within this sphere.

A problem does emerge here, however, in that it is unclear how a meaning-intention could ever be fulfilled unless we are actually able to get beyond this sphere of meaning to that which would fulfil the meaning-intention. For example, if perception is an act which fulfils, but if it fulfils on the basis of the interpretative *sense* of this perception, then this fulfilling act itself is still in the sphere of meaning, and as such it is a meaning itself in need of fulfilment. There is thus an epistemological infinite regress which is generated in that each fulfilling act is in turn in need of fulfilment, and thus of another fulfilling act, and so on *ad infinitum*; and as a result we cannot see how we can ever have adequate and complete fulfilment (i.e., knowledge). Hubert Dreyfus has recognized the infinite regress inherent in this position: 'a regress develops in which sense coincides with sense indefinitely. At each stage we arrive at a fulfilling meaning for an intending meaning, but at no stage does the fulfilling meaning imply a sensuous filling.'[58] Dreyfus follows this with an analysis of the efforts since Husserl to supply this 'sensuous filling' (in particular, Gurwitsch's[59]) in order to avoid the regress. Before turning to such issues ourselves, we want to examine this regress more closely in order to show that: (1) it is not isolated to Husserl's phenomenology, but can also be found in Frege; and (2) that Husserl was not unaware of this regress and made moves of his own to avoid it.

II

Earlier in this chapter we discussed a difficulty in Husserl's concept of the 'matter' of an act, of what Husserl also calls the 'interpretative sense' of an act. The problem follows from Husserl's claim that the interpretative sense determines not only *that* an act is directed to an object (i.e., it fixes a reference for this act), but also *what* this object is fixed as. The question arose concerning how two different interpretative senses (e.g., 'the victor at Jena' and 'the vanquished at Waterloo') were able to fix the same referent. Husserl's response to this question, as we saw, was that the objectively determined meaning, as with the objectively determined object, is to be considered as a transcendent unity. Meaning here is thus to be understood as a 'universal object,' as an ideal unity which allows for the possibility of a multiplicity of acts to mean the same thing. It was in order to support this position that Husserl then turned to the perceptual model to see how a transcendent unity (e.g., a perceived object) does in fact fulfil a multiplicity of acts.

This turn to the perceptual model, however, found us facing a new difficulty in Husserl's theory, a difficulty which seems to be a revised version of the ones which the turn to the perceptual model had sought to overcome. The problem here was in accounting for the role of sensations. On the one hand, the sensations appear to be *that* which an act of presentation takes up in an objectifying interpretation, and, on the other hand, the sensations appear to be *what* form this interpretation will take. This is compounded further when we see Husserl favouring the interpretation of sensations as the form of an act of presentation, as the 'interpretative sense,' and thus he reintroduces the unresolved difficulties concerning the interpretative sense itself. It therefore remains to be seen how the sense of an act (interpretative sense) is both *that* which is meant in the act and *what* that which is meant is meant as; and it is here that we can see most clearly Husserl's kinship to Frege.

The similarity between Frege and Husserl has been widely recognized, and much of recent interpretation of Husserl (this work included) has used this similarity in order to show that Husserl's philosophic concerns are not far removed from the concerns of the Anglo-American tradition which developed out of the work of Frege.[60] This similarity is most clear with respect to their theories of sense. They each claim that sense is ideal in that it is independent of the psychological states of individuals, and yet it is not objective, in the sense of real objects. The sense, as we saw in Husserl, is that which animates a 'mere expression,' a subjective utterance, and makes of it an expression that says *something*, that refers to an object; however, the sense is not that which is referred to, but mediates between a meaning-intention which is determined by this sense (i.e., interpretative sense) and the object (intentional object) which is what is intended on the basis of this sense and which ultimately comes to fulfil this meaning-intention. Frege, similarly, also claims that the sense of an expression is that which makes of a subjective act of expressing an act which refers to an object, and that this sense is neither the subjective act nor the object referred to: 'The reference of a proper name is the object itself which we designate by its means; the idea, which we have in that case, is wholly subjective; in between lies the sense, which is indeed no longer subjective like the idea, but is not yet the object itself.'[61]

This comparison we are making becomes even clearer when we see that Frege's notion of sense also has the same twofold function it does in Husserl's theory. The sense not only is *what* is expressed in an act as that which determines this act and makes it a meaningful act, but also designates or fixes the object *that* this act is directed towards, the reference of this act: 'A proper name (word, sign, sign combination, expression) expresses its sense, stands for or designates its reference. By means of a sign we express its sense and designate its reference.'[62] Furthermore, it seems that if our comparison of Frege and Husserl holds, then the difficulties which we found in Husserl's accounting of how the sense determines both that an act refer to an object and what this object is referred to as, then it should be the case that such a criticism might be made of Frege, and indeed this is the case. Kripke, in his book *Naming and Necessity*, makes just this sort of criticism against Frege. He claims: 'Frege should be criticized for using the term "sense" in two senses. For he takes the sense of a designator to be its meaning; and he also takes it to be the way its reference is determined.'[63] In other words, on the one hand, Frege takes the sense of an expression to be what is expressed, that which makes of an utterance a designating utterance (i.e., an expression), and Kripke concludes that, for Frege, this means that the sense is synonymous with a set of descriptions which determines *what* an object is designated as. In Husserl this was the aspect of the interpretative sense which determined what an object is intended as, with its 'properties, relations,' and so on. On the other hand, Frege takes the sense of an expression to be *that* which fixes the reference of this expression. In other words, as in Husserl, the sense also determines that an act be directed to an object, that there be a fixed reference which determines the directedness of this act. And since sense, as Kripke argues, is, for Frege, synonymous with a set of descriptions, the reference itself is therefore fixed on the basis of a set of descriptions.[64] Kripke comes down against both aspects of Frege's notion of sense; however, without turning our discussion to Kripke's criticism of 'description theory,' we want only to point out that the difficulties we have found in Husserl have also been found in Frege, and that this follows from their similar theories of sense. But there is another comparable difficulty common to Frege and Husserl, one which also follows from their theories of sense, and that is the infinite regress which is inherent in their theories.

We are now in a better position to discuss the regress we mentioned above: that is, as Dreyfus pointed out, sense infinitely coinciding with sense and never being fulfilled. This regress followed from Husserl's claim that we are always situated within the sphere of sense, that 'we live entirely in the consciousness of meaning'; however, it is now apparent from our discussion that meaning (or sense) is not itself an object for consciousness. It is through sense that we are conscious of objects, and conscious of them in a definite manner, but meaning itself is neither our subjective experience nor the object experienced. It is between the two and mediates their correlation. To make of this mediating sense an object, in the form of a representation or image, for example, would be to fall into a regress that Husserl was well aware of.[65] The sense is therefore never the object itself which is being expressed; however, there exists the possibility of turning to this sense in a new act (i.e., reflection) whereby it does become an object. For example, in the Sixth Investigation, Husserl claims that in perceiving, judging, and so on, the sense of these acts is not the object. The object is the perceived object or the state of affairs judged, et cetera; nevertheless, through reflection, we can turn to the sense of these acts. The resulting objects, Husserl claims, are the 'concept of perception' and the 'concept of judgment.'[66] This reflective act, however, as an act, must in turn have a sense which is different from the object, a sense which can be made the object of another act, and this act will also have a sense which can be made an object, and so on *ad infinitum*. It is this implicit regress which we believe to be the reason for the regress we mentioned earlier: sense will for ever coincide with sense because sense never coincides with the object.

This indefinite deferral of the coincidence of sense and its object, and the resulting infinite proliferation of sense coinciding with sense, appears to follow from Husserl's theory of sense; furthermore, extending our comparison with Frege, it appears that it is an intrinsic aspect of Frege's theory of sense as well. This has in fact been explicitly argued for by Carnap. In *Meaning and Necessity*, Carnap claims there is an infinite proliferation inherent within every naming-relation (i.e., the relation of a name to its reference on the basis of sense);[67] that is, Frege's theory of sense, as does Husserl's, implies an infinite regress. Carnap illustrates his point:

Let us start with a name n_1, say the sentence 'H_s.' According to Frege's method, there is an entity, e_1, named by this name; this is the truth-value of 'H_s.' And there is another entity, e_2, which is the sense of 'H_s'; this is the proposition that Scott is human. This proposition e_2 may also have a name; if we wish to speak about it, we need a name for it. This name is different from n_1 because the latter is the name of e_1 and hence, in a well-constructed language, should not be used simultaneously as a name of another entity. Let the new name be n_2. Like any name, n_2 has a sense. This sense of n_2 must be different from the nominatum of n_2; it is a new entity, e_3, not occurring in customary analyses. In order to speak about e_3, we need a new name, n_3. The sense of n_3 is a new entity e_4; and so forth *ad infinitum*.[68]

A question that needs to be asked at this point is whether or not the regress which is intrinsic to Husserl's and Frege's theory of sense is to be considered a fault in this theory, a fault which needs to be overcome. We hope to show that it is not a fault of a theory of sense that it result in a regress, but that it is of the very nature of sense itself.[69] In other words, we shall be coming down in support of Deleuze's claim that sense is at heart paradoxical, that it implies this regress (what Deleuze calls the 'paradox of regress').[70] A consequence of this is that sense is impotent and non-productive (an aspect of sense which we will find in Husserl's notion of the noema), nor can we ever express the sense of what we say (i.e., sense will never coincide with its object); but this also results in the power of language to speak about words, to double back upon language itself, to return to the source (Husserl's *Rückfrage*).[71] It is the power Husserl found in being able to return continually to the beginning, to launch again upon his quest to ground the science of phenomenology.

We shall now turn to an examination of Husserl's confrontation and recognition of this paradox of sense. We will see that Husserl neither accepted the paradox nor was unaware of it; rather, he continually attempted to assimilate the consequences of this paradox into his own system. His efforts in this regard are brilliant, and, because Husserl did want to ground the genuine and pure science of phenomenology, these efforts anticipate that which will fulfil this system and complete his efforts. The question concerning fulfilment thus returns once more.

III

In the Sixth Investigation, the question concerning fulfilment arises in the context of explaining how a sensuous intuition can fulfil a meaning-intention if the sensuous content is understood as interpretative sense, as form. Husserl thus recognizes that, although sensuous intuitions found meaning-intentions, they do not adequately found these intentions in that the intentions exceed that which is presented in sensuous intuition. Husserl gives an example of hearing a melody. In listening to a melody, that which is presented founds certain intentions. For example, in following the melodic line, I intend certain possible ways in which the melody might continue. I project future possibilities of a melody on the basis of what is given. The founding intuition of perceiving the melody (i.e., founding act of presentation) founds an intention which exceeds this intuition. In other words, Husserl accepts a paradoxical consequence of using the linguistic model in that meaning-intentions can be founded by that which does not found them. Husserl claims that 'we may say, in fact, with correct paradox that "indefiniteness" (i.e., the peculiarity of demanding an incompletely determined completion, which lies in a sphere circumscribed by a law) is a definite feature of such an intention.'[72] On the basis of the linguistic model, a founding act of presentation is necessary for a meaning-intention to have a content which is taken up and animated through an objectifying interpretation; however, this founding act of presentation is an inadequate founding act.

We have also discussed how the perceptual model was used to

explain both the founding act of presentation and the fulfilment of a meaning-intention. In the Sixth Investigation, however, we see that sensuous intuition neither adequately founds a meaning-intention (the meaning-intention exceeds that which is sensuously given) nor adequately fulfils such an intention. For example, a sensuous intuition which founds a linguistic expression, that is, a perceptual statement, neither adequately founds the word which expresses this intuition nor adequately fulfils the meaning-intention. As Husserl argues, 'the intention of the word "white" only partially coincides with the color-aspect of the apparent object; a surplus of meaning remains over, a form which finds nothing in the appearance itself to confirm it.'[73] That is, the intention of the word 'white' exceeds that which is given in that there is included in the expression an intention of a paper which *is* white, an intention of a substance which is white, and an intention of a 'white' which exceeds that which is immediately given (i.e., the various shades or things which could be perceived and yet be expressed by the word 'white'). As Taminiaux has noted, in the relationship between perception and a perceptual statement, 'the founded is in turn founder and excessive with respect to that upon which it is founded.'[74] A perception founds a sense which exceeds the givens of perception; consequently, we need to ask what can fulfil this founded which is excessive and founding with respect to this perception. Here we encounter what we have called 'the paradox of fulfilment': that is, an unfulfilled fulfilment. This is the paradoxical consequence of using the perceptual model to explain fulfilment on the basis of sensuous intuition, an intuition which fulfils an expression founded on this intuition when it does not fulfil it. In other words, the intention of the expression 'white' is meaningful (i.e., fulfilled, as opposed to an empty intention which, although meaningful, is a meaning derivative of an original intuition or act of presentation) only if there is the intuition of something 'white,' but this intuition does not fulfil or adequately found this intention. Husserl thus runs up against the regress pointed out above in that sensuous intuition founds and fulfils a meaning intention which in turn needs fulfilment (i.e., the regress of sense infinitely coinciding with sense). It is apparent, then, that Husserl recognized certain of the paradoxical consequences which followed upon his theory of sense; however, he sought to resolve the paradox through a theory of categorial intuition. Husserl turned to categorial intuition, for it became clear to him that sensuous intuition alone could not adequately fulfil meaning-intentions (e.g., linguistic expressions). Taminiaux was therefore correct to say that, since sensuous intuition 'cannot exercise the role of fulfillment, his problem is to extricate a non-sensuous intuitive field which might exercise this role.'[75] And it is precisely the field of categorial intuition which exercises this role.

Categorial intuition is a purely formal and non-sensuous act in that it directly intuits the form of a presentation rather than the 'matter' or sensed content of this presentation. For example, Husserl claims that categorial intuition is an act which takes up sensibility (here Husserl opposes sensations as stuff [Stoff] to sensations as 'matter,' as interpretative sense)[76] and gives it a categorial interpretation – that is, it intuits the form or category of this sensibility (e.g., 'white'). Thus Husserl claims that the 'fulfillment of categorial acts is founded on acts of sense. Mere sense, however, never fulfills categorial acts, or intentions which include categorial forms: fulfillment lies rather, in every case, in a sensibility structured by categorial acts.'[77] It is thus on the basis of sensuous intuition that one categorially intuits a concept (e.g., Being), but this intuition never fulfils these categorial acts (e.g., 'I can see color, but not being-colored ... being is absolutely imperceptible').[78] In other words, Husserl continues to accept the perceptual model in order to explain the fulfilment of an act, but it is the categorial form of fulfilment itself that is now used to explain the fulfilment of categorial acts. As Husserl argues, it is 'not in reflection upon judgments, nor even upon fulfillments of judgments, but in the fulfillments of judgments themselves [that] lies the true source of the concepts State of Affairs and Being.'[79] That is, it is not within the judging intention 'this paper is white' where one finds the concept Being (i.e., a meaningless, unfulfilable judgment will not present us with a concept of something which is; for example, the judgment 'this square is round' does not present us with the concept of something that is), nor is it in the sensuous fulfilment of this intention that one finds the concept Being – that is, one does not see 'being colored'; 'being is absolutely imperceptible.' Rather, Husserl claims that it is in the fulfilling of an intention, within the form of the fulfilment process itself, where the source of the concept Being lies. In other words, it is neither the contents of an act of judgment, nor the contents of a fulfilment, but the categorial form of a sensibility involved in the process of fulfilling an act: that is, it is in the presencing of the fulfilling wherein the concept Being is found. And this categorial form, as we have discussed, exceeds that which is given, and thus Being itself is a form which exceeds that which is given in sensuous intuition: thus Husserl claims that 'the form-giving flexion Being, whether in its attributive or predicative function, is not fulfilled as we said, in any percept.'[80] We thus see a similarity with Heidegger's notion of Being as the presencing of presence, the Being of beings, in that Husserl, too, implies Being as the 'presencing of fulfilling (i.e., presence),' as the Being which exceeds that which is given (being). Taminiaux notes that 'the excessiveness of Being over that which is, is recognized by Husserl, as we have seen, and it is this excessiveness that motivated Heidegger's fascination [with Husserl],'[81] and it is why Heidegger continued to find reason to study *Logical Investigations*.

This position of Husserl's, however, was offset by his continuing to explain the fulfilment of an act on the basis of an object: that is, on the basis of, in Heidegger's sense, being rather than Being. We see this most clearly in Husserl's discussion of the distinction between static and dynamic union. A static union, on the one hand, is characterized by the recognition (re-cognition) of an object (i.e., a being). We recognize an object through a given intuition (e.g., perception), but we immediately recognize this object as a *meaningful type* of object, as an object which can be named. In fact, for Husserl it is not that the object first appears and then there occurs the name or type of object that it is; rather, in recognition the object is immediately presented as a certain type of object, and as an object of expression it 'is clothed with the expression like a garment.'[82] This was especially clear in the case of demonstratives, as discussed above, in that the meaning-intention immediately implies its intuition and we have the 'conceptual thought playing the part of an intuition.'[83]

Dynamic union, on the other hand, is characterized by the consciousness of fulfilment whereby a meaning-intention and the fulfilling intuition are transitionally understood. That is, it is a meaning-intention which is in the process of fulfilment, the presencing of fulfilment (i.e., Being, in Heidegger's sense). The consciousness of fulfilment is thus a unity which is disjoined in time, a unity of a meaning-intention which is separated in time from that which is fulfilling it: 'In the dynamic relationship the members of the relation, and the act of recognition which relates them, are disjoined in time: they unfold themselves in a temporal pattern.'[84]

The union of an act of meaning and an act of intuition is therefore understood both in terms of *identity*, as the static union of a meaning-intention (e.g., expression) which is 'most intimately one' with the object recognized and given in intuition, and in terms of *difference*, as the dynamic union of a meaning-intention which is differentiated (disjoined) in time from the act of intuition which fulfils it. To put it another way, the static union expresses a temporal coincidence and identity, and the dynamic union expresses a temporal disjunction and difference. Husserl then claims that the dynamic relationship is more fundamental, and that the static union is only the result of the repetition (re-cognition) of the same dynamic union which over time produces an immediate recognition rather than a transitional recognition: 'In the static relationship, which represents the lasting outcome of this temporal transaction, they occur in temporal and material coincidence.'[85]

This static union is what we will call here 'the domestication of becoming and difference.' That is, the static relationship expresses the result of transforming the temporal difference of the dynamic union into the temporal identity and coincidence of static union. And it is precisely this transformation of difference and becoming into identity and being (i.e., object) that we refer to as 'domestication.' Consequently, following from domestication, Husserl is concerned, not with 'a coming into coincidence, but a being coincident.'[86] Ricoeur was thus correct to say that 'what interests Husserl in consciousness is not its genius, its power to invent in every sense of the term, but the stable, unified significations into which it moves and becomes established.'[87] Furthermore, although Husserl does claim that the static union is the result of a 'domestication' of the dynamic union, he nevertheless presupposes the identity of being, an object in general, as the condition which makes possible this domestication; and here we see Husserl offsetting his notion of being as the 'presencing of fulfillment' with a notion of being as an object in general, an object which ultimately conditions and determines the possibility of the presencing of fulfilment.

We see Husserl moving in this direction when he claims: 'Identity, it is plain, is not first dragged in through comparative, cogitatively mediated reflection: it is there from the start as experience, as unexpressed, unconceptualized experience.'[88] In other words, this means for Husserl that a meaning-giving act and an act of intuition, as acts, can be called acts in that each 'has its own peculiar intentional correlate, an objective something to which it is "directed."'[89] Husserl therefore bases an objective identification, whether a dynamic or static union of identification, upon an identifiable something which makes possible the relational identifications between a meaning-intention and an intuition. This is important for Husserl because, for example, when a name is applied to an object of intuition, we are referring to the intuited and named *object*, not to the identity of this object as something at once intuited and named. In other words, no act of relational identification is founded upon the experienced unity of a named object;[90] however, Husserl claims that 'the passage from a consciousness of unity to a relational identification always remains open, has a possibility guaranteed *a priori*, so that we are entitled to say that an identifying coincidence has been experienced, even if there is no conscious intention directed to identity, and no relational identification.'[91] The reason for this is that the relational identification (i.e., an act of identifying a meaning intention with an act of intuition, either statically or dynamically) is guaranteed *a priori* because, as an act, there must be the identity of something, of an object in general, which conditions and makes possible our experienced unity and consciousness of objects. In short, it is the condition which makes possible the intentionality of consciousness.

The same is true for what Husserl believes to be the most perfect form of identity, the most complete unity of an intention and its intuitive fulfilment: that is, self-evidence. Husserl claims that 'self-evidence itself is the most perfect synthesis of fulfilment. Like every identification, it is an objectifying act, its objective correlate being called being in the sense of truth.'[92] However, just as the experience of objective unity need not entail the act of identifying an object as the unity of an expressive act with an act of intuition (e.g., perception), so, too, we can experience self-evidence as the 'most perfect synthesis of fulfillment' without identifying this self-evidence as truth, as the adequate correspondence or fulfilment of an intention by an intuition. This is nevertheless guaranteed *a priori* by the self-identity of an object in general, by the identity of this object with itself (i.e., self-identity of Being as an object – as 'being,' in Heidegger's sense), and it is this self-identity which makes possible the act of identifying self-evidence, of perceiving the truth.

It is now clear how important the notion of an object in general is in Husserl's thought. It is that which explains fulfilment in every sense of the word, even its most ideal form as truth; and it is for this reason that, despite Husserl's moves in the direction of discussing the importance of the dynamic union, of the presencing of the fulfilment (i.e., 'Being,' in Heidegger's sense), he nevertheless continues to return to the notion of an object in general (i.e., 'being,' in Heidegger's sense) as what will explain fulfilment and allow it to pass.

This is apparent even within Husserl's discussion of categorial intuition when he utilizes the perceptual model[93] to explain the fulfilment of categorial acts. Husserl claims that it is on the basis of an object (as it was with a perceived object) that a categorial intuition is fulfilled. We thus have Husserl claiming, on the one hand, that the sensibility is structured and taken up by a categorial act; on the other, he argues that, 'if we are asked what it means to say that categorially structured meanings find fulfillment, confirm themselves in perception, we can but reply: it means only that they relate to *the object itself* in its categorial structure.'[94] In other words, it is because there is an object which fulfils an intuition that we are able to have a categorial intuition, and thus the concept Being. We therefore see Husserl repeating the difficulties mentioned earlier: that is, how a categorial act can take up a sensibility in order to determine *what* a categorial object is intended as, while maintaining it is *that* a categorially structured object is presented which enables us to intuit it as we do. Without resolving the ambiguities discussed earlier, Husserl's turn to the non-sensuous field of categorial intuition merely repeats them. In other words, the moves Husserl makes in order to resolve the paradox of sense in the end repeat the paradox. We see the paradox repeated here in that each categorial act structures (constitutes)[95] a sensibility on the basis of 'the (constituted) object itself in its categorial structure'; therefore, each constituting act requires a constituted object to work from, but each constituted object is itself the result of a constituting act, an act which in turn worked on the basis of a constituted object, and so on. Husserl's theory of categorial intuition does not resolve the paradox of regress.

One way to avoid this infinite regress, the regress of sense infinitely coinciding with sense, is to argue that it ends at a point where there is no difference between the sense of an object and the object itself. We saw that sense infinitely coincided with sense because sense never coincided with its object; therefore, if there is an instance where sense does coincide with its object, an instance which grounds all other instances of sense and object, then the regress will be resolved. This is precisely the move Husserl makes in analysing internal time-consciousness. The regress which followed from the irreducible difference between a *constituting* sense (interpretative sense) which determines *what* an object is intended as and the *constituted* object as *that* which is intended in any act will be resolved if there is something which is simultaneously constituting and constituted. And this is what Husserl believes to be characteristic of time-consciousness as a self-constituted unity: 'As startling (if not at first sight even contradictory) as it may appear to assert that the flux of consciousness constitutes its own unity, it is still true, nevertheless.'[96] Furthermore, it is on the basis of this self-constitution that Husserl moves to explain the role and place of sensations, an issue which, as we saw, remained problematic in *Logical Investigations*. Heidegger recognized the centrality of this theme, and, in his foreword to *The Phenomenology of Internal Time-Consciousness*, he claimed that 'the pervading theme of the present study is the temporal constitution of a pure datum of sensation and the self-constitution of "phenomenological time" which underlies such a constitution.'[97]

In the next chapter, we examine more closely Husserl's attempts to resolve the paradoxical consequences which arose from the theory of sense that he set forth in *Logical Investigations*. It will be on the basis of Husserl's discussion of the self-constitution of time-consciousness that he will then modify his theory of sense and attempt to further explain the fulfilment of sense by intuitive acts. Our discussion of the linguistic and perceptual models will continue to be our theme; however, we shall see that the noema which mediated between a linguistic intention and a sensuous intuition (i.e., the 'perceptual noema') needs to be understood in light of Husserl's attempts to resolve the paradoxical consequences which are implicit within *Logical Investigations*. That many interpreters have failed to see that the theory of the noema arose out of these efforts has resulted in opposing interpretations of the noema, and, in particular, of the perceptual noema.

II. The Perceptual Noema

In our discussions in chapter I, I have highlighted what Husserl believes to be an irreducible difference, a difference he continued to accept despite certain problematic consequences which he attempts to clarify through his analysis of time-consciousness. To illustrate this difference, Husserl used what we called the 'linguistic' and 'perceptual' models. By means of the linguistic model, Husserl demonstrates that what is experienced in attending to an expression is the sense or meaning of this expression, not the physical sounds or marks which carry this meaning. The experienced meaning (object) is given through physical means, but the meaning itself is independent of its manners of givenness and cannot be reduced to them; therefore, despite the need for the sense of an expression to be given or understood on the basis of a presentative act (e.g., speech, writing), the sense itself transcends these acts as that which is meant through them. In order to show how this transcendent meaning can be understood, and how it is possible that an object can be given in a variety of acts while continuing to be the same, Husserl turns to the perceptual model. In this model, for example, the same object can be perceived from a number of perspectives, and in so far as they are all perspectives of the same object, each of them (i.e., each perceptual act) is essentially related to the others. Yet this relation differs from that relation which holds between the sense of an expression and the expression of this sense. The latter is only contingently related to the sense which transcends it. One could imagine another expression (a number of acts) being used to express the same sense (i.e., object), but this is not the case with percepts if they are of one and the same object. The percepts (i.e., acts) cannot be other than what they are if the object is to remain the same, and thus perception is an example for Husserl of the intuitive grasp of a self-identical object. It is in this manner, then, that Husserl develops his understanding of the fundamental and irreducible difference between an experienced object as it is given in intuitive presentation (e.g., perceptually) and the manners in which this object is given as an intended object, as that which is signitively meant (e.g., linguistically).

A complication is added to this discussion, however, in that Husserl goes on to claim that the same matter can be taken up by both signitive acts and intuitive acts. For example, an expression which is intended to convey a meaning as the object of a signitive act can in turn be the object of an intuitive act. I can hear the sounds, or see a written word, without attending to the meaning, and yet the matter is the same whether it is taken up signitively or intuitively.[1] If one were to ask how it is possible that the same matter can be taken up in either an intuitive or a signitive act, and what the nature of this matter is which allows for these two different acts, Husserl admits that 'I can give them no further answer. We are facing a difference that cannot be phenomenologically reduced.'[2] In other words, both signitive and intuitive acts, as acts, require something to work from, something which will be taken up in the act, and, despite the fact that in both cases this matter can be the same, there is nevertheless an irreducible difference between the acts themselves. It is this difference which we have seen elaborated in our discussions of the linguistic and perceptual models. It is also this difference, what Husserl also identifies as the difference between *thinking* and *seeing*, which he believes has been inadequately explored and discerned within the philosophic tradition.[3] A reason for this, as Husserl admits, is that signitive (thinking) and intuitive (seeing) acts often use the same matter, and in the case of 'symbols' and 'symbolic thinking' there is even a commingling of these acts;[4] however, Husserl claims that these acts are, in principle, separable. More importantly, it is only in recognizing this possible separation and difference that one can argue against what Husserl calls a 'technization' of thought, a thought which has lost its intuitive foundations and become a technological skill of associating and using symbols. This critique of the technization of thought runs throughout Husserl's career, and it is the motivation behind his use of the linguistic and perceptual models.[5]

There was, however, an evident regress which our investigations of the linguistic and perceptual models revealed. It arose as a consequence of the irreducible difference between *sense*, which the linguistic model sought to explain, and *object*, which the perceptual model sought to explain. The result was an infinite regress of sense for ever coinciding with sense without ever being fulfilled, a regress which follows from the claim that sense never coincides with its object, that they are irreducibly different. On the one hand, sense is not the act itself, but the interpretative form of this act which determines *what* an object is intended as. On the other hand, sense is not the object itself, but the objective correlate of this act which determines *that* there is an object towards which this act is directed. For the sense to be an object itself would require a new act which has this sense as *that* towards which the act is directed; however, as an act there will be an interpretative form, a sense, which is in turn neither the act nor the object itself, but could become the object of another new act, and so on *ad infinitum*. In the period following Husserl's writings on time-consciousness, and in an unpublished manuscript quoted by Dagfinn Føllesdal, Husserl recognizes precisely this regress: 'The Sinn corresponding to an object is in its turn an object ... it can be made the object of a judgment ... As such it has a Sinn of the second level: the Sinn of a Sinn ... hence we come to an infinite regress, insofar as the Sinn of a Sinn may in its turn be made an object and then again has a Sinn and so on.'[6] This regress is not problematic for Husserl because, as he says in the same manuscript, it occurs within the unity of time-consciousness;[7] that is, it is within the unity of time-consciousness as a self-constituted unity that this regress occurs. Consequently, as mentioned at the end of chapter I, it is this self-constituted unity of time-consciousness where the coincidence of sense and object, the coincidence of constituting and constituted, ends the regress and is the non-regressive condition for the regress of sense that Husserl now recognizes. To clarify this point, and to see how this results in the notion of the noema, we shall turn now to a brief discussion of time-consciousness.

1. Self-Constitution

The irreducible difference between signitive and intuitive acts emerges in Husserl's writings on time-consciousness as the difference between that which is presented to consciousness and that which is 'presentified' to consciousness. In a present act of consciousness, for example, perception, an object is intuitively presented to consciousness as self-given, as a transcendent unity which can be perceived from a number of perspectives other than the one through which it is actually being perceived. Through an act of perception, I now perceive an object as present for consciousness. In recollection of this act, however, I bring this act before consciousness, and with this act the object is presented 'as if' it were present – it is 'presentified.' Recollection is therefore an act which Husserl claims functions like imaginative consciousness: they each posit an object that is not present, but is 'presentified' 'as if' it were present.[8] However, if it is through recollection that we are conscious of the past, then it would seem to follow that the status of the past itself would be no different from the status of an imagined object. The past could not be real, could not be presented, but could only be imagined or 'presentified.' This is a consequence Husserl did not accept, but it is one that Husserl believes Brentano did accept, and it is on the basis of his criticism of Brentano that Husserl formulates his theory of a 'presented' past which ultimately founds the 'presentifying' acts of recollection.

Husserl criticizes Brentano's notion that the past is present to consciousness only through imagination by claiming that the past itself is contained within the unity of a *present* consciousness as what 'has been,' or what Husserl calls a 'retention.' In other words, everything which is presented to consciousness is presented both as that which is now present for consciousness, what Husserl calls the 'primal impression,' and this same primal impression as modified, as presented in the mode 'has been,' but nevertheless *presented* within the unity of *the same present consciousness*. Using the perception of a melody as an example, Husserl claims 'when the tonal now, the primal impression, passes over into retention, this retention is itself again a now, an actual existent ... it is the retention of a sound that has been.'[9] In other words, that which is presented to consciousness is a primal impression, a perception which is then subject to the modification of retention such that it is now presented as what has been, a modified now. Husserl claims further that 'every actual now of consciousness is subject to the law of modification';[10] however, the retentional modification of this primal impression is not perceived, but is presented before the unity of a present (now) consciousness as what has been perceived, as what is not now perceived. In fact, Husserl claims that retention, as well as protention, which he defines here as primary remembrance and primary expectation, are the antithesis of perception: 'the antithesis of perception is primary remembrance, which appears here, and primary expectation (retention and protention), whereby perception and non-perception *continually pass over into one another*.'[11] There is thus an irreducible difference here which results for Husserl in an admitted infinite regress; however, it is a regress which occurs within the continuous unity of a single continuum, a continuum which is itself continuously modified. And it is the continuous modification of this continuum which is to be understood as the infinite regress inherent in the 'now,' where a 'now, which, as soon as we divide it further, immediately breaks down again into a finer now and a past, etc.'[12] That is, a now can for ever be broken down into a finer now and a past because the now and the past never coincide; yet they do occur within the single unity or continuum of consciousness, and it is this unity or continuum which is the non-regressive foundation for the regress.

Through this discussion of the unity of perception and non-perception within the continuity of consciousness, we find Husserl now able to clarify the ambiguous role of sensations as set forth in *Logical Investigations*. In the *Investigations*, sensations are understood both as the matter which is taken up by an objectifying act, the constituted given this act takes up, and as the matter which is the form (interpretative sense) of this act, the constitutive form of the act itself. In other words, Husserl does not adequately distinguish between a sensed content and the sensing of this content, between *what* an act takes up and *how* it takes it up. The result of not clearly making this distinction between the constituting and constituted elements of the act itself, as we saw, was an implicit regress in Husserl's position. In *The Phenomenology of Internal Time-Consciousness*, however, Husserl clearly makes the distinction between the constitutive flux of consciousness itself and the constituted elements within the immanence of this consciousness. Husserl argues that 'we must distinguish at all times: consciousness (flux), appearance (immanent Object), and transcendent object'; and he goes on to claim that 'that which in *Logischen Untersuchungen* is termed an "act" or an "intentional lived experience" is a flux in which an immanent temporal unity is constituted.'[13] In *Logical Investigations*, it was left unclear whether these immanent objects were constituted or not; consequently, these immanent objects presupposed a constituting act, but this act in turn presupposed an already-constituted object, and so on *ad infinitum*. However, in *The Phenomenology of Internal Time-Consciousness*, Husserl turns to an analysis of an absolute consciousness (i.e., what he calls 'a flux') which does not presuppose a constituted object.[14] In fact, Husserl claims that subjective time itself is an object constituted by an absolute consciousness, that 'subjective time is constituted in absolute, timeless consciousness which is not an Object.'[15] Husserl thus understands absolute consciousness to be the primal source for all immanently constituted objectivities, and it is a consciousness which does not entail any already-constituted objects. As John Brough has remarked in discussing Husserl's formulation of an absolute consciousness, it entails a break from Husserl's earlier analysis of 'acts' as set forth in *Logical Investigations* (what Brough calls, as mentioned in the previous chapter, 'the schematic interpretation'), and in so doing he 'draws a sharp distinction within consciousness itself between two dimensions, one constituting in the ultimate sense, the other constituted but still immanent.'[16] In order to understand what Husserl means by a 'constituted but still immanent' aspect of consciousness itself, and thus to clarify the notion of an immanent object (which emerges later as 'noema'), we need to return to a discussion of retentional modification.

Husserl repeatedly points out that an immanent objectivity needs to be distinguished, first, from the things of experience in objective time, for example, our experience of things in the world persisting through time; and we then need to distinguish it from 'the absolute temporally constitutive flux of consciousness,'[17] the flux which constitutes this immanent objectivity. Husserl claims that the latter 'is something which we name in conformity with what is constituted, but it is nothing temporally "Objective."'[18] In other words, one cannot attribute temporal qualities such as duration and persistence since these are qualities that pertain to temporal objectivities; consequently, as Husserl claims later, 'there is no duration in the primordial flux,' and since it is on the basis of duration that one is able to say of something that it persists, it also follows that 'to the essence of flux there can be nothing persistent in it.'[19] This absolute flux, however, does constitute duration and persistence, and it is on this basis that Husserl argues for the constituted nature of the data of sensation.

By claiming that the data of sensation are themselves constituted, Husserl is simply saying that, for a datum to be perceived and apprehended as such, it needs to persist in some way before consciousness. In order for something to be seen, this something must be present in time, it must persist long enough to be apprehended as a datum; and since persistence and duration are themselves constituted unities, it is clear why Husserl claims that we must 'take into account that the data of sensation which play their role in the constitution of a transcendent object are themselves constituted unities in a temporal flow.'[20] In other words, for something to be apprehended there must already be something for this apprehension, an already-constituted datum which apprehension takes up. This pre-given datum is precisely the matter which, as discussed in chapter I, an act takes up and gives an objectifying interpretation. Here Husserl defines apprehension in much this same way when he claims it is the 'animation of the datum of sensation'; however, Husserl is now accounting for the constitution of this datum of sensation, and thus is attempting to resolve the regress implicit within his position in *Logical Investigations*.

In clarifying his claim that the datum of sensation must be constituted before the animating apprehension can begin, that it does not emerge simultaneously with this apprehension, Husserl argues that, 'in the moment in which the apprehension begins, a part of the datum of sensation has already expired and is only retentionally retained.'[21] In other words, the primal impression is given to an animating apprehension as something which both *is* and *has been*; that is, as something (a unity) which has persisted within a duration of time. The datum of sensation is therefore a temporal unity before being apprehended, and it is this temporal unity, as a datum which has been retained, which is what is given to an animating apprehension of this datum as an object. Apprehension thus animates not only the momentary phase of the primal impression, 'but also the total datum, including the interval which has expired';[22] that is, the total datum is a unity of persistence, a primal impression that has been retained, and it is this unity which conditions the apprehension of an 'Object.'

Husserl, following through on the claim that the animating apprehension does not occur simultaneously with the datum apprehended, also claims that a perceived 'object' does not arise simultaneously with its perception. In other words, there is a temporal *difference* between the beginning point of perception (i.e., the datum of sensation) and the beginning point of the object (i.e., the animating apprehension of this datum). For example, we do not perceive our sensations, say, red sensations; we perceive only objects, but we perceive objects only if there are sensations already given to perception. There is thus an irreducible temporal difference between a perceived external object and the datum of sensation which precedes this perception. This difference, however, is appropriate only for the perception of transcendent objects, and, when Husserl turns from the perception of external objects to the internal perception of *immanent objects*, we find him claiming that there is a simultaneity of the perceiving and the perceived.

The reason Husserl argues for the simultaneity of the perceiving and the perceived with respect to internal perception is that the original primal impression, the momentary phase which is retained, is itself primordially constituted by a consciousness which does not apprehend this immanent content. If the consciousness which constituted this primal impression were to apprehend this impression, then it would in turn require an already-given content to be animated by this apprehension, and thus we would again have a regress that Husserl wanted to avoid. In order to avoid this, Husserl claims that the absolute consciousness is not an apprehending consciousness, and that the immanent objects constituted by it reflect the way in which this consciousness constitutes its own unity, a unity which is not itself an object apprehended, and as such it is an object or content that is, for Husserl, 'unconscious':

> One may by no means misinterpret this primal consciousness, this primal apprehension, or whatever he wishes to call it, as an apprehending act ... If one says that every content attains consciousness only through an act of apprehension directed thereon, then the question immediately arises as to the consciousness in which we are aware of this act, which itself is still a content, thus the infinite regress is unavoidable. However, if every 'content' necessarily and in itself is 'unconscious' then the question of an additional dator consciousness becomes senseless.[23]

Husserl therefore recognizes the difference between an immanent constituted object and the absolute consciousness which constitutes this object (i.e., the difference between the perceiving and the perceived); however, he then claims that this simply demonstrates the two types of intentionality which characterize this absolute consciousness. There is what Husserl calls 'vertical intentionality,' an intentionality which intends the unity of an object that stands above the flux of consciousness (i.e., the unity of immanent objects, such as the immanent temporal unity of the datum of sensation); and there is 'horizontal intentionality' which intends the unity of the flux of consciousness itself,[24] and yet it is within the same absolute flux of consciousness that these two intentionalities occur: 'It is the one unique flux of consciousness in which the immanent temporal unity of the sound and also the unity of the flux of consciousness itself are constituted.'[25] The absolute consciousness thus constitutes itself, constitutes its own unity, and is therefore the coincidence of constituting and constituted, which is the coincidence we claimed Husserl needed in order to avoid the regress discussed in chapter I: 'As startling (if not at first sight even contradictory) as it may appear to assert that the flux of consciousness constitutes its own unity, it is still true, nevertheless.'[26]

We also see these two intentionalities reflected in two fundamental types of retentional modification. Husserl argues that there must be two types of retentional modification, for 'if in this flux lived experiences which are not "internal perceptions" are to be possible [i.e., if there is to be a difference between perceiving and perceived], there must be retentional series of two kinds. Thus with the constitution of the flux as unity through "internal" retention [i.e., horizontal intentionality] there must in addition be a series of external ones [i.e., vertical intentionality]. The latter series constitutes Objective time (a constituted immanence, external with regard to the former but still immanent).'[27] Put more simply, if there is to be the consciousness of an objective unity, for example, consciousness of a sound which has just been, then there must in turn be the consciousness of the unity of the consciousness which perceived this sound that has just been; and since it is the self-constitutive nature of absolute consciousness which entails these two fundamental intentionalities, it is therefore the condition for the perception of any external and transcendent object (i.e., it is the differentiating condition for the difference between the perceiving and the perceived).

A further consequence of the self-constitutive nature of absolute consciousness, of a consciousness that constitutes its own unity, is that it is implicitly a self-consciousness. In other words, if absolute consciousness constitutes its own unity, then it constitutes its own form; consequently, the form of time-consciousness itself is a constituted form, and it is constituted as a pre-immanent temporality in that it is the form the experience of subjective time will take (i.e., the form of immanent and objective time), but is not this experience itself. Absolute consciousness thus constitutes its own unity as the form of time-consciousness, as the form which makes possible an immanent objective time, and as a result time-consciousness itself will imply the self-consciousness of this absolute consciousness. As Husserl argues,

> the flux of the immanent, temporally constitutive consciousness (i.e., time-consciousness) not only *is*, but is so remarkably and yet so intelligibly constituted that a self-appearance of the flux necessarily subsists in it, and hence the flux itself must necessarily be comprehensible in the flowing. The self-appearance of the flux does not require a second flux [i.e., no regress], but qua phenomenon it is constituted in itself.[28]

Absolute consciousness is the self-constituting flux which is not itself temporal, does not endure or persist; rather, it constitutes the form of temporal objectivity, and consequently constitutes subjective time itself ('Subjective time is constituted in absolute timeless consciousness, which is not an object'). This form is not an object, but is a pre-immanent temporality and is therefore a constituted content which is 'unconscious': that is, it is not an apprehended object, but is the form which makes possible the apprehension of an object. Consequently, Husserl takes time-consciousness to be a peculiar type of consciousness which takes this pre-temporal form as its object, and as such constitutes an immanent objective time which is implicitly a reflection upon the form constituted by absolute consciousness (i.e., self-consciousness). In other words, our experience of subjective time occurs within the pre-immanent temporality of absolute consciousness. We can in principle reflect upon this pre-immanent temporality (i.e., the constituted form) and take it as an immanent objective time for time-consciousness, but this in turn will occur within the pre-immanent temporality of absolute consciousness, and so on. It appears we have reached another regress.

This infinite regress, however, is not one which Husserl will find troublesome; on the contrary, he ultimately claims that it is of the nature of absolute consciousness that it be infinitely open to reflection, that its horizon is an infinite horizon. For example, Husserl claims that, in attending to a sound, this sound appears with a given duration, and this duration is, as mentioned earlier, a unity constituted by consciousness. The sound thus appears as an objective unity which appears in time, yet we can reflect upon the temporal form of the constitutive series itself and take this for our object. In other words, we have returned to the issue of the continuous modifications of the continuum and the infinite regress of the 'now' which can forever be divided into a finer now and a finer past. We now see that what Husserl ultimately means by this continuum wherein the infinite regress of the now occurs, is the self-constitutive nature of absolute consciousness whereby the constituted forms taken up by time-consciousness are implicitly self-consciousness, a self-consciousness and reflection which is forever open and possible. As Husserl states in Appendix VI:

> We have, therefore, a continuous consciousness, of which every point is a stable continuum. This continuum, however, is again a temporal series to which we can attend. Thus the business begins afresh. If we fix any point of this series, it appears that a consciousness of the past must pertain to it, which consciousness refers to the series of past series, and so on.
>
> Even if reflection is not carried out *ad infinitum* and if, in general, no reflection is necessary, still that which makes this reflection possible, and, in principle possible *ad infinitum* must be given.[29]

Husserl thus recognizes and accepts this infinite regress as an essential possibility of consciousness to reflect upon itself, to be open to further determinations, to be, as Husserl discusses this in the *Crisis*, the horizon of 'infinite tasks.'[30] But the question remains, however, concerning the relationship between this absolute self-constituting consciousness and perceptual consciousness. Although Husserl has discussed the constituted nature of the datum of sensation, he has discussed this datum only as a constituted temporal unity, as a datum whose temporal duration allows it to be apprehended as a datum, and as the datum of an object. Even if we accept this as a necessary condition for the perception of an object, this still does not shed any light on why the datum is apprehended in the particular way that it is (i.e., why it is fulfilled in the particular way that it is). For example, why is there a perception of a red object rather than a green object? Why is there the perception of a circle rather than an ellipse? And what criterion determines whether what I remember is something that actually happened, something that I justifiably believe to have occurred in the past, or simply an imagined memory about something that didn't really happen? In other words, even though absolute consciousness entails the coincidence of constituting and constituted, and as such is the non-regressive differentiating condition which makes possible the irreducible differences between constituting and constituted, perceiving and perceived, sense and object, and hence is the condition for the regress, the question still remains how a subject can, in fact, attain intuitively fulfilled and objective knowledge. How does this transcendental coincidence of sense and object resolve the difficulty of accounting for how an actual subject can obtain the coincidence of sense and object? We thus once again encounter the question of fulfilment: how do immanent objects get fulfilled in the ways that they do, and does this in turn allow Husserl to account for the possibility of intuitively fulfilled and objective knowledge? To see how he goes about answering these questions, and to clarify the relationship between perceptual consciousness and the absolute consciousness of 'infinite tasks,' we turn now to Husserl's work in *Ideas*, in particular, to his discussion of morphological essences.

2. Morphological Essences

Husserl's discussion of morphological essences develops from a distinction he makes between the descriptive contents and concepts of natural science and the ideal contents and concepts of exact science. In the first case, the natural scientist develops concepts which may be apprehended on the basis of sensory intuition. For example, Husserl claims such concepts as 'notched, indented, lens-shaped, umbelliform, and the like'[31] are concepts which cannot be exactly determined: there is a vague and inexact flux within which something may be accurately described as 'lens-shaped.' However, Husserl claims that these vague concepts, what he calls 'morphological concepts,' do not express a defect on the part of the descriptive sciences which they should attempt to overcome; rather, these concepts are 'flatly indispensable to the sphere of knowledge they serve, or, as we may also say, they are within this sphere the only concepts justified.'[32] In other words, although one may not be able to determine or define exactly a concept such as lens-shaped, or roundness, there is nevertheless no ambiguity in our perceiving something as such. We perceive something as lens-shaped, as round, and we perceive this unambiguously. It would therefore be more accurate to say that the morphological concepts are anexact, that they are *essentially and not accidentally inexact*;[33] that is, they are not inexact, in the sense of sensible things, because they can be rigorously and essentially applied. One will unhesitatingly apply the concepts; however, these morphological concepts are not exactly defined either. When one attempts to determine this concept in a precise manner that is independent of its being perceived, then the vagueness becomes apparent.[34] It is for this reason Husserl argues that, on the basis of sensory intuition, these morphological concepts are 'directly apprehended, and, vague as they are, conceptually or terminologically fixed.'[35] In other words, Husserl claims that 'morphological essences, as correlates of descriptive contents,'[36] are the objective correlates which can be 'conceptually or terminologically fixed,' and as such morphological essences are constitutive of the 'only concepts justified' within the descriptive natural sciences. The descriptive natural sciences therefore begin and end their efforts with that which is seen.

In the case of the exact sciences, however, their concepts express something which is ideal, 'something which one cannot "see."'[37] In other words, unlike the descriptive student of nature, the scientist of ideal concepts – the geometer, for example – is uninterested in the actual forms which can be intuited through the senses. The geometer is not concerned, for example, with the sensory intuition and concept of 'roundness'; rather, he is concerned with the ideal concept of the 'circle,' a concept which is never intuited by the senses. It is for this reason that Husserl believes the geometer cannot help the descriptive scientist: the concepts of the geometer are not to be found in any description. There is, however, an interesting relationship between these two sciences in that the ideal concepts of the one express the 'ideal "limits"' which cannot on principle be found in any sensory intuition, to which on occasion morphological essences "approximate" more or less.'[38] That is, the ideal concepts express a limit reached after an infinite number of determinations, determinations only finitely carried out by the descriptive sciences which only more or less approximate this limit. These ideal concepts are thus to be understood as the invariant poles of an infinite determination which Husserl claims 'have the character of "Ideas" in the Kantian sense.'[39] We thus see emerging here an accounting of the infinite tasks that followed upon the regressive nature of time-consciousness; that is, Husserl believes these infinite tasks have an ideal correlate, an 'Idea' in the Kantian sense, which is the invariant pole that can be infinitely determined. In fact, Husserl claims that we can 'apprehend in a certain way ... the stream of experience as a unity also ... after the fashion of an Idea in the Kantian sense.'[40] In other words, the unity of the absolute flux, a flux forever opened to reflection within time-consciousness, can be grasped as the invariant pole or unity of these reflective determinations.[41]

The distinction between morphological and ideal essences appears, on the one hand, to resolve some of the difficulties mentioned earlier concerning a 'sensuous filling.' We saw that as long as sensuous intuition was understood in light of its interpretative sense, its abstractable form, it would in turn require a fulfiling intuition, and thus arose the regress of sense infinitely coinciding with sense. One way to avoid this regress, as was mentioned, would be to have a sensuous form that coincided with its intuitive content (which is what is meant by a 'sensuous filling'). The morphological essence seems to do just this. The morphological essence is a sensuous form which can be directly apprehended by sensory intuition, and the resulting vague concept is precisely the expression of a form which coincides, however vaguely, with its intuitive content. On the other hand, since Husserl places the morphological essence in relation to an ideal essence which it simply 'approximates, more or less,' then it appears that Husserl has simply repeated the same difficulties. If the morphological essence approximates the ideal essence, then it must in some way anticipate this essence; in other words, there must be an anticipatory or ideal structure to the morphological essence, a structure abstractable from its vague content, and a structure which makes possible the ideal passage to the limit, a limit which fulfils this abstractable structure.

The ambiguity here can be made clearer if we note that Husserl uses the notion of a Kantian Idea in both an omnitemporal and supratemporal sense, whereby the Idea has a history which is both immanent and transcendent, a history that reflects the horizontal and vertical intentionalities discussed in the previous section. The Idea is thus manifest within the processes of determination, within the flux of consciousness, and in this way is the anticipatory ground and condition for the passage to the limit; and the Idea is the limit which transcends these determinations and processes, and is that which validates and fulfils these processes. In the first instance, Idea is understood as the unity of the flux itself, the unity immanent to consciousness (i.e., horizontal intentionality). In the second instance, Idea is understood as the unity which transcends the flux (i.e., vertical intentionality). The morphological essence reflects both aspects: it is both an Idea more or less approximated within the processes of description, and the anticipation and condition for transcending these processes of description, for the Idea as the invariant pole of an infinite determination.

It can now be seen that morphological essences bring in the ambiguities we examined earlier concerning sensations. On the one hand, sensations appeared to be simply the matter which is taken up by an act, the material which receives an objectifying interpretation, and as such they were understood as the already-constituted pre-given which is necessary for an objectifying act. On the other hand, sensations also appeared to be the 'interpretative sense' of the act, the form of the interpretation itself which can be expressed and understood by those who had not perceived that which is being expressed. In the same way, morphological essences appear to be an already-constituted ideality which anticipates and more or less approximates the exact essence which is grounded thereby. The ideation which apprehends an exact essence as a Kantian Idea, as the invariant pole of an infinite determination, does so by taking up and going beyond this pre-given morphological essence. Morphological essences are also idealities which can themselves be directly apprehended, they can be 'conceptually and terminologically fixed,' and they are also 'flatly indispensable to the sphere of knowledge they serve.' In other words, morphological essences are both constitutive, in the sense that they are constitutive of the concepts and terms which found, despite their anexact and vague nature, the sphere of knowledge associated with descriptive natural science, and they are also the constituted givens upon which the exact sciences such as geometry are founded. Husserl, however, does not clarify how the morphological essences themselves are constituted, just as earlier he did not clarify how the sensations were constituted; consequently, in so far as morphological essences are both constituting and constituted, Husserl, as Derrida has shown, attempts to avoid an infinite regress in explaining the origin of geometry.[42] Despite this move, however, morphological essences implicitly have the same unresolved ambiguity that characterized the earlier discussion of sensations, and thus it seems the same regressive difficulties we found in the earlier case would also apply here. However, and perhaps in recognition of the difficulties inherent here, Husserl turns to a clarification of the nature of sensations, or sensory matter, and their role in acts of consciousness.

In *Ideas*, Husserl continues to understand sensations as the matter taken up by an animating and objectifying interpretation. He claims, and we will discuss this in more detail when we turn to the perceptual noema as set forth in *Ideas*, that the sensile element, what he calls *hyle*, is the material stratum of an intention animated by a meaning-bestowing stratum, and it is through this animation that 'out of the sensile element, which contains in itself nothing intentional, the concrete intentional experience takes form and shape.'[43] The meaning-bestowing stratum thus in-forms the material stratum; however, Husserl reminds us that this duality between the *hyle* and the informing (what he calls *morphe*) occurs 'within the stage of constituted temporality ... (and that this) ... must always be borne in mind.'[44] In other words, the material stratum itself is constituted on the basis of temporality, and, consequently, as discussed in the previous section, what must be 'borne in mind' is that the sensory matter does not pose difficulties if we understand that it, too, is constituted within time-consciousness. As a result, Husserl now recognizes the earlier ambiguity concerning sensations, and now argues that 'we need a new term which shall express the whole group [i.e., the group of sensory elements that play their part as functioning materials in, for example, sentiment, will, perception] through its unity of function and its contrast with the formative characters.'[45] *Hyle* is precisely the term he uses to cover the sensory elements or material as a whole, and *morphe* is the term he uses to delineate the form given by the meaning-bestowing stratum. In other words, Husserl is clearly distinguishing here between the sensed content (*hyle*) and the sensing of this content (*morphe*). He then goes on to claim that the *morphe*, or the meaning-bestowing stratum which in-forms the *hyle*, is an intentional phase, a phase of consciousness, and is best understood by the term 'noetic phase,' 'noesis' and 'noetic' being used derivatively from the

Greek word for mind or spirit: *Nous*. In other words, the *hyle*, as the material phase, and the noetic phase comprise for Husserl the 'proper components of intentional experiences,'[46] and thus of consciousness (or *Nous*) itself.

The analysis of the proper components of consciousness, the material and noetic phases, is, for Husserl, important for phenomenology to do; however, he recognizes that the meaning-bestowing stratum is not what readily appears for analysis. That is, the meaning is ordinarily passed over by a consciousness that is directed towards *that* which is meant. This was clear with respect to speech: one does not attend to the sounds themselves, or to the animation of these sounds, but simply to that which is expressed. Husserl continues to accept the generalization of this case (i.e., the linguistic model) as it applies to consciousness generally; consequently, Husserl claims that 'consciousness is just consciousness "of" something; it is its essential nature to conceal "meaning" within itself.'[47] The ultimate task of phenomenology, therefore, will be to study that which consciousness is a consciousness 'of,' the objective unities intended by consciousness on the basis of the noetic and material stratum. The problem will then be to study 'how objective unities of every region and category "are consciously constituted"';[48] how a multiplicity of actual and possible consciousnesses, working from a material stratum and 'following essential laws,'[49] constitute the objective unities which transcend the consciousness 'of' them.

In discussing this problem earlier (cf. chapter I), we saw how the perceptual model was used to explain the manner in which an object determines the essential relationships between a multiplicity of acts as the objectivity which ultimately fulfils these acts. Now, however, and following upon the distinctions made in *The Phenomenology of Internal Time-Consciousness*, we see that this object is to be understood as an immanent object, as a constituted object within the immanence of consciousness itself (i.e., a transcendence in immanence). To put it another way, the immanent object is the 'of something' that is the correlate of consciousness itself, its intentional correlate, and it is this object which it is the task of phenomenology to reveal. To define this immanent yet transcendent object, Husserl introduces the term 'noema': 'the correlative noematic content, the noema.'[50] Therefore, the question concerning the object that fulfils a multiplicity of acts, the question of the 'meaning that fulfills,'[51] and thus the difficulties we have continued to encounter concerning the problems of explaining fulfilment (i.e., objective knowledge) are approached by Husserl in *Ideas* through an analysis of the noema.

3. The Noema

In discussing the twofold function of morphological essences, we brought to light an ambiguity. On the one hand, morphological essences are directed towards sensible things, towards an immediate sensuous intuition of form. This understanding of morphological essences seemed to account for the sensuous filling that was needed for the fulfilment of sense, or what was needed in order to get beyond the infinite coincidence of sense with sense to that which would concretely fulfil sense. On the other hand, morphological essences are directed towards an ideal limit, towards the Kantian 'Idea' as the pole of an infinite determination. Following upon Husserl's analysis of time-consciousness and the emergence of infinite tasks, we see Husserl emphasizing this latter role of the morphological essence: that is, its role as the anticipatory structure of exact essences.

This same ambiguity seems to characterize speech. Speech seems at times to coincide with its sense, to be a concrete sense; for example, inflections of voice (e.g., sarcasm, questioning, doubting) and gestures (e.g., pointing, hushing someone) appear to be the coincidence of sense with that which fulfils and presents this sense. But speech is also directed to a meaning which is independent of its manifestation, a meaning that can be presented with great variability (e.g., different tones of voice, accents, and languages) and yet be presented as the same. It is clear, however, as was the case with morphological essences, that Husserl emphasizes the latter over the former. With respect to the former, Husserl infrequently mentions inflection, gestures, and so on, and their relationship to sense, but in *Logical Investigations* he does say that, although they may sometimes come in to play with meaning, 'in the vast majority of cases they are not parts of an expression *qua* expression, i.e., not its significant parts; they are only parts of the expression as a sensuous phenomenon.'[52] Furthermore, Husserl claims that we are, for the most part, directed towards the sense, that we live in the meaning expressed rather than the physical manifestation of the expression. Consequently, following through on the linguistic model, our attitude with respect to speech is one that is *reduced* to the meanings alone. Similarly, in generalizing this notion to consciousness generally, Husserl seeks to reduce all consciousness to the meanings of this consciousness. This latter approach Husserl calls the 'phenomenological reduction,' and it is an attitude we are already in when attending to speech (i.e., we thus see both the emphasis Husserl places on the independence of meaning from its concrete manifestations and the use of the linguistic model in justifying this emphasis). Andre de Murault, in referring to *Ideas*, argues along these lines that, for Husserl, the 'reduction is implicitly carried out – simply performed and not yet made explicit – as soon as language is considered on its own account.'[53]

This phenomenological reduction is, first and foremost, a method whereby what is posited as transcendent is reduced in order to reveal that which is immanent: in other words, that which cannot be so reduced. For example, we have seen that, in an expression, one is attending to the meaning being expressed and not to the physical sounds; therefore, these physical sounds can be reduced to reveal the more fundamental meanings. However, in attending to everyday speech, we already are, paradoxically, situated in the sphere of meaning in that, with successful communication, we hear what is meant, not the sounds. With successful communication we are therefore already in the reduced sphere of meaning. What we have here, then, is the consciousness of the meaning expressed, the meaning as an object for consciousness; however, for Husserl, the reduction is to be extended beyond what is already done in expression to include all objects posited as existing independently of consciousness. For Husserl, this entails a reduction of 'formal logic and the entire field of Mathesis';[54] in other words, the laws of logic themselves are not to be posited as existing independently of consciousness, or, to put it another way, they are to be reduced to reveal their nature as a correlate of consciousness, as an immanently constituted object of consciousness. Husserl claims, then, that the phenomenological reduction entails a 'suspension' (what he calls *epoche*) of existence, a suspension of the positing of the existence and independence of objects, and as a result of this suspension, or *epoche*, we are to be concerned with objects merely as correlates of consciousness, not as objects posited as existing.

Prior to the reduction, Husserl claims we are in the 'natural standpoint.' That is, we posit the existence of the world (e.g., the things of the world such as physical objects, mathematical objects, logical laws) as something which is independent of our consciousness of this world. I can perceive this table, understand a mathematical theorem, and these exist independently of my consciousness of them. I can return to them again and perceive them as the same. After the reduction, however, these objects are not posited as independently existing objects, but are grasped merely as the correlates of consciousness 'as such', as the immanent yet transcendent objects of consciousness. In order to alert us to the

difference between something meant 'as such,' as a correlate of consciousness, and something as meant in the natural standpoint, Husserl
uses quotation marks:

> ... to make what is meant as physical thing as such, namely as correlate
> (something perceived as such with regard to perception, something named
> as such with regard to the naming), the object of research, to make asser-
> tions about what belongs eidetically to these sorts of physical-thing inten-
> tions as such – that is not to explore physical things, physical things as
> such. A 'physical thing' as correlate is not a physical thing; therefore the
> quotation marks.[55]

These assertions which are made about the correlate, assertions modified in their meaning by the use of scare quotes, are assertions concerned precisely with what Husserl calls the 'noematic correlate.' In
other words, they are assertions concerning the relationship between
consciousness and its object, but concern this object only in so far as it is
immanent to consciousness itself, in the sense discussed earlier of an
immanent object which is a transcendence in immanence (the 'of something' correlate of consciousness). For example, in the case of perception, Husserl claims that 'the objective relation between perception and
perceived is suspended [i.e., suspension of positing the perceived as
existing, as being] and yet a relation between perception and perceived
is obviously left over, a relation which in its essential nature comes
before us in "pure immanence" ... on the ground of the phenomenologically reduced experience of perception.'[56] There is therefore an immanent meaning to perception, a meaning that, for example, can be
grasped independently of its actually being perceived, and it is this
meaning that Husserl calls the 'noematic correlate,' the 'noema,' or the
perceived as such: 'We must everywhere take the noematic correlate,
which (in a very extended meaning of the term) is referred to as "meaning" (Sinn) precisely as it lies "immanent" in the experience of perception, of judgment, of liking, and so forth.'[57]

Since the noematic correlates are what is 'left over' within a phenomenologically reduced experience, what remains after the natural standpoint is suspended (the 'disconnecting' or 'bracketing' of positing
existence [epoche]), and if this is what phenomenology is to take as its
'object of research,' then it becomes crucial for Husserl to demonstrate
the possibility of the phenomenological reduction itself. Husserl must
show that there is a possible consciousness which does not posit the

existence and being of its objects, a consciousness which is neutral with respect to being or non-being; in other words, Husserl must explain the possibility of a consciousness that is not doxic, that is not implicitly functioning in the mode of belief. Husserl recognizes the importance of doing this and claims that a neutral consciousness is 'of the highest importance and occupies a position all by itself ... and its correlates ... contain nothing that can be posited, nothing that can be really predicated; in no respect does the neutral consciousness play towards that of which it is aware the part of belief.'[58]

As an example of such a neutral consciousness, Husserl gives the perception of Dürer's engraving *The Knight, Death, and the Devil*.[59] In the perception of this engraving as something which depicts something, the engraved print is perceived, on the one hand, as an existent, as an engraving among many in a portfolio, let us say; on the other hand, in perceiving the engraving, our attention is directed towards that which is being depicted in the engraving – to the knight on horseback, death, and the devil. This depicted object is, in turn, depicted as a reality, as the flesh-and-blood knight on horseback (though it could just as well be depicted as a non-reality, as a mythological creature, etc.). The 'depicted as such,' however, has one side turned towards the depicting object 'within which in the black lines of the picture there appear to us the small colorless figures, "knight on horseback," etc.,' and it has one side turned towards the depicted object, towards 'the knight of flesh and blood, and so forth.'[60] The 'depicted as such' is nevertheless not to be identified with either side, and is ultimately neutral with respect to both the depicting and the depicted objects. A depicting picture-object is thus perceived neither as that which is depicted nor as the picture-object itself, as a physical thing. In other words, our normal perceptual consciousness which posits a real perceived object is suspended with respect to a depicting picture-object. In perceiving a depicting picture-object, we see neither an object nor that which is depicted, but the 'depicted as such.' As Husserl goes on to argue, the perception of a depicting picture-object is thus the result of a 'neutrality modification of the normal perception ... [whereby] ... this depicting picture-object stands before us neither as being or as non-being, nor in any positional modality.'[61] The depicting picture-object, as an object, is posited neither as being nor not-being; rather, it has, as Husserl goes on to say, a 'quasi-being' which is transcended in the service of depicting.

Another example of neutral consciousness can be seen in the perception of an expression (e.g., hearing an expressed proposition). As in the case of a depicting picture-object, an expression is perceived as something which expresses or *means* something, and is, on the one hand, perceived as a physical manifestation; however, since Husserl claims that in expressing we are paradoxically within the attitude of the phenomenological reduction, and because this attitude is what Husserl wants to show as possible for consciousness generally, it would be more accurate to say that one hears an expressed proposition. This is clear if we recall that Husserl extends the reduction to include the positing of being to all objectivities, for example, propositions, formal logic, and that in our naturally reduced sphere of language we do hear and posit propositions in this manner. On the other hand, in hearing an expressed proposition, our attention is directed towards that state of affairs which is designated by the proposition. The expressed or 'meant as such,' however, the noema, is neither the expressed proposition nor the designated state of affairs. The noema is thus presented neither as the proposition itself nor as the state of affairs itself; in other words, the normal consciousness which posits its objects is 'suspended' with respect to the noema: the noema is presented neither as the proposition expressed nor as the state of affairs in the world designated by the expression, but it is the 'expressed as such.' The noema, as neutral with respect to propositions and states of affairs (i.e., objects), thus emerges for Husserl as a solution to the regress which followed the irreducible difference between sense and object. That is, the noema is to be understood as the neutral 'quasi-being' which turns one side to propositions as *what* the proposition expresses, the sense or expressed of the proposition, and turns one side to the state of affairs as an attribute of the state of affairs, as *that* designated by a proposition. However, as a neutral 'quasi-being,' the noema is not to be identified with either or both, thus avoiding the regress; rather, and analogous to the depicting picture-object, it is the 'quasi-being' exhausted in its making expression possible (i.e., the noema is both the sense of the proposition and the attribute of the state of affairs, but, as neutral, it is not to be posited, *nor does it posit*, either of these). The noema is, as a result, understood by Husserl to be the neutral, sterile, non-productive, and yet necessary condition for the expressibility of consciousness, for the possibility of intentionality in general to achieve expression: 'The stratum of expression – and this constitutes its peculiarity – apart from the fact that it lends expression to all other intentionalities, is not productive. Or, if one prefers: its productivity, its noematic service, exhausts itself in expressing.'[62]

With this understanding of the noema, we can see how it emerges within Husserl's continuing efforts to confront the paradoxical consequences which followed from the irreducible difference between sense and object. For example, we saw Husserl move to resolve the regress of sense infinitely coinciding with sense by arguing for the self-constitutive nature of absolute consciousness. In this way we saw that subjective time was itself constituted as the immanent form, the '"unconscious" content' (cf. above, section 1), which was implicitly the self-reflection of this absolute consciousness, a content which is not apprehended as reflective content (thus it is 'unconscious'), but conditions and leaves forever open the possibility of reflection. In the same way, the noema is constituted as an immanent form, as an 'unconscious' content which is not apprehended in the manner of an object, a manner which implies a regress;[63] however, this noematic content conditions and leaves for ever open the possibility of apprehending an object. The noema is, as mentioned above, that which 'lends expression to all other intentionalities': or, to put it another way, the noema is the immanent constituted content, the immanent objective correlate, which lends its objectivity to all objectifying acts, to all positings of existence, and thus is the condition for the 'Natural Standpoint' itself.

The neutrality of the noema does appear, then, to develop along the lines of Husserl's efforts in *The Phenomenology of Internal Time-Consciousness* to resolve the regress of sense coinciding with sense by arguing for a notion of a content immanently constituted within consciousness itself; however, if the neutrality of the noema is an immanent content constituted within consciousness, and if this is a neutral consciousness, then consciousness itself must be, as an essential possibility, neutral. This is precisely what Husserl claims to be the case. He claims that there is an *irreducible difference* at the heart of consciousness itself, that 'consciousness generally, of whatever kind and form it may be, is traversed by a radical cleavage.'[64] This cleavage reflects an essential possibility of consciousness whereby an experience which is not from the start lived 'as if' an ego brought it about can be modified such that it is being lived as if an ego brought it about. What this means, for Husserl, is that there is a radical cleavage between a doxic and a non-doxic consciousness.

A consequence of this irreducible difference, Husserl claims, is 'two fundamental possibilities connected with the way in which consciousness is brought about within the modus cogito.'[65] On the one hand, there is the cogito, 'a "real," "really positing" cogito,' and, on the other hand, there is 'the "shadow" of an act, an act improperly so-called, a cogito that does not "really" posit.'[66] In other words, there is the cogito which is a 'really positing' cogito, a doxic cogito, that posits objects as 'real'; and there is the cogito which does not 'really' posit, or what I will call the 'para-doxic cogito,' in that it does not posit its objects as 'real.' Husserl then claims the noema is not to be understood in this latter case as it usually is, but as 'counter-noema';[67] that is, the objective correlate of the para-doxic cogito is a non-'real' correlate that 'exactly corresponds with' the 'real' correlate of the cogito: thus he calls it a 'counter-noema.' This exact correspondence is one between an act that 'really' posits and this *same* act (an act 'improperly so-called') that does not 'really' posit. In other words, the cogito and its parallel counterpart are to be understood as the same, as having the same content, yet differ only in their positing, or doxic, quality. This is analogous to the irreducible difference between signitive and intuitive acts where these acts took up the same matter; so, too, in this case the doxic and para-doxic cogito may have the same content (i.e., its noetic phase and noematic content, what we will see below as 'noematic *Sinn*'). Furthermore, in the same way that every signitive intention implies or intends the possibility of its intuitive fulfilment, so, too, does every para-doxic cogito imply the possibility of being a doxic cogito. As Husserl argues, 'every cogito is in itself either a primary form of doxic positing or not. But by virtue of a system of laws, which again belong to the essential nature of consciousness in its basic generality, every cogito can be transferred to a primary positing of a doxic type.'[68]

To clarify what Husserl is saying here, and some of his terminology as well, we shall look at an example of a 'primary positing of a doxic type.' A positing act, or an objectifying act, is simply an act which posits an object. For example, if we are conscious of a melody, our consciousness posits this melody as an object 'of' consciousness. The melody is the object towards which our conscious experience is directed. Husserl then claims that our positing acts have a qualitative character, what he calls its 'thetic-character.' I not only posit the melody as an object, but posit it in a certain way, and as a definite type of object, such as pleasing, as a melody, and so on. If I find the melody pleasing, then my consciousness is directed in a particular way to this object, what Husserl calls here 'a pleasure-noesis.' In other words, there is a quality or thesis to the noetic phase of consciousness such that we are not only conscious, but conscious in certain and definite ways. Consequently, as an objective noematic correlate of the pleasure-noeses, there will be the experience 'of something' as pleasing, what Husserl calls the 'noematic *Sinn*' of this experience. However, this experience might be neutral; that is, we might not posit the 'being' or 'reality' of this pleasing something, and thus not posit what is experienced as 'real.' This positing therefore does not have a doxic quality or thesis, yet there remains the essential possibility that the positing can be transferred to a 'primary positing of a doxic type.' In other words, there is the essential possibility of an experience 'of something' as pleasing to become an experience 'of something' that *is* pleasing. The modification that takes place after the transfer to a doxic positing is that the objective correlates of consciousness acquire an ontic character (i.e., they are posited as 'being real'). There thus emerge two senses of the noematic correlate to be discerned here. On the one hand, there is the noematic correlate of the pleasure-noeses, or what Husserl calls the 'noematic *Sinn* of the act'; on the other hand, there is this noematic *Sinn* in its mode of givenness: that is, whether the noematic *Sinn* is given in a 'really positing' act, what Husserl calls the 'full noema,' or whether it is given in an act that is not a 'really positing' act, what we have discussed as the counter-noema. In Appendix XIX to *Ideen I*, Husserl recognizes that this distinction results in an ambiguity with respect to the noematic correlates, or the noema: 'There is a two-way ambiguity in the notion of noema: 1) The *Sinn*, the so and so determined object as such (noematic *Sinn*). 2) The *Sinn* in its mode of givenness (full noema).'[69]

This ambiguity, however, follows from the distinction Husserl makes between acts that are 'really' positing and those that are not. In other words, the noematic *Sinn* is the fundamental content either taken up by a doxic cogito, and thus we have the full noema, or taken up by a para-doxic cogito, and thus we have the counter-noema. The full noema is therefore the objective correlate of an act that 'really' posits, of an act that posits something as 'real.' As a result we can distinguish between a sense through which a being is intended (full noema) and a sense through which it is not (counter-noema), and, as this theme is developed in the fourth part of *Ideas*, it represents a transition in Husserl's thought to the problem of the constitution of Being, of the relationship of sense to Being. For example, by distinguishing between a neutral, para-doxic cogito, and the primary doxic cogito, Husserl: (1) shows in what way the noema (noematic *Sinn*) is neutral and yet is the essential possibility of expression, of being taken up within a doxic cogito, and this further elaborates the manner in which the noema as neutral 'lends expression' to intentionality generally; he then goes on to claim: (2) the noema is the sense of an act that posits 'reality,' that reality is given through the sense of an act. In other words, Husserl distinguishes between the content of the noema, the noematic *Sinn* as the 'meant as such,' and the object or 'reality' intended by the noema through this content, and in doing this he recognizes that there is a parallelism between the structure of acts (noeses) and the structure of sense (noemata), an 'essential parallelism of the two structures that had not yet been clearly grasped (i.e., in *Logical Investigations*).'[70]

What Husserl failed to do in *Logical Investigations* was to distinguish between the sense of the act which determines *what* an object is intended as, its immanent content, and the sense that designates an object as *that* towards which the act is directed. Since Husserl did not clearly delineate between these two aspects of the sense of an act, we found Husserl beset with the difficulty of explaining how, if sense determines both the nature of an act and the object of this act, one could ever get beyond sense to that which would fulfil it. Or, to put it another way, how can Husserl avoid the regress of sense infinitely coinciding with sense? He circumvented this regress in *The Phenomenology of Internal Time-Consciousness* by founding it upon the self-constitutive nature of absolute consciousness, a consciousness whereby an infinitization resulted, with the accepted regress of consciousness being forever opened to reflection: that is, consciousness itself conditions the 'infinite task' of reflection as a result of its self-constituted nature. This infinite task, or the openness to the infinite determinations of reflection, appears now in *Ideas*, with the discussion of morphological essences, as the Kantian 'Idea,' as the invariant pole of an infinite determination. Now, however, in returning to the sense of the act, to the noema, and in finally making clear the distinction between the content of the noema (noematic *Sinn*) and the object intended by the noema, we find Husserl employing again the Kantian 'Idea.' The Kantian Idea appears here as the determinable X, as the same 'determinable X which is intended by different noemata, and, in the case of a thing, of a perceived thing in the world, Husserl claims that it is determinable "*in infinitum.*" The "and so forth" is an absolutely indispensable phase in the thing-noema.'[71] However, despite the fact that all transcendent objects are essentially inadequately perceived, including 'all realities which are included under the rubric Nature or World ... which cannot be given with complete determinacy,' Husserl nevertheless claims that 'as "Idea" (in the Kantian Sense), the complete givenness is nevertheless prescribed.'[72]

This distinction between the content and object of the noema, however, as a distinction within the sense of the act itself, seems to transfer the difficulties from the realm of acts to the realm of sense. For example, earlier the question was how an act, on the basis of the sense of this act, determines both *what* is intended and *that* something is intended; now the question is how the sense of an act, the noema, determines both *what* an object is meant as, that is, the 'meant as such,' and *that* an object, a determinable X, is there for consciousness. In the first case, the problem was in explaining how we could get beyond the sense of an act to that which fulfils this sense; similarly, what needs to be explained now is how we can get beyond the noema to the reality, the X as completely determined, which will fulfil it. As Ricoeur has noted, within the fourth part of *Ideas* we find Husserl clearly presenting 'the central difficulty of the Husserlian notion of constitution, the difficulty of bringing the theme of sense-giving into coincidence with the theme of self-givenness.'[73] In other words, the difficulty is in bringing the noema into coincidence with reality, with a completely self-given Being; and it is this coincidence with reality, or showing how a completely determined and objective knowledge is possible, which is the problem we have continued to encounter.

Husserl never resolves this difficulty; rather, he posits the Kantian 'Idea' as the invariant pole of an infinite determination, an Idea which 'prescribes the possibility' of being completely self-given, the possibility of a noema becoming and being coincident with reality. As a result, we can see that the Kantian 'Idea' is for Husserl an ideal object, an object as the pole of an infinite determination, and it is this 'Ideal' object in general which conditions the possibility both of an infinite number of determinations of the same object and of a completely determined and adequately self-given object. In other words, the perceptual model that was used in order to explain fulfilment is now being used in a Kantian manner: that is, rather than a perceived object being the model to explain a multiplicity of acts of the same object, and explain the adequate fulfilment of these acts, we have now an ideal object, an object as the 'Ideal' and invariant pole.

This Kantian 'Idea,' the invariant object of an infinite determination, is, as we have seen, a consequence of Husserl's attempts to overcome the paradox of regress. Furthermore, as a means of resolving the regress which arose out of the irreducible difference between sense and object, we find this Object in general mediating between the sense and the object, with one side turned towards the sense and another turned towards the object. For example, as the sense of an act, as the immanent content within consciousness itself, we find this Kantian Object turned towards this flux of consciousness as that which we are able to 'apprehend in a certain way ... the stream of experience as a unity also ... after the fashion of an Idea in the Kantian sense.'[74] And as the object of an act, as that which consciousness is a consciousness 'of,' we find the Kantian

Object turned towards the object as that which 'as "Idea" (in the Kantian sense)' has a complete determination and givenness which is 'pre-scribed.'[75] We have also seen Husserl further developing his response to the paradoxical consequences in our discussion of the neutrality of the noema. There we saw that the noema had one side turned towards the expressed proposition as the sense of this proposition, and it had one side turned towards the designated state of affairs as an attribute of this state of affairs. However, in order to justify this neutrality, Husserl needed to make further distinctions within the noema, distinctions which in the end entailed the notion of the Kantian Idea. This notion was brought in, as we have been arguing, in order to avoid unwanted paradoxical regresses.

It seems clear, then, that the concept of the Kantian 'Idea' is crucial to Husserl's phenomenology, and especially so considering the importance it plays in reconciling his phenomenology with the paradoxical conse-quences of the infinite regress. The noema also reflects Husserl's efforts in this regard; for example, the noema as neutral is that which has one side turned towards the sense of a positing act (e.g., as the sense of an expressed proposition) and another side turned towards the object pos-ited (e.g., as the attribute of the state of affairs). The noema is not to be *identified* with either – it is neutral with respect to posited identity and being – nor does it posit identity and being (i.e., as neutral it is 'not pro-ductive'); furthermore, the reason Husserl argues for a neutral con-sciousness (what in *The Phenomenology of Internal Time-Consciousness* was 'unconscious content') is precisely to avoid an infinite regress that is not ultimately founded upon a non-regressive, self-constituted conscious-ness. In other words, the neutrality of the noema needs to be understood in light of Husserl's continuing efforts to avoid certain paradoxical consequences.

This has not been done, for the most part, and as a result we find the noema actually being *identified* with either the side of sense, for example, the noema as a proposition, or *identified* with the side of the object, for example, the noema as an attribute of a state of affairs. Nowhere is this more apparent than in the diverging interpretations that are to be found in Gurwitsch, Kerns, and Cairns, on the one hand, and Føllesdal, Miller, Smith, and McIntyre, on the other. For example, Izchak Miller claims that 'the noema is, in fact, a certain kind of proposition,'[76] and this Miller admits is simply his further explication of Føllesdal's claim that 'the noema is an intensional entity.'[77] Gurwitsch, on the other hand, claims that the 'noema ... [is] ... the object as it is meant ... the object in the perspective, orientation, illumination and role in which it presents itself.'[78] In other words, the noema is an attribute of an object, the object as it is given, and, in the case of the perceptual noema, Gurwitsch claims: 'It turns out to be the perceived thing, just as it presents itself through a concrete act of perception – namely, as appearing from a certain side, in a certain perspective, orientation, etc.'[79] To further clarify these positions, and to elaborate how they result from a failure to appreciate the emergence of the noema as that which sought to resolve the paradox of regress, we turn then to a discussion of the perceptual noema.

4. The Perceptual Noema

The important role of perception within Husserl's phenomenology cannot be emphasized enough. On the one hand, perception is the ground from which all our judgments, sciences, and knowledge take shape; it is our 'primordial dator intuition.'[80] On the other hand, perception, as inner or immanent perception, is the end which validates and justifies our knowledge, judgments, and sciences; it is, in other words, the perception of truth itself.[81] Perception is thus literally the alpha and the omega of Husserl's phenomenology; consequently, it is no wonder that much critical attention has been focused upon Husserl's theory of perception, and, in particular, upon the *sense* of perception: that is, the perceptual noema.

If, as we have been arguing, the noema is understood as the neutral 'quasi-being,' as that which is neither the expressed or posited sense (e.g., an expressed proposition) nor the object or state of affairs designated by this sense; or, if it is understood as neutral, as non-productive, and non-positing, then we see that the noema is turned towards both the intentional act as the sense of this act (e.g., the sense expressed in an expressed proposition) and the object of this act as that which is being intended or meant (e.g., the attribute of the state of affairs designated by a proposition). However, since the noema has largely not been interpreted within the light of its neutrality, a neutrality motivated by the effort to circumvent an epistemological infinite regress, there has been, subsequently, a tendency in the literature to affirm only one of the two contrasting senses affirmed by the noema. For example, the noema is identified either with the expressed proposition or with the object designated; and it is precisely this ambiguity which is most clearly revealed in the literature concerning the perceptual noema.

This ambiguity regarding the perceptual noema can be found even in the way the original German has been translated. For example, in section 89, immediately following the section where the noema is defined as the 'meant as such,' and where the perceptual meaning, the perceptual noema, is defined as the *'perceived as such,'* we find Husserl, in what is now a famous example, clarifying the relationship of the perceived as such to an actual tree being perceived. Within this context, Husserl's original German reads as follows: 'Der Baum schlechtin, das Ding in der Natur, ist nichts weniger als dieses Baumwahrgenommene als solches, das als Wahrnehmungssin zur jeweiligen Wahrenehmung unabtrennbar gehört.'[82] W.R. Boyce Gibson's 1931 translation of this sentence reads as follows:

> The *tree plain and simple*, the thing in Nature, **is as different as it can be from** this *perceived tree as such*, which as perceptual meaning belongs to the perception, and that inseparably.[83]

Frederick Kersten's 1982 translation is markedly different:

> The *tree simpliciter*, the physical thing belonging to Nature, **is nothing less than** this *perceived tree as perceived* which, as perceptual sense, inseparably belongs to the perception.[84]

Boyce's translation implies that the perceptual noema is simply the way the tree is *taken* by the perceiving act itself; in other words, the perceptual noema is to be understood as the sense of the perceiving act, the sense which determines *what* we take the perceived object to be. The perceptual noema is therefore understood to be the conceptual or propositional sense which determines precisely the way the perceived is taken.[85] There is also ample textual support to back up this interpretation. For example, in *Ideas*, Husserl claims: 'Whatever is "meant as such," every meaning in the noematic sense (and indeed as noematic nucleus) of any act whatsoever can be expressed conceptually (durch "Bedeutungen").'[86] And, in *Ideas III*, Husserl claims that 'to posit significations (i.e., something as meant) and to posit objects (i.e., something as present) are two different things: the noema in general is, however, nothing further than the universalization of the idea of signification to the total province of the acts.'[87]

Kersten's translation implies that the perceptual noema is the way the tree is *given* to the perceiving act; that is, the perceptual noema is to be understood as a perspective upon the perceived itself, as that through which the perceived object is given in the perceiving act (i.e., *'perceived tree as perceived'*). The perceptual noema is here understood as a percept, as *that* which is given in the perceiving.[88] There is also textual support for this interpretation. For instance, in *Ideas*, Husserl asks: 'What is the "perceived as such"? What essential phases does it harbor in itself in its capacity as noema? We win reply to our question as we wait, in pure surrender, on what is essentially *given*.'[89] Furthermore, following through on the idea that the perceptual noema is the way the perceived object is given, and if we consider that a perceived object is given only through a single perspective, then this perspective should entail other possible perspectives upon the same object. This is precisely what Husserl claims is the case: 'In the noema of the act of perception, i.e., in the perceived, taken precisely as characterized phenomenologically, as it is therein an intentional object, there is included a determinate directive for all further experiences of the object in question.'[90]

An important distinction needs to be noted here. It is one thing to say that the noema 'can be expressed conceptually,' that the noema can be understood in the manner of 'the idea of signification,' but it is something else entirely to say that the noema *is*, at bottom, a concept, that it is itself a signification (e.g., a proposition). Similarly, it is one thing to say that the noema is 'what is essentially given,' that the noema gives an object in the manner of a 'determinate directive,' but it is also something entirely different to say that the noema *is* an attribute or percept of the object as given. In our discussion of the neutrality of the noema, we have sought to explain that the noema, although turned towards the act and the object, is not to be *identified* with either side; nevertheless, the perceptual noema has been largely identified with one side or the other. On the one hand, if we adopt terminology that Hubert Dreyfus has employed,[91] the perceptual noema is understood as a *concept*; and, on the other, the perceptual noema is understood as a *percept*. We will examine each briefly.

Concept Theory

Interpretations of Husserl which claim the noema is to be understood as a type of concept or intensional entity develop this interpretation for roughly two reasons. First, Husserl himself continued throughout his career to compare the role of the noema with that of linguistic meaning – what we call the 'linguistic model.' Consequently, the interpretation of the noema as an intensional entity seems simply to follow certain indications left behind by Husserl. For example, Husserl claims that 'whatever is "meant as such," every meaning in the noematic sense of any act whatsoever can be expressed conceptually.'[92] Second, this interpretation places Husserl's thought solidly within the analytic context of linguistic analyses regarding meaning. Føllesdal then will claim that, 'given all the philosophical discussion of meaning in the linguistic sphere, it may be illuminating and helpful for understanding Husserl to be told that the noema is a generalization of the notion of meaning (*Bedeutung*) to the realm of all acts.'[93] In other words, since Husserl understands the noema in the manner of linguistic meaning as generalized to all acts (i.e., the linguistic model), then it would be helpful to analyse the noema in a manner similar to that done with linguistic meaning; consequently, in doing just this, Føllesdal's first thesis in his article 'Husserl's Notion of Noema' is that 'the noema is an intensional entity, a generalization of the notion of meaning (*Bedeutung*).'[94]

In developing this interpretation, Føllesdal goes on to claim that the 'noematic *Sinn* is that in virtue of which consciousness relates to the object.'[95] The noematic *Sinn*, or the content of what is meant in an act, or what an object is taken to be, determines precisely the manner in which this act is related to the object. For example, in a judgment such as 'The murderer is in this very room,'[96] the content of this judgment, the noematic *Sinn*, which determines the manner in which this act is related to the object, is precisely the content: 'The murderer is in this very room.' However, this content is presented in a definite way, in this case as a judgment, and thus, as Føllesdal points out, this noematic *Sinn* has a noematic character, or a thetic-character which is the mode of presentation of this content. In this example the noematic character is the mode of judging: '*I judge that* the murderer is in this very room.' The noematic *Sinn* could also have been presented in the mode of questioning, doubting, and so on;[97] consequently, since it is a noematic *Sinn* which is presented in various ways by different types of acts, it is therefore that which is the condition for its being expressed, for its being taken up in the mode of judging, stating, expressing, and so on.

Ronald McIntyre and David Woodruff Smith draw a similar conclusion and claim that, if 'linguistic meanings are noematic *Sinne* expressed,' then 'the noematic *Sinne* of any act is in principle expressible in language.'[98] Considered in the light of Husserl's comment quoted above (i.e., the noema is the condition which 'lends expression to all other intentionalities'), this thesis, what they call the 'expressibility thesis,' appears to be reasonable. However, we have been arguing that the

noema, or noematic *Sinn*, is neutral, non-productive, and is to be identified neither with an object nor with an expression or proposition. The
noematic *Sinn* is therefore the condition not only for relating to objects,
but for relating to our expressions and propositions as well, for positing
the sense of these propositions as objects, and thus it is the condition for
the non-vicious regress of the sense of an act being for ever open to the
possibility of being the object of a new act, an act with a sense similarly
open, and so on *ad infinitum*. This is so because, as the non-productive
and neutral condition which relates propositions to states of affairs in
the world, or intuiting acts to intuited objects, the noema is not identified when one identifies one side or the other; consequently, one can
indefinitely identify the sense of an act without ever identifying the
noema. This is the sense in which the noema is the condition for the possibility of the non-vicious regress. Føllesdal recognizes this regress, and
in fact quotes from Husserl's essay 'Noema und Sinn' to show that Husserl himself was aware of it;[99] however, for Føllesdal this means only,
and he quotes Husserl again, that 'the *Sinn* cannot be a real component
of the object.'[100] In other words, the regress moves away from the world,
and from objects in the world, in the manner of unchecked abstraction;
consequently, the *Sinn*, or noema, which becomes the object of each further abstraction, 'is as different as it can be from'[101] an actual object.

Accepting the conclusion that the noema 'is as different as it can be
from' an actual object, are we then justified in claiming that the noema is
an intensional entity, that it is, as Izchak Miller argues, 'a certain kind of
proposition'?[102] On the one hand, the full noema, the noema as the
immanent object of a *positing* consciousness, can be seen as a certain
type of proposition. The content of this positing consciousness is precisely the noematic *Sinn*, the *Sinn* taken up in various *positing* modes
(i.e., noematic characters), and as full noema it can be seen to be of propositional form: for example, I judge that (noematic character) the murderer is in this very room (noematic *Sinn*). On the other hand, if
Husserl's phenomenological reduction entails the possibility of a neutral *non-positing* consciousness, then there is, as we have argued, the
noema as the 'quasi-being' which conditions the possibility of expression, of a positing consciousness. Føllesdal, among others, does not recognize the significance of this neutral noema within Husserl's thought, a
noema whose neutrality was meant by him to circumvent the vicious
epistemological regress and account for the possibility of the regress
wherein the sense of a proposition can in turn be an object of a new
proposition, a proposition which in turn has its own sense, and so on. In

other words, Føllesdal does not recognize the non-identifiable, non-productive, non-positing noema; consequently, since the regress shows that the sense as intended by consciousness, as posited by consciousness, is not an actual object, he concludes that this posited sense must be a conceptual, propositional, and intensional object.

The perceptual noema is in turn analysed in light of this conclusion. For example, Izchak Miller, in his book *Husserl, Perception, and Temporal Awareness*, argues that perception is a special case of meaning, what he calls 'singular meaning.' For example, in the proposition 'I expect I will see ... ,' the proposition expresses the noema of expectation; that is, the noematic correlate (the thesis) or mode of presentation is 'expectation,' and the noematic *Sinn* of this proposition, the determinative content, is the content 'I will see ...' Miller then claims, 'I will see ...' is the noema of the expected act, not the noema of expectation. In other words, what one expects to see is not the same thing as expecting to see it. The noematic *Sinn* of 'I will see ...,' however, is not in turn a noema; it is a singular meaning, a straightforwardly meant content which is not meant in a propositional form, but is meant directly. That is, in seeing that which is expected, a friend, for example, this friend is not posited in the form 'I see my friend' (i.e., propositional form); rather, one is singularly and directly presented with the perception of their friend, and this is what Miller means by calling it a 'singular meaning.' However, for Miller, this singular meaning is only the content of a full noema, of a noema which *is* in propositional form (e.g., 'I will see ...'), and in the example discussed here it is the content of a content [e.g., '(((I expect)((I will see)(singular meaning)))']. This content is also understood to be an abstract content, and is not to be confused with the singular perspective of an object, for example. Furthermore, since Miller recognizes only the noematic *Sinn* (content) as the content of a positing consciousness, and does not recognize the neutral non-positing consciousness, he is led to conclude that even this singular meaning is *always* an embedded content, always embedded in the noemata of a positing consciousness, and that these noemata are *'nothing less than'* propositions: 'It should be kept in mind that noematic Sinne, whether singular or propositional, are always embedded in noemata, and a noema – I have been maintaining all along – is always a proposition.'[103]

Percept Theory

There is indeed a tendency in Husserl's writings to interpret the meaningful nature of acts as just a more general form of linguistic meaning, but this is a tendency of which Aron Gurwitsch is critical, especially when it is used to explain the sense of a perceptual act: that is, the perceptual noema. Gurwitsch claims, to the contrary, that linguistic meaning is to be understood as a 'more narrow'[104] form of meaning apprehension than that associated with perceiving. In other words, Gurwitsch thus emphasizes the sense of acts in terms of that which is intuited, that which is given, and believes that this remains true to the phenomenological reduction. Husserl, however, did not in Gurwitsch's eyes remain true to the reduction because of his continued emphasis upon linguistic meaning. For instance, in *Logical Investigations*, Husserl claims that a consequence of the linguistic model was that all acts had to have a matter which carries the meaning intended by this act, just as an expressed meaning depends upon physical sounds,[105] but the meaning itself is independent of this matter. In applying this to perception, however, a problem arises in explaining how the sensations are both the matter taken up by an act and the sense of this act itself. Without getting into specifics, we want simply to note that Husserl recognized this problem and sought, in *The Phenomenology of Internal Time-Consciousness*, to resolve it. In short, Husserl claims the datum or matter of perception is itself constituted by an absolute, self-constituted consciousness.[106] But it is precisely this move to an absolute self-constituting consciousness (i.e., the pure transcendental ego) which Gurwitsch claims is no longer true to the method of the phenomenological reduction. He claims, 'there is no place in the body of phenomenological doctrines for the pure or transcendental ego,'[107] and that 'the ego, like all other objects, falls under the phenomenological reduction.'[108] Consequently, if one is to remain true to the phenomenological reduction, the transcendental ego will *not* be something which remains, something that is given to an intuition which can be described; rather, a true phenomenological reduction would 'get rid of that paradoxical and contradictory entity.'[109]

Gurwitsch's rejection of the transcendental ego entails the further rejection of Husserl's distinction between *hyle* and *morphe*, for, if the transcendental ego emerges as a means of accounting for both the matter as taken up by an act (i.e., the constituted pre-given, or *hyle*) and the matter as the sense of this act (i.e., the 'interpretive sense,' or the constitutive form, *morphe*), and if this distinction is no longer accepted, then the problematic consequences will not occur either, and it will no longer be necessary to argue for a self-constituting absolute consciousness. This is exactly the move Gurwitsch makes.

In *The Field of Consciousness*, Gurwitsch recognizes that Husserl's distinction between *hyle* and *morphe* involves the problematic consequence of accounting for the sense-datum of perception as both the carrier of meaning (i.e., formless matter, or *hyle*) and the attribute of the object as given (i.e., the form, or *morphe*, of this sense datum).[110] For this reason, Gurwitsch is critical of the idea that perception entails the animation of some amorphic material, or that there is a formless matter (i.e., the *hyle*) in-formed by an animating act (i.e., the *morphe*). Gurwitsch asks rhetorically: 'is not that given in direct sense-experience so qualified by the different implicit ideas involved [i.e., *morphe*] in either percept [e.g., Duck or Rabbit in Jastrow's Duck-Rabbit] that the two percepts cannot be asserted to contain identical elements?'[111] Is it even possible to abstract a formless matter out of what is given in consciousness, a matter which is identical within different conscious experiences? Gurwitsch claims this cannot be done, that the sense-datum is given everywhere and always as a formed or structured sense-datum, and he argues that 'a separation between *hyle* and *morphe* is not even abstractly possible.'[112]

Following through on this line of criticism, Gurwitsch contends that the only thing that does remain identical across differing experiences is the form and structure of these experiences themselves, or what he calls the 'inner horizon' (developing a notion put forth by Husserl in *Experience and Judgment*). If there is a change within this horizon, it will effect the experience as a whole, including what 'is given in direct sense experience':[113] that is, the sense-datum. This concept of the 'inner horizon' ultimately emerges as Gurwitsch's theory of the sense of perception, the perceptual noema, as a gestalt. Perception is not a matter of a formless given being taken up by an interpreting act; rather, the sense-datum and form are mutually interdependent: the form as a whole is functionally dependent on the parts (i.e., the sense-data), and the parts are functionally dependent on the whole which determines their role. For example, the notes of a melody are defined in terms of the functional significance they have within the melody as a whole. One does not hear the notes as independent entities strung together, but hears them as related to, and in the context of, the notes which precede and follow one another in the playing of the melody. Furthermore, one does not hear a melody unless there are notes functionally related to one another, and, if one were to change one of the notes, the whole melody itself would be changed as well. And it is as a structured whole, a gestalt, that Gurwitsch interprets the perceptual noema or, what is the same for him, the percept.[114]

Gurwitsch understands the perceptual noema, or the percept, as a complex and structured unity, a unity where all the parts – that is, noemata – are functionally dependent upon one another. In perceiving an object, for example, there is the possibility of other perspectives, of seeing sides that are not given, and this is a possibility given within the actual perspective itself; consequently, Gurwitsch claims that 'every visual perception of a material thing has its perceptual sense or meaning co-determined by the presence and intervention in this perception of items not seen.'[115] The perceptual noema is therefore a 'complex unity of meaning,'[116] a unity determined by its functional relation to other noemata, that is, to the other perspectives. As a unity, however, the perceptual noema is not to be understood as something unified by some act, as some matter which receives a unifying form or structure; rather, the unity of the perceptual noema is, for Gurwitsch, an intrinsic unity: 'the unity of the percept (or perceptual noema) is intrinsic unity in that its parts and components are dependent upon each other for their individual qualification.'[117] The sense of a perceived thing is not the result of an organizing of properties and qualities, an organization carried out by means of some 'supervenient coordination.'[118] The sense of the perceived thing is intrinsic to the perceived itself: 'the sense is incorporated and incarnated in the very appearances themselves.'[119] It is thus the intrinsic structure of the perceived thing itself that conditions the possibility of various perspectives of this thing, and it is also the condition for the different perceptual noemata that are functionally dependent on one another in so far as they are all aspects or appearances of the same object. In the end, the complex and structured unity of the perceptual noema is therefore the complex and structured unity of the perceived thing, and for this reason Gurwitsch claims the perceptual noema 'turns out to be the perceived thing, just as it presents itself through a concrete act of perception – namely, as appearing from a certain side, in a certain perspective, orientation, etc.'[120] And again: 'The perceptual noema denotes the material thing perceived from a given standpoint, in a determinate orientation with regard to the perceiving subject, under a certain aspect, etc.'[121]

Conclusion

The relationship between concept theory, percept theory, and the problem of accounting for objectivity can now be further clarified. For instance, with concept theory's emphasis upon Husserl's use of the linguistic model, and without fully recognizing his efforts to resolve the problematic consequences of using this model, this theory is led to the conclusion that, if the noema 'can be expressed conceptually,' and is understood in the manner of 'the idea of signification,' then it therefore is, at bottom, a concept, a signification or proposition. This position does not account for Husserl's efforts to avoid the epistemological regress by arguing for a neutral, non-positing noema, nor does it account for the regress whereby the sense of an act can be the posited object of another act, an act with a sense that can likewise be posited, and so on *ad infinitum*. Føllesdal quotes Husserl's recognition of this latter regress, but then goes on to claim that this shows only that the noema, or sense (*Sinn*), is not a real component of the object. Although this is certainly true for Husserl, this does not mean, however, that the noema must therefore be an intensional entity, some type of concept or proposition. Husserl's moves, in *The Phenomenology of Internal Time-Consciousness*, and later, in *Ideas*, to argue for a neutral consciousness are done precisely in order to avoid this either/or, this false dilemma that the noema is either an object or an intensional entity, a proposition. The noema, rather, is the neutral and non-productive 'quasi-being' which is neither a proposition nor a thing. In essence, the concept theorists have not considered the possibility that the noema is simply the neutral, non-productive boundary between propositions and things, a boundary with one side turned towards propositions and the other towards things; consequently, since they see that the noema is not a thing, they conclude that it must be a type of *posited sense*, that is, a proposition or concept.

On the other hand, percept theory emphasizes the role of perception at the expense of the linguistic model. Gurwitsch recognizes the difficulties of maintaining the linguistic model, and recognizes the move to the transcendental ego, 'the paradoxical and contradictory entity,' but he rejects this paradoxical entity, and, with it, the distinctions that motivated the move to it. Gurwitsch's position also does not account for Husserl's own efforts to explicate the infinite correlation of sense and object on the grounds of the neutral, non-positing noema, a noema that is the paradoxical condition which allows for the differentiation between percept and concept, but which is to be identified with neither. As a result, Gurwitsch believes he is faced with an either/or: either one has to accept such 'paradoxical and contradictory' entities, or the noema is, ultimately, the perceived thing itself. Percept theory has therefore not recognized the possibility that the noema is simply the neutral, non-productive, non-posited boundary between propositions and things, a neutral boundary which is the condition of possibility for the correlation between sense and object. Because this has not been recognized, and following from his either/or, Gurwitsch concludes that the perceptual noema is 'nothing less than' the perceived, *posited object*.[122]

The concept and percept theories of the perceptual noema represent the two contrasting senses of the noema understood as neutral, and in each case they fail to appreciate the ongoing effort of Husserl to account for the non-vicious infinite regress while avoiding a vicious epistemological regress (e.g., Hume, as discussed above). Concept theory accepts the non-vicious regress only in so far as it shows that the noema is not an object; percept theory rejects Husserl's paradoxical solution, and is left claiming that the perceptual noema is 'nothing less than' the perceived thing. We have been trying to show, however, that the noema arose through Husserl's efforts to circumvent the epistemological regress and account for the possibility of objectivity, an objectivity characterized by the fundamental and irreducible difference between sense (e.g., signitive acts) and object (e.g., intuitive acts). The noema is subsequently understood as the neutral condition for the possibility of the differentiation and correlation of sense and object, and hence is for Husserl the key to explaining objectivity. As the neutral, *non-positing* boundary between sense and object, the noema allows for their interaction in that it has a side turned towards each without itself being identified with either. The noema can be understood, then, to function much as geographic boundaries do: that is, they do not exist as anything but that which differentiates between one country or territory on the one side, and another country or territory on the other. As a boundary it is not to be identified, or *posited*, with either side, yet it is the condition for differentiating and identifying each side. Furthermore, it is only after the two sides of an irreducible difference are identified (i.e., posited) that one can then have the regress which arises with their infinite correlation; consequently, the neutrality of the noema, or paradoxa, is the condition for the regress, and it is in this way that Husserl's transcendental phenomenology can be understood in light of an encounter with, and an attempt to explicate, paradox.

This continuing encounter with paradox that we have found to be implicit throughout Husserl's work becomes, in the work of Maurice Merleau-Ponty, an explicit theme. Merleau-Ponty, unlike Gurwitsch, does not claim that remaining true to the phenomenological reduction entails the rejection of paradox and paradoxical entities; rather, Merleau-Ponty claims that the phenomenological reduction teaches us the 'impossibility of a complete reduction,' and that the world is at heart 'paradoxical.'[123] In Merleau-Ponty's later work, he goes on to say that 'the schizophrenic and the philosopher each knocks himself against the paradoxes of existence'; on the one hand, the schizophrenic 'is ruled by his failure which expresses itself only in a few enigmatic phrases'; on the other hand, the philosopher 'leaves behind a furrow of expressive acts which enable us to rediscover our situation.'[124] Husserl's notion of the noema is, as we have tried to show, one such example of an expressive act left in the wake of Husserl's encounter with paradox. However, Husserl continued to encounter and contend with paradoxes until the end of his career, and even more explicitly than in the works we have discussed here. For example, in *Cartesian Meditations*, Husserl attempts to reconcile the paradox of an-other absolute self-constituting consciousness that is constituted by one's own absolute consciousness, yet, nevertheless, is other. And, in *The Crisis of European Sciences*, Husserl encounters the paradox of a part of the world, human subjectivity, constituting the world of which it is a part. Limited space prevents our discussing in detail all these issues; however, before turning to Merleau-Ponty, we will briefly examine the problem of the other in Husserl's phenomenology, a problem which directly influenced and motivated Merleau-Ponty's departure from Husserl. This discussion should show that Husserl: (1) continued to try to reconcile his encounters with paradox with his efforts to ground and establish the science of phenomenology; and (2) his moves in the Fifth Cartesian Meditation demonstrate a recognition on his part of certain inadequacies in his theory of the noema, in particular, the manner in which the noema is related to objectivity; or, to put it another way, the relation between noema and truth. After all, Husserl's efforts to ground the science of phenomenology were, in the end, meant to put the traditional sciences back on the road to truth.

PART TWO

Merleau-Ponty

III. The Middle Path

Husserl's philosophic career was dominated, as he himself admits, by the attempt to elaborate the correlation between experienced objects and the manner in which these objects are given as intended objects.[1] For example, in speech one experiences the meanings that are intended, the sense of what is being said, but this experienced object (sense) depends upon its being given in some manner – that is, being given in an act of expression which intends this sense. Husserl will thus argue for what he believes to be a fundamental and irreducible difference between signitive acts (i.e., acts which intend or give an object) and intuitive acts (i.e., acts that experience or are given an object). Husserl criticized Kant, as we saw,[2] for not recognizing this difference; that is, for not accounting for the pre-logical objectivation of consciousness (i.e., the givenness of objects to intuition), an object-ivation that is the condition for a signitive concept (i.e., category), for a concept that intends an object. The problem for Husserl, therefore, is to show, on the one hand, how intuitive acts lay the foundation for signitive acts, and, on the other hand, show how signitive acts are fulfilled by intuitive acts. In other words, the problem is to elaborate the correlation between signitive and intuitive acts, and it is precisely this elaboration which Husserl recognized to be the dominant theme of his work.

In our discussion of this theme, we saw that the correlation between signitive and intuitive acts is mediated by the sense of the act or by the consciousness of meaning. That is, the sense of an intuitive act founds a signitive act which intends this sense; and the sense of a signitive act is fulfilled by an intuitive act if the latter act gives that which was intended or meant. The question then arises concerning the nature of this sense. It is clear that, for Husserl, the sense of an act, or the meaning immanent to consciousness, is not to be identified with this act, with the subjective processes of consciousness itself. To do this is simply a form of psychologism that Husserl wanted to avoid: that is, Husserl does not want to reduce the meaning of acts, for example, logical reasoning, to the acts themselves, or to the states of psychological subjects (à la Mill). Husserl also does not want to claim that the sense or meaning of an act is a transcendent and independent object. Not only does this position entail a Platonic Realism that Husserl was against, but, if one claims that an object is known only through the sense of an act, and if this sense is itself an object, then we have an example of an epistemological infinite regress; that is, the regress of knowing an object only when we know another object, an object which is in turn known only when we know another, and so on ad infinitum.[3]

To avoid this regress, Husserl argues that in intuition an object is known directly or 'straightforwardly.' In perception, for example (i.e., the perceptual model), one perceives an object as a unity of perceptual aspects, as a whole which is open to further inspection, but this object is nevertheless directly perceived as a unity. Perception is therefore an example of how one can be directly presented with objects, and thus Husserl also avoids the regress which is generated when one claims that an object is known only indirectly through other objects. There is, however, a problem which we saw emerge out of this position. This followed Husserl's claim that it is the sense of an act which mediates the correlation between signitive and intuitive acts, or that 'we are always situated in the sphere of sense.' If this is so, then it was difficult to see what Husserl took to be the sense of a perceptual act, the meaning of perceptual consciousness. On the one hand, Husserl seems to claim that the constituted sensations of an object are determinative (i.e., the sense) of what object we see; and, on the other, he claims that it is the abstract form or concept which determines what we see. However, if Husserl claims that the sense of perceptual consciousness is the sensations, or the constituted givens of an object, then he would be arguing that an object is known only through another object (sensations or impressions), and thus the regress would result. But if Husserl claims that it is an abstract form or concept, then it is difficult to see how we could get beyond the sense of perception to the object perceived. As Dreyfus pointed out, there results here an infinite regress of sense infinitely coinciding with sense. Since the perceived object is determined on the basis of an abstract sense, and since perception was brought in as an example of how an object can be directly given, or how we can avoid the regress, then the fulfilment of an intended sense by an intuited object is not explained. It is only the fulfilment of the sense of one act by the sense of another that has been explained, and thus the effort to show how something can be known or intuited directly, or how the sense of an intending act can be fulfilled by an intuitively given object; this effort does not show how sense can coincide with its object, how sense can be fulfilled. Consequently, since it is the object which is to be known directly through sense (i.e., object as fulfilment, as adequation of knowledge), Husserl has thus not been able to avoid the epistemological infinite regress.

Husserl did make moves, as we showed, to resolve these difficulties. For example, in order to avoid the regress of sense infinitely coinciding with sense, Husserl, in *The Phenomenology of Internal Time-Consciousness*, claims that this regress is grounded in an absolute consciousness, a consciousness where sense and its object do coincide. Husserl thus claims that, 'as startling (if not at first sight even contradictory) as it may appear to assert that the flux of consciousness constitutes its own unity, it is still true, nevertheless.'[4] In other words, the vicious epistemological regress, the regress that is generated when sense never coincides with its object, and when, as a result, sense only coincides with sense, is overcome at the level of the absolute consciousness (or what in *Ideas* Husserl calls 'the pure transcendental ego'). At this level consciousness *is* the coincidence of sense and its object; or, as Gurwitsch claims, it is 'that paradoxical entity.' Furthermore, this paradoxical entity is the differentiating condition which makes possible the regress of sense infinitely coinciding with sense; that is, it is the condition which makes possible the distinction between an intended sense (i.e., a signitive act) and a given sense (i.e., an intuitive act). Husserl will then conclude that this paradoxical entity is the condition which opens consciousness to nonending reflection: 'Even if reflection is not carried out *ad infinitum* and if, in general, no reflection is necessary, still that which makes this reflection possible (i.e., the absolute or "paradoxical" consciousness), and, in principle possible *ad infinitum*[,] must be given.'[5] Thus the paradoxical nature of this absolute consciousness avoids the vicious epistemological regress, and is subsequently interpreted to be the condition for the nonvicious regress of reflection, for the possibility of for ever taking consciousness as an object for consciousness.

An important consequence of this paradoxical consciousness, of a consciousness that constitutes its own unity, is that it explains how there can be a constituted object immanent to consciousness itself. That is, if consciousness constitutes its own unity, then there is a constituted object that does not transcend consciousness; and it is precisely this immanent object which Husserl uses in order to take a middle path between psychologism and Platonic Realism. In other words, this immanent object is not the constituting act of consciousness itself, for it is a constituted object. On the other hand, this immanent object is not transcendent, in the sense that 'real' objects transcend our consciousness of them; rather, this immanent object is to be understood as a transcendence in immanence, or what Husserl later calls the 'objective correlate of a constituting consciousness.' It is therefore in *The Phenomenology of Internal Time-Consciousness* where the concept of an immanent object is first formulated; yet, despite this move, the question remained whether this absolute consciousness resolved the question of how an actual subject comes to have an intuitively fulfilled and objective knowledge. In attempting to explicate Husserl's possible response to this question, we explored this concept of an immanent object as developed in *Ideas*, where Husserl uses the term 'noema' to refer to the objective correlate of a constituting consciousness (i.e., noesis-noema).

In our discussion of the noema, we saw that Husserl claims it is neither a positing nor a posited entity. As an objective correlate, the noema is not to be confused with the constituting or positing acts of consciousness, and, as a transcendence in immanence, it is not to be confused with an object posited as transcendent. The noema should be interpreted, therefore, to be the differentiating condition which makes possible both the positings of consciousness and the posited objects for consciousness. We also argued that the noema, as was the case for the absolute consciousness, is paradoxical. In other words, the noema is simultaneously subjective and objective, immanent and transcendent, but is not to be identified with either side. For example, in discussing the perceptual noema, we saw that a failure to recognize the paradoxical nature of the noema led to an identification of it either as a posited sense, as a sense immanent to a *positing* consciousness (i.e., concept theory), or as a *posited* object, as the aspect or manner in which a transcendent object is given (percept theory). We argued, on the contrary, that the noema should be understood as the paradoxical entity which is the differentiating condition that makes possible the distinction between positing sense and posited object. In short, the noema is the differentiating condition between an immanent sense and a transcendent object (i.e., the noema as boundary), and is thus the condition for the infinite coincidence of sense with sense that is a result of this irreducible difference.

These discussions have shown paradox to be an important theme in Husserl's philosophy. On the one hand, it is the paradox of an absolute self-constituting consciousness which is used to avoid the vicious epistemological regress, the regress that was generated when one claims that an object can be known only through another object (i.e., sense). On the other hand, it is the paradoxical nature of the noema which conditions the correlation of positing sense and posited object; or, to put it another way, the noema is the differentiating condition for the signitive/intuitive distinction. It is therefore a fundamental paradox, or an entity that is at bottom paradoxical, which emerges in Husserl's thought as that which makes possible an irreducible difference (i.e., between constituting and constituted, signitive and intuitive); and this is precisely what we mean when we say that the absolute consciousness, or the noema as boundary, is the paradoxical entity that is the differentiating condition.

To claim that the absolute consciousness and the noema are paradoxical is not to say that they are contradictory. To be contradictory would presuppose the identity of the opposed and contradictory elements. The understanding of paradox that we have in mind is, rather, that of a differentiating condition which makes possible the contradiction of opposed identities. This was the sense in which the noema was described as the boundary between a posited sense and a posited object. That is, as paradox we claimed the noema can be rightly seen to affirm both the sense of a positing consciousness and the sense of a posited object. We can then define paradox here as the simultaneous affirmation of two contrasting senses; however, these contrasting senses are not contradictory, as the differentiating-condition paradox (e.g., the noema) is what makes possible the identifications of a posited sense and a posited object. In other words, the noema is the neutral, non-positing condition which cannot be identified with either of the two sides it makes possible. It was for this reason that we claimed our understanding of paradox could be more accurately defined as paradoxa – it is the differentiating and non-positing (non-doxic), neutral, and non-identifiable condition for the identifications that lead to the contradictions upon which the traditional understanding of paradox is based.

It was with this interpretation of the noema as paradoxical that we approached the percept and concept theories of the perceptual noema. Both these theories attempted to identify the perceptual noema – concept theory identified the perceptual noema with a posited sense, and percept theory identified it with a posited object. Our claim, to the contrary, is that, as the paradoxical differentiating condition, the noema is non-identifiable and non-positing, and is furthermore that which makes possible the identifications of posited sense (concept theory) and posited object (percept theory). We thus claim that both percept theory and concept theory fail to recognize this paradox, and it is for this reason that we find two contrasting interpretations. In other words, there is a tendency to affirm and identify only one of the two senses of the paradox (e.g., posited sense/posited object), and as a result there is the sharp contrast between percept theory and concept theory.

This tendency to affirm only one of the two senses of the paradox is, in essence, a denial of the paradox. It is the denial of paradox as differentiating condition, as non-identifiable, in favour of a condition that is identifiable (e.g., noema *is* a proposition; noema *is* a percept). Another example of this tendency, and what we believe Husserl himself does, is to argue for the identity of a mediating third. That is, the two senses affirmed by the paradox are seen to be mediated, or correlated, by the identity of a third entity (e.g., the noema). For example, and this returns us again to the dominant theme of Husserl's work, the noema is interpreted to be that mediating identity which correlates the positings of consciousness (i.e., manners of givenness, or signitive acts) with the posited objects of experience (i.e., experienced objects, or intuitive acts). And this is seen most clearly in *Ideas*, where the noema is understood to mediate between a fundamental positing consciousness (i.e., Urdoxa), and the reality that is the invariant pole of this positing (i.e., object in general, or the identifiable X). This interpretation of the noema, however, also denies the paradox; that is, it denies the noema as the non-identifiable, non-positing, differentiating condition, and claims that the noema is the mediating identity between two already-identified entities (i.e., the dualism of a fundamental positing consciousness and a posited reality). Thus, despite Husserl's moves in the direction of taking the noema as the paradoxical differentiating condition, the understanding of the noema that ultimately emerges runs counter to these moves. As a result, Husserl's affirmation of a fundamental dualism between an absolute positing consciousness and the reality that is the correlate of this consciousness becomes especially problematic when he attempts to account for the relationship between them, or as he attempts to elaborate their correlation. And as we turn to Merleau-Ponty and Ricoeur's analysis of Husserl's work, we will see that they claim Husserl's dualism leaves this elaboration necessarily inadequate.

1. Merleau-Ponty's 'Noematic Analysis'

In his excellent book on Husserl, *Husserl: An Analysis of His Phenomenology*, Paul Ricoeur claims that 'in the final analysis *Ideas I* undertakes the task of constituting the "relation" of the noema as "sense-intending-a-being."'[6] In other words, the noema, as Ricoeur interprets it, is understood to be that which mediates the relation between a constituting or intending consciousness and the reality or being that is the constituted 'given' for this consciousness. Thus the noema as 'sense-intending-a-being' exemplifies the Husserlian theme of elaborating the correlation between an intending act and an intuitive act; or, as Ricoeur continues, it exemplifies 'the central difficulty of the Husserlian notion of constitution, the difficulty of bringing the theme of sense-giving into coincidence with the theme of self-givenness.'[7]

The difficulty here for Ricoeur, and a difficulty which follows Husserl's understanding of noema as 'sense-intending-a-being,' is that the coincidence Husserl hopes to achieve is, in principle, impossible for the simple reason that Husserl presupposes an irreducible difference between a constituting consciousness and a constituted self-given object (i.e., the dualism of positing consciousness and posited reality). Thus the dualism that is a consequence of the interpretation of the noema as a mediating identity, as 'sense-intending-a-being,' results in the irremovable difficulty of elaborating the correlation between the intending of sense and the fulfilment of this sense in the self-givenness of a directly presented object. In short, Husserl's understanding of the noema does not resolve the epistemological regress, and thus his theory of the noema does not show how an actual subject can obtain the coincidence of sense and object (i.e., intuitively fulfiled and objective knowledge).

The regress that Husserl's move to an absolute self-constituting consciousness sought to resolve returns when the noema itself is not interpreted as a 'paradoxical entity.' That is, when the noema is interpreted to be a mediating identity, then the problem is to explain the nature of the reality that is being posited through the noema. In other words, rather than trying to elaborate how the sense is fulfiled by a self-given object, the problem now is to explain how the noema is fulfiled by the reality (or object in general) it intends. Ricoeur will thus claim that Husserl's moves in *The Phenomenology of Internal Time-Consciousness*, as well as in the Third Cartesian Meditation, fall short. The reason is that these moves entailed the presence of a constituted self to a constituting self, a presence that is typified in Husserl's analysis of time-consciousness. In the Third Meditation, for example, as was the case in his earlier work on time-consciousness, Husserl claims that his analysis should ascend 'from the lowest objective basis. To be the lowest objective basis is the continual function of immanent temporality, *the flowing life that consti-tutes itself in and for itself.*'[8] With the move to the noema, however, the coincidence of self with self is no longer adequate. Now the problem is to account for the coincidence of self with the reality that transcends the self, with the reality intended through the noema. In other words, the problem that now emerges as central to Husserl's project is the problem of the other; or, as Ricoeur notes, 'if evidence does not make us get beyond ourselves, the whole burden of otherness rests on the otherness of the Other.'[9] To put it another way, if the move to the noema does not resolve the epistemological regress, then Husserl must account for the otherness of the other, for that which transcends the self, in order to elaborate adequately the noema's mediating correlation between con-sciousness and reality. The task, therefore, is to show that 'transcenden-tal subjectivity *is* intersubjectivity.'[10]

Merleau-Ponty also concludes that Husserl's key problem is to show that 'transcendental subjectivity is intersubjectivity';[11] however, his rea-sons for this differ somewhat from Ricoeur's. In particular, whereas the problem for Husserl, as Ricoeur sees it, is that of constituting reality, or the noema's relation to the reality it intends, the problem for Merleau-Ponty is that reality is always already given: 'The problem of the world, and, to begin with, that of one's own body, consists in the fact that it is all there.'[12] As a result, Merleau-Ponty claims that the phenomenologi-cal reduction's attempt to reduce the world to the 'world-as-meaning,' or to the world as the correlate of a constituting consciousness, presup-poses the world as an already-given and constituted unity, as the unity which makes possible the reduction.[13] Merleau-Ponty therefore claims that 'the most important lesson which the reduction teaches us is the impossibility of a complete reduction.'[14] Consequently, Merleau-Ponty claims that, rather than attempting to describe the world or reality as the product of a constituting consciousness, Husserl should have remained true to a '"noematic reflection" which remains within the object and, instead of begetting it, brings to light its fundamental unity.'[15] In other words, instead of attempting to elaborate the unity of the world in terms of a correlation between a constituting consciousness and the consti-tuted givens for consciousness, Merleau-Ponty claims that phenomenol-ogy should reveal the unity of the world that is always already there.

The noema, therefore, is not for Merleau-Ponty, as it was for Husserl, the mediating identity between the subject and the world; rather, the noema is the unity that is the condition which makes possible the distinction between subject and world. The problem for Husserl, as Merleau-Ponty sees it, is that he did not remain true to his moves towards understanding the noema as the differentiating condition. As a result, the difficulty for Husserl is to account for the unity of the world, or for the unity of subjects in a world; that is, the problem is to show that 'transcendental subjectivity is intersubjectivity.' However, as long as Husserl continues to try to reduce the world and others to the level of a constituting consciousness, and as long as the noema is understood as 'sense-intending-a-being,' then Husserl will be confronted with the paradox of explaining how part of the world, a human subject, constitutes the whole world as well as others. For Merleau-Ponty, on the other hand, if you understand a proper noematic reflection to be the revealing of an already-given unity – the unity of self, other, and world – and as a unity which is the condition for differentiating between self, other, and world, then one can see that 'transcendental subjectivity is intersubjectivity,' and that this unity is the condition for the distinction between self and other. It is therefore to the already-given unity of the world that Merleau-Ponty will look in his efforts to resolve the difficulties he will see emerge in Husserl's account of the other. To do this, Merleau-Ponty believes, is simply to be true to the phenomenological reduction: 'The best formulation of the reduction is probably that given by Eugen Fink, Husserl's assistant, when he spoke of "wonder" in the face of the world.'[16] That is, the impossibility of the phenomenological reduction reveals the wonder we have in the face of a world that is always already there.

To clarify further Merleau-Ponty's point of departure from Husserl, we will discuss in more detail the problems that Merelau-Ponty and Ricoeur believe exist in Husserl's account of the other.

2. The Problem of 'the Other'

In Ricoeur's interpretation of Husserl's argument for the other, he stresses Husserl's effort to reconcile the reduction of the natural attitude to a correlate of a constituting consciousness with the recognition that the other is meaningful and cannot be reduced to one's self. In attempting to do this, Ricoeur claims that this task is recognized to be paradoxical. In particular, Ricoeur claims that Husserl's strategy of reducing the phenomena of world and others to the 'sphere of ownness' is, for Husserl, a 'recognition of the paradox as a paradox.'[17] We thus find Husserl claiming that, 'in this pre-eminent intentionality there becomes constituted for me the new existence-sense that goes beyond my monadic very-ownness; there becomes constituted an ego, not as "I myself," but as mirrored in my own ego, in my monad.'[18] In other words, the paradox here is that, although there is only one subject, that is, 'this pre-eminent intentionality,' there is an-other subject, a subject that mirrors this subject. This mirroring is the condition which is the sense (i.e., 'existence-sense') of the consciousness of the other. However, this is a purely formal condition and sense, and the other is here simply 'an analogue of my own self';[19] therefore, this formal condition or sense needs to be fulfilled. We need to account for the other as other, as a subject that cannot be reduced to the self.

To account for the fulfilment of the sense of the other, Husserl turns to analogy. The other is hence perceived as an other subject because the expressions and behaviours of the other's body are analogous to the expressions and behaviours of one's own body, the body which is the constituted object for our consciousness, for our 'pre-eminent intentionality.' Husserl is straightforward on this point:

> Since, in this Nature and this world, my animate organism is the only body that is or can be constituted originally as an animate organism (a functioning organ), the body over there, which is nevertheless apprehended as an animate organism, must have derived this sense by an *apperceptive transfer from my animate organism*, and done so in a manner that excludes an actually direct, and hence primordial, showing of the predicates belonging to an animate organism specifically, a showing of them in perception proper. It is clear from the very beginning that only a similarity connecting, within my primordial sphere, that body over there with my body can serve as the motivational basis for the *'analogizing' apprehension* of that body as another animate organism.[20]

This does not resolve our earlier problem, however, and only shifts it from the level of consciousness to the level of objects constituted by consciousness. In other words, if we can know the other only on the basis of an antecedent understanding (i.e., the knowledge of one's own body), then again the other is being reduced to the self, to 'this pre-eminent intentionality,' and thus the account of the other as Other remains inadequate.

Ricoeur argues that, despite these difficulties, Husserl does not seem to find them unpalatable. The reason for this, Ricoeur claims, is that, through imagination, the analogical presentation of the other becomes freed from one's actual experience. In other words, our recognition of the other moves beyond what we actually experience to what we can possibly experience, a possibility that is revealed through the free variations of imagination. For example, although I am here and the other is there, I can imagine myself being there: it is an imagined possibility or variation of myself. Ricoeur argues that, as a result, 'I pair the Other not only to my actual experience but to my potential experiences as well; by imagining what I would see from over there, I advance further into the analogous existence of the Other.'[21] The other is thus freed from being known only through one's own actual experience, and since the other can be recognized with what is not actual, with what is not actually presented to consciousness,[22] then we can see why the other is not problematic for Husserl. In essence, through the imagination we can recognize as meaningful that which is not present, or, to put it another way, the otherness of the Other.

There is a problem here, however, and it is a problem familiar to Husserl. For example, in *The Phenomenology of Internal Time-Consciousness*, Husserl states that, for Brentano, not only is the past known only through the imagination, but the very idea of time itself has its origins in 'the sphere of phantasy.'[23] In other words, for Brentano one is constantly within the present, and to be conscious of the past one must, in a present moment, bring to consciousness something that is not present. Brentano claims that this, however, is an act of imagination (i.e., presenting something as not present), and further that it is this act which opens us to the very conception and consciousness of time. Husserl, on the other hand, asks whether 'the past really appears in this consciousness (i.e., time-consciousness) in the mode of phantasy,'[24] and argues, in the end, that such a position is 'very questionable.'[25] His reason for this conclusion is that he does not want to reduce the past to the status of an imagined object. The past is something that Husserl believes can actually be presented, and thus he is opposed to the claim that the past is ultimately indistinguishable from an imagined object. But is this not exactly what Husserl is doing with respect to the other? Isn't Husserl reducing the other, the other as not-self, to the status of an imagined object?

It seems clear that this is what Husserl is doing. Consequently, if one wants to claim that an other is actually presented, not merely imagined, then Husserl's argument for the other is open to the same criticism that Husserl himself made of Brentano, and his failure to recognize this criticism reflects his commitment to the phenomenological reduction, to reducing the world and the other to the constitutions of a 'pre-eminent intentionality.' Husserl is thus unable to reconcile this commitment with the fact that the other as other *is* meaningful, that the other cannot be reduced to the self. Ricoeur recognizes this difficulty and concludes that, 'according to the idealistic requirement of constitution, the Other must be a modification of my ego'; and that this is never reconciled with the descriptive claims of phenomenology whereby 'the Other never ceases to exclude himself from the sphere of "my monad."'[26] In other words, Husserl is never able to show that 'transcendental subjectivity *is* inter-subjectivity.'

What Husserl should have done, and this is precisely what he did to circumvent Brentano's assertion that the past is only imagined, is to claim that there is a fundamental unity of self and other. That is, just as Husserl claims that there is, within the unity of time-consciousness, both past and present, so, too, should he have claimed that there is a unity wherein there is both self and other. He couldn't do this, however, because the unity he recognizes is always the unity of a constituting consciousness; consequently, the other could be understood only as something that is part of this unity (i.e., its mirrored part, or its analogue), and not something that is truly other. It is therefore the unity of consciousness which aids Husserl in resolving the difficulties he saw in Brentano, but it is this unity which creates problems for Husserl when he attempts to account for the Other. As Merleau-Ponty argues, in recognition of this difficulty,

> positing another person as an other myself is not as a matter of fact possible if it is consciousness which must do it. To be conscious is to constitute, so that I cannot be conscious of another person, since that would involve constituting him as constituting, and constituting in respect to the very act through which I constitute him. This difficulty of principle, posited as a limit at the beginning of the fifth Cartesian Meditation, is nowhere eliminated.[27]

Merleau-Ponty does recognize an effort on Husserl's part to argue for a fundamental differentiating condition that is to be identified neither with self or other nor with 'a consciousness which is neither self nor other.'[28] This we saw in our discussion of the absolute consciousness, the consciousness that is both constituting (self) and constituted (other). Despite this move, however, it is within the unity of this consciousness that an other consciousness is to emerge, and this, Merleau-Ponty claims, is, in principle, impossible. In other words, as long as the paradoxical unity of self and other, constituting and constituted, is a unity of consciousness, then Merleau-Ponty believes that it will be impossible to account for the other as Other, for the other that transcends our consciousness. What is needed, therefore, is a subject that is neither self nor other, consciousness nor object; a subject that is the differentiating condition for self and other, consciousness and object. In short, what is needed is an understanding of paradox that is not a paradox of consciousness, and it is precisely Merleau-Ponty's move to a phenomenology of the lived body that is intended to do just this: 'This subject which experiences itself as constituted at the moment it functions as constituting is my body.'[29] In other words, just as Husserl, in order to resolve problems he saw in Brentano, argued for a *consciousness* that is simultaneously constituting and constituted, so, too, does Merleau-Ponty, in order to resolve problems he saw in Husserl, argue for a *body* that is simultaneously constituting and constituted.

3. Paradox and the Middle Path

We are now in a better position to understand Merleau-Ponty's critique of Husserl's theory of the noema. Merleau-Ponty claimed, as quoted earlier, that Husserl should have remained true to a '"noematic reflection" which remains within the object and, instead of begetting it, brings to light its fundamental unity.'[30] In other words, since the noema emerges in Husserl's thought as the mediating identity between a constituting consciousness and the reality that is the invariant pole, Husserl is unable to account for the coincidence of this consciousness with reality. In particular, he is unable to show that transcendental subjectivity is intersubjectivity. The reason for this, as we argued, is that, for Husserl, unity is always a unity of consciousness; consequently, his account of the other as Other, that consciousness which transcends one's own constituting consciousness, remains inadequate. However, had Husserl revealed a unity that is not simply a unity of consciousness, but a unity wherein consciousness and object, self and other, are present, then he would have avoided these difficulties. Therefore, as Merleau-Ponty works through his noematic reflection, he claims that it reveals the body, and the world, as the unity which is the condition (i.e., differentiating condition) for self and other, consciousness and object.[31] That is, Merleau-Ponty's noematic reflection reveals the already-given unity of the world and one's body, a unity that is both constituting and constituted; or, as Merleau-Ponty argues, this reflection reveals the 'world as strange and paradoxical.'[32]

Another consequence of this paradoxical world is that it resolves the epistemological infinite regress. Just as Husserl's theory of an absolute consciousness, that paradoxical entity, was seen to avoid the regress in that it was the coincidence of sense and its object, so, too, does Merleau-Ponty's claim that the world, and one's body, is paradoxical resolve the regress. For Husserl, however, the regress reappeared when the noema was interpreted as the mediating identity between consciousness and reality; that is, Husserl was unable to account for the coincidence of consciousness (e.g., sense or self) and reality (e.g., object or other). Merleau-Ponty, on the other hand, by claiming that the always-already-given unity of the world is the paradoxical differentiating condition, will be able to circumvent the regress. Furthermore, just as the paradoxical differentiating condition of the absolute consciousness resolved, for Husserl, the vicious regress and replaced it with the non-vicious regress of reflection, Merleau-Ponty's claim that the body and the world is this differentiating condition will also replace the vicious epistemological regress with the non-vicious regress of being for ever open to the world, a world or reality that is infinite and inexhaustible.[33]

We can thus see that Ricoeur was wrong to say that Merleau-Ponty's theory of the body 'is entirely in the service of a philosophy of finitude.'[34] Ricoeur was correct to say that, whereas Husserl's philosophy was 'an effort to subordinate the understanding of the natural attitude more and more to the phenomenological reduction and to clarify the reduction by the transcendental constitution of the world,' Merleau-Ponty's philosophy, to the contrary, subordinated the reduction to the natural attitude, to 'the assurance that the world is always "already there."'[35] Ricoeur is not, however, correct to conclude that this commits Merleau-Ponty to a philosophy of finitude. The reason is that Ricoeur failed to recognize that, although Merleau-Ponty's move to resolve the epistemological infinite regress did entail grounding it in an already-given world, this grounding nevertheless results in another regress, the regress of being infinitely opened to this inexhaustible world. As a result, Ricoeur's claim that Merleau-Ponty, because of being entirely committed to a philosophy of finitude, is unable to account for 'the devotion to universality and to truth,'[36] is seen to be unjustified. The infinite plays an important and crucial role in Merleau-Ponty's thought, a role we will explore further in the next chapter.

Before turning to this subject, however, we want to conclude by emphasizing that Merleau-Ponty's phenomenology of the lived body continues to confront the issues that were of concern to Husserl. Thus, Merleau-Ponty's claim that the lived body is that paradoxical entity, that differentiating condition, is analogous to our claim that the noema is the paradoxical differentiating condition. In addition, Merleau-Ponty also takes the lived body, and, in particular, the lived body as a perceiving body, to be that entity which is neither positing or posited: 'the perception of our own body and the perception of external things provide an example of non-positing consciousness.'[37] Consequently, the perceiving body is to be identified neither with a positing or posited subject nor with a positing or posited object. As the paradoxical differentiating condition, the perceiving body is the boundary between the body as object and the body as subject. In other words, Merleau-Ponty's analysis of the body allows him, as Husserl attempted to do, to take a middle path between psychologism and Platonic Realism. And it is the charting of this middle path that is to characterize Merleau-Ponty's entire philosophic career. Thus even in Merleau-Ponty's first major work, *The Structure of Behavior*, he uses the term 'behavior' because he claims it is 'neutral with respect to the classical distinctions between the "mental" and the "physiological".'[38] In other words, Merleau-Ponty claims that behaviour cannot be reduced to either a physiological objectivism or a psychological subjectivism, and, in setting forth his concept of 'structure,' he attempts to chart a middle path between naturalism (i.e., physiological-causal, psychologism, object-ivism) and idealism (i.e., intellectualism, Platonic Realism, subject-ivism). This is precisely Merleau-Ponty's announced strategy: 'By going through behaviorism, however, one gains at least in being able to introduce consciousness, not as psychological reality or as cause, but as structure.'[39]

We turn now to an analysis of Merleau-Ponty's efforts to take this middle path.

IV. From Psychology to Phenomenology

1. Paradox and 'Structure'

Through a study of behaviour, Merleau-Ponty grapples with many of the problems we have been discussing. The two problems that are of particular concern for us are the problem of the other, or that independent object which is the condition for the fulfilment of objective knowledge (e.g., the other as the condition for objectivity, for the intersubjective objectivity of the scientific method), and the problem of the epistemological infinite regress, the regress which emerged in Husserl's thought as he attempted to resolve the first problem. In chapter I, for example, we saw that Husserl's efforts to explain the coincidence of an intending act with a fulfilling intuition resulted in a regress in that these acts were determined on the basis of their sense (i.e., determinative sense), and that this sense was in turn open to the possibility of being an object for another act, an act likewise determined by a sense, and so on. In other words, the object that fulfils an intention is given only through the sense of an intuitive act, but the sense of this act is in turn a sense that can be fulfilled by another act, by an act that takes this sense as its object, as the objective determination or fulfilment of its sense; but this determination is itself one that is in need of determination in that it, too, has a sense in need of fulfilment; and so on *ad infinitum*.[1]

Husserl's solution to the regress involved arguing for an absolute consciousness, for a consciousness that is both constituting and constituted, or is the paradoxical coincidence of sense and object ('that paradoxical entity'). The regress returned, however, when Husserl took the noema to be the mediating identity between consciousness and reality, and thus Husserl was again unable to resolve the problem of that object which fulfils an intention (e.g., the other). It was in response to these difficulties that Merleau-Ponty argued for the paradox of the world and one's body as the differentiating condition for self and other, sense and object. In short, the role of paradox becomes central to Merleau-Ponty's attempt to resolve the problem of the other, or what he calls in *The Phenomenology of Perception* the 'problems of transcendence':

> The problem of the existential modality of the social is at one with all problems of transcendence ... the question is always how I can be open to phenomena which transcend me, and which nevertheless exist only to the extent that I take them up and live them ... how the presence to myself (*Urpräsenz*) which establishes my own limits and conditions every alien presence is at the same time depresentation (*Entgegenwärtigung*) and throws me outside myself.[2]

Within the context of *The Structure of Behavior*, this problem of transcendence appears as the problem of whether behaviour is simply an objective physiological phenomenon, or whether there is a consciousness and subjectivity in behaviour that cannot be reduced to physiology. In other words, the problem is to explain how behaviour is simultaneously objective and subjective; or, to put it another way, how can we reconcile the interiority of subjectivity (*Urpräsenz*) with the exteriority (*Entgegenwärtigung*) of physiological causality? The solution lies in Merleau-Ponty's concept of structure – that is, the structure of behaviour is such that a physiological explanation of behaviour 'cannot be formulated without being transformed into consciousness and without presupposing existence for-itself'; and behaviour cannot be 'reduced to consciousness without presupposing the world and the situation in the world.'[3] And as Merleau-Ponty's critique of behaviourism in *The Structure of Behavior* reveals the impossibility of reducing behaviour either to the status of consciousness or to that of an object, he claims that we must not overlook the fundamental reason for this impossibility; that is, the paradox that is constitutive of structure: 'By following this short route [i.e., by simply criticizing behaviourism] we would have missed the essential feature of the phenomenon [i.e., of behaviour], the paradox which is constitutive of it: behavior is not a thing, but neither is it an idea.'[4] It is structure. Thus, in Merleau-Ponty's first approach to the problem of transcendence, we see that paradox plays a key role. Furthermore, the paradox that is constitutive of structure is the differentiating condition that is to be identified neither with things (objects, physiology) nor with ideas (subject, sense, consciousness). Structure is what makes these distinctions possible.

With this emphasis upon structure, we can see clear similarities between Gurwitsch's and Merleau-Ponty's approach to phenomenology. In particular, they each incorporate aspects of gestalt theory into their work. For example, Gurwitsch claims that the noema, as discussed earlier, is simply the manner in which the object presents itself, this object being understood to be 'a systematically organized multiplicity of manners of appearance and presentation.'[5] In other words, the perceived object, this perceived object as meant,[6] and the perceiving subject,[7] are all understood as systematic and organized structures. Put in the language of gestalt theory, 'the whole is the system of functional significances mutually dependent upon and attuned to one another.'[8] At the level of structure and gestalt, therefore, there is a coincidence of sense and object: that is, the sense is simply a part of a greater whole (e.g., perceptual noema as aspect or percept of the object).

Gurwitsch's turn to gestalt theory can thus be seen to be an effort to avoid the regress that was generated when sense never coincides with its object. We discussed this in greater detail in an earlier chapter; however, we can now see that Merleau-Ponty's turn to gestalt theory is similarly motivated. For example, in discussing meaning as it relates to perception, Merleau-Ponty claims that

> the meaning which I ultimately discover is not of the conceptual order. If it were a concept, the question would be how I can recognize it in the sense data, and it would be necessary for me to interpose between the concept and the sense data certain intermediaries, and then other intermediaries between these intermediaries, and so on. It is necessary that meaning and signs, the form and matter of perception, be related from the beginning and that, as we say, the matter of perception be 'pregnant with its form.'[9]

In other words, the perceived is not a formless mass moulded by an intellectual synthesis via concepts (recall our earlier discussion of the *hyle/morphe* distinction); on the contrary, the perceived is a structured unity from the beginning. It is an always-already-given whole or gestalt.

Despite these similarities between Gurwitsch and Merleau-Ponty, however, there is a fundamental difference. On the one hand, Gurwitsch rejects paradox, and, in particular, he rejects, as discussed earlier, Husserl's positing of an absolute consciousness (i.e., 'that paradoxical entity'). As a result, Gurwitsch's analysis, and, in particular, his theory of the perceptual noema, were seen to emphasize the perceptual noema as a percept of the given *object*. This theory, however, is susceptible to Husserl's criticism that, as a form of objectivism, it fails in the end to account for, or even understand, subjectivity or spirit. As Husserl puts it, 'they [gestalt theorists] remain caught up in objectivism; and this is especially true of the new reformers in psychology, who think that the fault lies entirely in the long dominant prejudice of atomism and that a new era has dawned with holistic psychology.'[10] He argues that gestalt psychology, because it is committed to a naïve objectivism, fails to account for the very conditions of objectivity itself: that is, spirit. In other words, by reducing spirit to a structured or 'pregnant' matter, gestalt theory is simply, Husserl would argue, a more sophisticated psychologism.

Merleau-Ponty, on the other hand, even though he does speak of a matter 'pregnant with its form,' is nevertheless concerned with discerning the conditions of objectivity, and, in the end, the condition for structure itself. And this condition is, as we have been arguing, paradox as the differentiating condition, the condition which makes possible the positing of objects and subjects. It is therefore the affirmation of the paradox that is constitutive of structure that allows Merleau-Ponty, on the one hand, to be concerned with the conditions for objectivity (and thus this is analogous to Husserl's paradox of absolute consciousness which is the condition for objectivity), and, on the other hand, to utilize the concept of structure and gestalt without being susceptible to Husserl's criticism. And with this understanding of structure and paradox, Merleau-Ponty believes that many problems can be resolved: in particular, the problem of the other, and the problem of the infinite regress.

2. Behaviour

In *The Structure of Behavior*, Merleau-Ponty's concept of structure first appears as the solution to the problem of the infinite proliferation of neural connections. For example, if each novel situation required a pre-established neural connection that this situation triggers, Merleau-Ponty claims that there would then need to be an infinite number of neural connections to account for the simplest of actions. Merleau-Ponty gives the example of an itch that needs to be scratched, and the indefinite number of positions that the arm could have to move from in order to scratch this itch.[11] Merleau-Ponty argues that there is not, however, the necessity that each new stimulus require a new neural connection. The reason is that it is the situation itself which 'governs the novel distribution of innervations.'[12] That is, the meaning of the situation, or the situation's general form or structure, is what can properly be understood to be the stimulus: 'the genuine stimulus is the ensemble as such.'[13]

It is therefore the structure or form of a situation, the stimulus as an ensemble, which triggers the response of the subject. The subject thus need not be capable of establishing an infinite number of connections in order to be able to respond to any novel stimulus. Subsequently, Merleau-Ponty claims that it is not the stimulus of perception which constitutes the perceived object. If this were so, then there would again need to be an infinite number of neural connections to process all possible stimuli.[14] Merleau-Ponty therefore claims that 'it is not the real world which constitutes the perceived world';[15] that is, it is not the stimulus. What constitutes the perceived world, rather, is a unity of functioning, a general form or structure – a gestalt.

Merleau-Ponty thus recognizes an irreducible difference between the unity of functioning and the parts of an objective physiological process – that is, the difference between perception understood as a unity of functioning, or as a gestalt, and perception understood as an external relationship of parts (i.e., its neural connections). This latter understanding will never explain the whole, the unity of functioning, and furthermore it generates a regress, because, no matter how many parts are used to explain this unity of functioning, they will never coincide with, or fully legitimate, this functioning. In other words, each determination of a behaviour is in turn open to another determination, and so on, until we find that we need an infinite number of neural connections to account for behaviour. The question here, however, is whether this is a vicious regress or not. On the one hand, a vicious regress is not started by claiming that behaviour, as well as the world, is for ever open to an infinite number of determinations. It is like saying that one can never count all the natural numbers. On the other hand, if a behaviour is to be accounted for in terms of pre-established nerve pathways and reflex arcs, and if that which regulates the inhibition and control of these nerves is itself understood in terms of pre-established reflex arcs, then, as Merleau-Ponty argues, the explanation of this behaviour will never be found. Each regulation will require a higher-order regulation, and this in turn will require an even higher one, and so on *ad infinitum*.[16]

To avoid this regress, Merleau-Ponty will make a distinction between physical and vital structures, a distinction which further reflects his recognition of an irreducible difference between the unity of functioning and objective physiological processes. A physical structure and system is one that is defined by its relationship to the external events with which it comes into equilibrium. For example, an analysis of the body as a physical structure would correlate a given system of neural connections with an actual environment, or with the external events (i.e., stimuli) that gave rise to this system. With a vital structure, on the other hand, its 'equilibrium is obtained, not with respect to real and present conditions, but with respect to conditions which are only virtual and which the system itself brings into existence.'[17] For example, an instinctive reaction to a stimulus is not simply a response to an external event; it is, rather, a response that Merleau-Ponty claims expresses as 'a unity of signification,'[18] a unity of functioning that cannot be decomposed into individual practices. That is, the animal lives in a milieu that is more than a set of externally related and present events, but is a milieu which is the unity that prompts all actions, whether actual or virtual: 'the reactions of an organism are understandable and predictable only if we conceive of them, not as muscular contractions which unfold in the body, but as acts which are addressed to a certain milieu, present or virtual: the act of taking a bait, of walking toward a goal, of running away from danger.'[19]

A vital structure thus cannot be reduced to a physical structure, and it is precisely the attempt to do this that generates the regress we spoke of. If a behaviour (i.e., a vital structure) is known only through its observed parts or aspects (i.e., physical structure), and if these parts or aspects are in turn known only through other parts and aspects, then there is generated the regress Merleau-Ponty wants to avoid. However, if a vital structure cannot be reduced to a physical structure, then we need not attempt to reduce the unity of behaviour to its observed parts. What we need to do, rather, is to understand that these observed parts express a 'unity of signification,' or each observed part is itself expressive of the unity or totality (i.e., vital structure) that conditions it. 'The totality,' Merleau-Ponty argues, 'is not an appearance; it is a phenomenon.'[20] In other words, the *appearances* of a 'physical structure' are externally related to each other in a relationship of cause and effect, and the *phenomena* of a 'vital structure' are intrinsically related to the unity or totality that they express.

There is here, as Merleau-Ponty admits, a paradox, the paradox of a unity or totality that is given only through a part or aspect. In other words, the phenomena of a vital structure are paradoxical in that these observed parts or aspects express the unity and totality of this structure.

For example, in perception the perceived object is given only through one of its aspects; however, in perception itself (i.e., perception as a vital structure and activity), this object expresses a unity of functioning, a unity of signification such that one perceives the object as a totality, and not as an aspect. This is also true of an observed behaviour in that the unity and totality of the subject are present in each of their individual actions, just as an object is present through each of its aspects. Thus one need not deduce or determine the unity of behaviour on the basis of its observed parts, for this unity is paradoxically present in each of its parts. In *The Structure of Behavior*, Merleau-Ponty recognizes this paradox but claims that 'this is not the place to analyze further the paradoxical relation of the "aspects" to the thing, of the "manifestations" to that which is manifested.'[21] The reason for this is that, in *The Structure of Behavior*, Merleau-Ponty intended to show the need for an accounting of structure, and he did this through a critique of behaviourism. To turn to an explanation of the phenomena of vital structures themselves, however, would entail doing phenomenology: 'In order to indicate both the intimacy of objects to the subject and the presence in them of solid structures which distinguish them from appearances, they will be called "phenomena"; and philosophy, to the extent that it adheres to this theme, becomes a phenomenology, that is, an inventory of consciousness as the milieu of the universe.'[22]

It is precisely this theme, and the paradox of perception (i.e., the paradox as constitutive of structure – the vital structure of perceiving), that becomes the concern of Merleau-Ponty in *The Phenomenology of Perception*.

3. Virtual Reality: The Human/Animal Distinction

To do phenomenology, however, one must be able to grasp the same unity from a multiplicity of perspectives. In other words, the same totality or structure is to be grasped through a series of perspectival changes. In perception, for example, an object can be perceived as the same despite the changing perspectives that one might have of this object. The reason, as alluded to earlier, is that the perceived is freed from the stimuli, or 'it is not the real world which constitutes the perceived world.'[23] It is, rather, the unity or structure of functioning (i.e., vital structure) which perceives an object as the unity of possible perceptions. But to perceive the phenomena of vital structures *as* phenomena, and not as appearances, entails being able to be freed not only from the stimuli themselves, but also from one's own vital structure – that is, one is able to identify with another structure. For example, one must be able to identify with another perspective, or grasp what an object would look like if one were 'over there' instead of 'here.' There is thus a distinction between perceiving an object as a physical structure, as a structured and systematic set of appearances, and perceiving an object as a vital structure, as phenomena. The first can be done by any vital structure, or by an animal where it is the unity of the milieu that prompts their actions, both actual and virtual (e.g., possible perceptions of the same object); the second is possible only if one can grasp oneself as an object, as the intended goal of an action. In other words, humans can grasp themselves as a vital structure, as an object, and thus can perceive the phenomena of these structures. Humans are thus able to perceive phenomena, or the unity and totality of an object through an aspect of this object, and it is this ability which opens humans to the use of symbolic forms, or to the possibility of expressing and perceiving the same theme or totality in a number of ways: 'It is this possibility of varied expressions of a same theme, this "multiplicity of perspective," which is lacking in animal behavior.'[24] In short, only humans are capable of using symbols, and of doing phenomenology.

A further consequence of this ability to use symbolic forms is the ability to recognize the other as Other. In other words, humans recognize an other ego or subject, a subject that is a unity or totality, through the aspects and behaviours that are perceived. Put another way, the recognition of the other is a variation of the paradoxical relation between the aspects or manifestations and that thing which is manifested. Therefore, the other is present in each of their behaviours, in each of their manifestations; or, as Merleau-Ponty puts it in *The Phenomenology of Perception*, 'there is nothing hidden behind these faces and gestures.'[25] The other is what they present to others, and, conversely, the self or ego is what it presents to others: 'I must be the exterior that I present to others, and the body of the other must be the other himself. This paradox of the Ego and the Alter are possible only provided that the Ego and the Alter Ego are defined by their situation, and are not freed from all inherence.'[26]

In other words, the self or ego is already other in that it is the exterior that the other sees, and the other, likewise, is the exterior that one sees. There is thus a paradox of the lived body in that it is at once self and other, interior and exterior, and it is this paradox which is constitutive of the self–other structure (i.e., paradox as the differentiating condition of self and other): 'Everything transpires as if the other person's intuitions

and motor realizations existed in a sort of relation of internal encroachment, as if my body and the body of the other person together formed a
system.'[27]

Merleau-Ponty claims that 'for Husserl ... it is well known that there is
a problem of other people, and the alter ego is a paradox'; however,
since Merleau-Ponty claims that it is the body which experiences this
paradox – that is, 'it experiences itself as constituted at the moment it
functions as constituting'[28] – then it is the experienced body which is the
basis for identifying oneself and others. The experienced body is thus
the differentiating condition for self and other without being identified
with either. In fact, Merleau-Ponty emphasizes childhood as the time
prior to the identification of self and other, yet the time that nevertheless
conditions the recognition of self and other. He argues that 'psychogene-
sis begins in a state where the child is unaware of himself and the other
as different beings.'[29] The child is, in other words, unable to perceive
itself or others as an abstract object, as a vital structure, and, as was the
case with animals, is unable to use symbolic forms. The child and the
animal are completely defined by their *actual* situation, by their milieu,
and they are unable to grasp a possible situation that they, as a vital
structure, can be in. They are thoroughly literal: 'The child is, in fact, the
situation and has no distance from it. The situation is taken in its most
immediate meaning, and all that happened before is nothing, canceled
from the time when a new situation arises.'[30]

Children do, however, eventually learn to recognize themselves and
others. Merleau-Ponty argues, following Lacan, that this occurs when
the child learns to recognize the objectification of itself, when the child
comes to recognize that it is the exterior it presents to others, or when
one comes to see one's self, as self, in the mirror: 'The child's problem is
... of understanding that the image in the mirror is *his* image, that it is
what others see of him, the appearance he presents to other subjects; and
the synthesis is less a synthesis of intellection then it is a synthesis of
coexistence with others.'[31]

To do this requires that the child, first, *identify* itself in a mirror and,
then, recognize that this mirror is *different* from itself. In other words, the
image in the mirror becomes a symbol that re-presents one's body. In
short, with the mirror stage, or what is called the 'specular image,' the
child first acquires the ability to recognize symbols, and it is this recognition that leads to the identification of other selves (i.e., selves that are
represented through the appearance, or facial gestures, they present). Yet
this is an ability Merleau-Ponty claims is never completed, and, as a

result, we are always susceptible to setbacks. There will be times, for example, when we fail to differentiate between ourselves and others, between our desires and others' desires, between our will and the will of others.[32]

This ability to recognize and use symbols, an ability Merleau-Ponty claims sets humans apart from animals, is also reflected in the animal's relationship to its image in the mirror. Merleau-Ponty argues that an animal's reaction to its specular image 'is very different from that of children.' In particular, the animal does not see itself in the image, but 'it is like a second animal facing him.' Even the chimpanzee, Merleau-Ponty claims, does not get to the point where the image in the mirror becomes a symbol of its self, or body.[33] An animal, therefore, although a vital structure, is unable to transpose this structure unto another object, whether a mirror or another animal (i.e., identifying with the other 'over there'); consequently, because it lacks the ability to carry out this transposition, or this ability to recognize and use symbols, an animal is unable to recognize an other as a possibility of itself, and itself as a possibility of an other. An animal's world is one limited to that which is actual; as a result, it cannot perceive one situation to be a symbol for another situation. For example, a gesture is not seen to be a symbol for something this gesture is not: 'this pointing gesture, which animals do not understand, supposes that we are already installed in virtual space – at the end of the line prolonging our finger in a centrifugal and cultural space.'[34] In other words, an animal cannot respond to something that is not actually there, to something that is only virtually there, or only there as symbolized.

A couple of problems emerge with this analysis that need to be addressed. First, Merleau-Ponty had earlier claimed that the milieu is that which prompts an animal's actions, both actual and *virtual*. For example, a bird hears a sound and flies off as if the sound were actually a threat; a fish takes the bait as if the lure were an actual fish; and KoKo uses sign language to ask for food. It appears, then, that animals are to some degree 'installed in virtual space,' and it also seems that Merleau-Ponty's own analyses bear this out. Why does he then go on to claim that only humans are installed in virtual space, and that therefore only humans can recognize and use symbols? The second problem is that Merleau-Ponty's argument for the other seems to bring in the difficulties we saw with Husserl's account. For example, Merleau-Ponty claims that 'the other's body is a kind of replica of myself, a wandering double which haunts my surroundings more than it appears in them.'[35] That is, one knows the other as a double of one's self, or as an imaginative trans-position of one's self (i.e., what would it be like if I were over there?). But is this not simply reducing the other to the self, or, at best, to the status of an imagined object (à la Husserl)? There is evidence, even in Merleau-Ponty's late writings, which supports the claim that, for Merleau-Ponty, the other is known only on the basis of self-knowledge; that is, the other as self, not the other as Other: 'The reason why I have evidence of the other man's being there when I shake his hand is that *his hand is substituted for my left hand*, and my body annexes the body of another person in that "sort of reflection" [i.e., reflection = right hand touching left hand] it is paradoxically the seat of.'[36] And again in this same essay, he states: 'I see that this man over there sees, as I touch my left hand while it is touching my right.'[37]

Merleau-Ponty does indeed claim that an animal, situated in its envi-ronment, is prompted to both actual and virtual actions. However, these virtual actions nevertheless entail a connection to something actual – for example, the bird to the sound, the fish to the lure, and KoKo to his hun-ger. Therefore, although the action is virtual, it is not freed from an actual stimulus. With humans, on the other hand, their virtual actions are prompted by a recognition of the virtual *as* virtual. For example, one responds to a pointing gesture because it is recognized as virtual, as something directed towards a space that is not the space of the gesture. Thus the relationship between the respondent and that space which is being pointed to (i.e., virtual space) is indirect: it is established by means of the gesture. In other words, humans are capable of indirect communi-cation.[38] Furthermore, as freed from being directly linked to an actual stimulus in order to be communicated, this indirect communication gen-erates the possibility of infinite reiteration. The messages can be indi-rectly communicated indefinitely: A sees X and tells B about it; B tells C; C tells D; and so on *ad infinitum*. The first word (e.g., the word of God) thus makes possible its infinite transmission – the infinite task of com-munication. And it is precisely this origin – the first word that broke the silence and opened the infinite horizon of expression; the first painting that opened the infinite horizon of painting – that becomes a central theme in Merleau-Ponty's philosophy.

Perception is also a founding and originating act in that it, too, opens an infinite horizon, a horizon of inexhaustible possibilities. Conse-quently, to perceive the virtual *as* virtual entails seeing something as infinite, as the infinite possibilities of perceiving this same thing; possi-bilities that are only *virtually* present within the actual perception of an object. This is precisely what Merleau-Ponty understands to be the paradox of perception: 'Perception is here understood as a reference to a whole which can be grasped, in principle, only through certain of its parts or aspects ... Perception is thus paradoxical.'[39] And it is this paradox of the infinite within the finite that also opens us up to others, to the perception of the other as Other, as an absolute unity that transcends all we do or ever can know of them: 'Just as the perception of a thing opens me up to being by realizing the paradoxical synthesis of an infinity of perceptual aspects, in the same way the perception of the other founds morality by realizing the paradox of an alter ego, of a common situation, by placing my perspectives and incommunicable solitude in the visual field of another and of all others.'[40]

Although our contact with others is always of a finite and limited nature, we experience the other as the unity of infinite possibilities, as an absolute – that is, the other as Other. For Merleau-Ponty, consequently, an absolute divinity is to be understood, not by looking beyond man, but by looking at man: 'Nietzsche's idea that God is dead is already contained in the Christian idea of the death of God.'[41] That is, the death of Jesus, a man, is the death of an absolute – namely, the death of God. And even in *The Structure of Behavior*, we find Merleau-Ponty already saying something similar: 'A face is a center of human expression, the transparent envelope of the attitudes and desires of others ... This is why it seems impossible for us to treat a face or a body, even a dead body, like a thing. They are sacred entities, not the "givens of sight."'[42]

The claim that humans are set apart from animals because they perceive the virtual as virtual is therefore intimately related, as we can see, to the claim that humans also perceive the other as Other; consequently, the second problem concerning Merleau-Ponty's account of the other becomes even more pressing. That is, the problem of accounting for the other without reducing it to the self. In *The Structure of Behavior*, this problem is not resolved; however, in *The Phenomenology of Perception*, Merleau-Ponty turns to an investigation of that event which opened us to a perception of the other as Other, and this in turn entails an investigation of the conditions that make possible the perception of the virtual as virtual. Put another way, Merleau-Ponty's work turns towards an analysis and description of phenomena as phenomena – he turns to phenomenology. And since it is as an object of perception that the virtual is *seen* as virtual, and the other as Other, then it is understandable that the work which follows *The Structure of Behavior* is *The Phenomenology of Perception*.

4. The 'Primacy of Perception'

Merleau-Ponty's liberal reference to and reliance upon the facts of psychology, linguistics, and so on, to support and argue for his various philosophical positions appears to run quite counter to the spirit of phenomenology as understood by Husserl, who is clearly opposed to just this sort of move. Facts, as Husserl argued in *Logical Investigations*, can achieve, at best, only an approximate truth; therefore, a 'factual science,' and, in particular, psychology, can produce only 'statements about approximate regularities of coexistence and succession.'[43] In contrast to this, Husserl claims that direct intuition, or inner intuition, does give us certain indubitable, non-probablistic truths: 'Insight [direct intuition] justifies no mere probabilities of their holding, but their holding or truth itself.'[44]

Husserl will remain consistent to this position throughout his career. In *Ideas*, he will bracket the natural world of factual, probablistic knowledge, and claim that the phenomenological reduction reveals the fundamental truth to be a pure constituting consciousness (i.e., the pure transcendental ego). And even in 'The Origin of Geometry,' Husserl bemoans the fact that the self-givenness of intuition often gives way to a non-intuitive, technization of thought; that is, thought as a type of game which merely follows certain factual rules: 'in every individual life from childhood up to maturity, the originally intuitive life which creates its originally self-evident structures through activities on the basis of sense experience very quickly and in increasing measure falls victim to the seduction of language ... [that is] ... life lapses into a kind of talking and reading that is dominated purely by association.'[45]

Merleau-Ponty's use of arguments which utilize certain facts (e.g., the mirror-stage in his argument for the other) is therefore not in line with Husserl's rejection of facts in favour of the self-given evidence of intuition, or with the evidence that is revealed through the phenomenological reduction. In other words, Merleau-Ponty does not continue Husserl's effort to reduce the world of the natural standpoint – that is, the world as transcendent – to the world-as-meaning, or the 'world as such.' In fact, Merleau-Ponty claims that such a reduction presupposes the very transcendence it hopes to explain and legitimate. That is, the phenomenological reduction presupposes a fundamental relationship between the subject and the world, a relationship that is prior to, and the condition which makes possible, the positings of a thetic and doxic consciousness. Merleau-Ponty thus argues that the very transcendence of this world must retain a meaning in the eyes of 'reduced' consciousness, and transcendental immanence cannot be simply its antithesis ... [therefore] ... The natural attitude itself emerges unscathed from the complaints which can be made about naturalism, because it is 'prior to any thesis,' because it is the mystery of a *Weltthesis* prior to all theses. It is, Husserl says in another connection, the mystery of a primordial faith and a fundamental original opinion (Urdoxa).[46]

In our earlier discussion of the noema as the mediating identity between a fundamental positing consciousness (i.e., Urdoxa as the positing and belief in a world) and the reality that is the invariant pole of this positing (i.e., Object in general, or world), we saw that this dualism of subject (Urdoxa) and object was a result of not interpreting the noema as the differentiating condition (i.e., as paradoxa) which makes possible such a dualism. It was as a result of this dualism that we saw Husserl unable to resolve the epistemological infinite regress, that is, unable to account for the fulfilment of this fundamental positing (Urdoxa) by the self-given object (i.e., the world). And a sign of this failure, as Merleau-Ponty understands it, is precisely Husserl's claim that there is a fundamental belief, or 'a primordial faith,' in this world, a faith in a world that is prior to the thesis or positing of the world; in short, a faith that is the condition for the natural standpoint itself (i.e., natural standpoint as the *thesis* of the natural, transcendent world). In other words, Husserl's failure to resolve the epistemological regress appears, for Merleau-Ponty, as the failure of the phenomenological reduction – that is, the failed attempt to reduce the world to, *or make it coincident with*, an absolute constituting consciousness, and it is the fundamental belief in this world – Urdoxa – which makes such an attempt possible. For this reason, Merleau-Ponty claims that 'the most important lesson which the reduction teaches us is the impossibility of a complete reduction.'[47]

The *Phenomenology of Perception* will be, consequently, an investigation that reveals the impossibility of the reduction, or a phenomenological reduction that reveals, as Merleau-Ponty says, quoting Eugen Fink, 'the wonder in the face of the world.'[48] The failure of the phenomenological reduction is not, for Merleau-Ponty, a sign of phenomenology's inadequacy, but the recognition of a fundamental experience that is the condition for the natural attitude (i.e., for positing consciousness). And this experience is precisely the 'mystery of a primordial faith (Urdoxa),' the already-always-given ground and horizon of all our experiences. As a result theoretical consciousness is, as Merleau-Ponty argues, simply a variation upon this already-given world: 'Every evocation of possible worlds refers to a way of seeing our own world. Every possibility is a variant of our reality, an effective possibility of reality ... [and this will] make explicit that "world's thesis prior to every thesis and theory".'[49] In other words, there must first be a world that is given in experience before we can begin to speak of possibilities of this world, or posit theories concerning this world.

There is an interesting parallel here with Kripke. Kripke also claims that 'we begin with the objects, which we have, and can identify, in the actual world. We can then ask whether certain things might have been true of the objects.'[50] For example, 'it is because we can refer (rigidly) to Nixon, and stipulate that we are speaking of what might have happened to him (under certain circumstances), that "transworld identifications" are unproblematic in such cases.'[51] In other words, it is because we are already given and can designate an object that we can then speak of possibilities of this object, possibilities of identifying this object in different circumstances. This claim is analogous to Merleau-Ponty's that it is because we are already given a world as the horizon of our experience that we can then posit and designate possibilities of this world (i.e., theorize). And the motivation for this claim is also similar to that of Kripke's. Kripke, as discussed earlier, claims that it is the already-given (i.e., rigidly designated) object that allows for us to speak of different descriptive properties that *this* object might have, and thus his causal theory of reference emerges in contrast to the theory that claims the reference is determined by its description, or by its descriptive properties. The difficulty with description theory, Kripke argues, is that it results in a false dilemma: either the object is behind the bundle of descriptive properties or it is nothing but these descriptive properties. In each case, however, the difficulty was to explain how an object could be referred to by means of an indefinite series of descriptions, both factual and counter-factual.[52]

The problem for Merleau-Ponty, similarly, is to explain how an object can be given and identified if it is given only through one of an infinite number of possible aspects or perspectives. Merleau-Ponty is thus also confronted with a dilemma: either the object is behind the aspects or perspectives that it presents (i.e., Kant's thing-in-itself) or it is nothing but the aspects it presents (i.e., Berkeley's phenomenalism). Merleau-Ponty's solution to this problem is to say, analogous to what Kripke says, that the world is the already-always-given ground and horizon that make possible the perspectives we can have of *this* world: 'the natural world is the horizon of all horizons, the style of all possible styles, which guarantees for my experiences a given, not a willed, unity underlying all the disruptions of my personal and historical life.'[53] Furthermore, it is this horizon that is the already-given 'mystery of the world,' the mystery of a world that is always given, yet never given completely:

> when I say that I see the ash-tray over there, I suppose as completed an unfolding of experience which could go on *ad infinitum*, and I commit a whole perceptual future. Similarly, when I say that I know and like someone, I aim, beyond his qualities, at an inexhaustible ground which may one day shatter the image that I have formed of him. This is the price for there being things and 'other people' for us, not as the result of some illusion, but as the result of a violent act which is perception itself.[54]

In other words, the givenness of the world is, as Husserl recognized, a matter of faith, a faith and commitment to an unknown future; and it is this faith, Merleau-Ponty argues, that characterizes perception: 'Perceiving is pinning one's faith, at a stroke, in a whole future of experiences, and doing so in a present which never strictly guarantees the future; it places one's belief in a world (i.e., *Urdoxa*).'[55] And this perceptual faith is intimately related to the paradox of perception; that is, perception gives us an object despite the fact that this object is not given completely, that there is much that remains to be seen, and that future perceptions may destroy the object we thought we saw, the object upon which we had pinned our faith.[56] Perception not only gives us a world, but also gives us more than what is actually given, and this paradox of perception leaves open the possibility of disruption, or the possibility of a violent overthrow of our future expectations. The possibility of this overthrow, furthermore, adds support to Merleau-Ponty's claim that the phenomenological reduction cannot reduce transcendence to immanence, even if it is a transcendence in immanence. In other words, the paradox of perception leads Merleau-Ponty to claim that, although an object may be given to a perceiving subject only in a certain manner (i.e., through a part or aspect), this object is nevertheless given as transcendent to this givenness. Merleau-Ponty concludes from this that 'there is a paradox of immanence and transcendence in perception. Immanence, because the perceived object cannot be foreign to him who perceives; transcendence, because it always contains something more than what is actually given. And these two elements of perception are not, properly speaking, contradictory.'[57]

There is not a contradiction in the usual sense because Merleau-Ponty does not take paradox to be an expression that describes a contradictory state of affairs between two posited and identifiable elements. It is, rather, the condition that makes possible such positings and identifications; or, as we have defined it, it is *paradoxa*. Merleau-Ponty thus argues that a fundamental paradox or contradiction is not a damning one if it is the condition that makes possible the identifications and distinctions that give rise to contradictions. Merleau-Ponty claims that 'I wish only to point out that the accusation of contradiction is not decisive, if the acknowledged contradiction appears as the very condition of consciousness.'[58] A distinction needs to be made, therefore, between 'the sterile non-contradiction of formal logic and the justified contradictions of transcendental logic.'[59] In other words, if an investigation reveals a paradox (i.e., the phenomenological reduction that shows 'the world is paradoxical'), it is justified if this paradox is the fundamental differentiating condition that makes possible consciousness and the posited identifications and differentiations that are the result of this consciousness. In short, it is justified if it reveals paradoxa.

To understand perception as paradoxa, therefore, entails, as we have argued, understanding it as the differentiating condition which makes possible the positings of a thetic consciousness. 'Primary perception,' consequently, 'is non-thetic,'[60] or the paradox of perception is to be identified neither with a positing subject nor with a posited object – neither idealism nor realism. Merleau-Ponty's effort to take the middle path will thus emphasize the transcendental contradiction (i.e., paradoxa) which makes possible the dualisms of subject–object, idealism–realism, immanence–transcendence. A proper transcendental phenomenology will therefore disclose a world and body that is paradoxical, a world and body that is always already there. Or, to put it another way, the impossibility of a complete phenomenological reduction shows that the problem is precisely to understand our openness to the world, the body, and others; and this is a problem not only for phenomenology, but also for psychology.[61] And if paradox is the fundamental transcendental condition (i.e., paradoxa), then it should not be surprising to find a theoretical consciousness (i.e., a positing or thetic consciousness), whether in philosophy or psychology, confronting the paradox that is its condition. In other words, philosophy and psychology will each confront the paradox that conditions the openness of a subject to a world – for example, the paradox of perception. As a result, the transcendental differentiating condition of paradoxa makes possible both Husserl's rejection of facts in favour of the phenomenological reduction which reduces the world to the *constituting subject* and the empirical sciences and their attempt to account for the givens of the *constituted world* (i.e., the facts). For Merleau-Ponty, therefore, the transition from psychology to phenomenology is a natural one: they each tackle with the problem of accounting for the relationship between the subject and the world, and, as Merleau-Ponty moves to transcendental phenomenology, he continues with the effort to reveal the conditions that make this relationship possible. Therefore, to clarify Merleau-Ponty's position, and to further our understanding of paradoxa, we turn now to a discussion of Merleau-Ponty's phenomenology and its place within the tradition of transcendental philosophy.

V. Merleau-Ponty and the Transcendental Tradition

1. Phenomenology as Transcendental Critique

As we concluded our discussion of Merleau-Ponty's first major work, *The Structure of Behavior*, we saw that Merleau-Ponty had not adequately accounted for the other, for the other *as* Other. In order to give such an accounting, what was needed was an analysis of that event which made possible the perception of the other as Other; or, to put it another way, an analysis of that event whereby there is an experience of phenomena as phenomena. That is, Merleau-Ponty needed to do phenomenology.

With Merleau-Ponty's move to phenomenology, the nature of this event became clearer – it is perception itself that is the event which opens us to being, and it does so through the paradoxical synthesis of an infinite series of aspects. This paradox of perception also accounts for our experience of phenomena as phenomena, that is, the experience of a whole or unity in each of its parts (i.e., phenomena). Furthermore, the paradox of perception enables Merleau-Ponty to take a middle path between Kant's transcendentalism and Berkeley's phenomenalism. And in taking this middle path, Merleau-Ponty is able to avoid an unnecessary either/or (or what Kripke analogously referred to as a 'false dilemma'): either the object is behind the aspects it presents (e.g., Kant's thing-in-itself) or it is nothing but these aspects (e.g., Berkeley's phenomenalism). By claiming that there is a fundamental paradox or transcendental contradiction which is the condition for experiencing objects, Merleau-Ponty still continues to accept the Kantian claim that there is the necessity of a transcendental foundation of the relation of consciousness to its objects; yet he holds that the paradoxical nature of this relation is such that these objects are presented only through their aspects. The thing-in-itself is given, paradoxically, as phenomenon.

When Merleau-Ponty discusses Kant's transcendental philosophy, therefore, he will question precisely his claim that there is a thing-in-itself that is given in advance, a completed being (i.e., a completed infinite synthesis) that one never perceives as such, but is completed none the less. In other words, Merleau-Ponty will criticize Kant for presupposing this completed being when, ultimately, the problem is to understand the emergence of a completed being to consciousness, to a consciousness that perceives only a part or aspect of this being (i.e., phenomena). Thus transcendental phenomenology differs from Kantian transcendental philosophy in that it is 'a study of the advent of being to consciousness, instead of presuming its possibility as given in advance. It is striking how transcendental philosophies of the classical type never question the complete disclosure which they always assume done somewhere.'[1]

And the effecting of this complete disclosure is, for Merleau-Ponty, possible because of the paradoxical nature of perception: that is, a completed being given through a part or aspect, or as 'phenomenon.' A proper and truly radical transcendental philosophy, therefore, should, as Merleau-Ponty argues, take 'itself as a problem.'[2] In other words, a transcendental philosophy should not presuppose as completed the conditions of thought, but should take as its problem our very access to these conditions. Thus, rather than presupposing a completed being, or the complete and infinite disclosure of being, a radical transcendental philosophy (i.e., transcendental phenomenology) will take as its problem the very possibility of this completion and disclosure. In short, a radical transcendental philosophy should strive to be a presuppositionless philosophy; or, the conditioned should not be used as the model to explain the conditions. For example, Merleau-Ponty would claim that a being as it is disclosed to perception is being unwittingly used as the model to explain the condition which makes this perception possible (e.g., the thing-in-itself). In recognition of this, Merleau-Ponty turns to an analysis of the conditions of perception itself, and, as we saw and will expand on later, this condition is a fundamental paradox.

Merleau-Ponty's criticism that the conditioned is being presupposed and used as the model to explain the conditions is rather common. In Kant's argument against Hume's position, for example, he makes a similar criticism. Kant argues that Hume's claim that the idea of causality is a conditioned idea, conditioned by an association of ideas (i.e., contiguity), presupposes, in the end, the conditioned idea of causality itself. In order even to be able to have an experience of contiguity, this experience presupposes, Kant claims, the very idea and form of causality itself (i.e., causality as *a priori* category). Hume, as Kant sees it, presupposes the conditioned (i.e., idea of causality) and unwittingly uses it as the model in explaining the conditions (i.e., contiguity).[3] And it is Kant's critique of Hume's presuppositions that leads him to seek the proper conditions for thought, conditions that presuppose nothing from experience, but are the very possibility of experience. In other words, Kant's criticism of Hume's presuppositions becomes a transcendental critique.

Kant's own philosophy, however, also becomes subject to this transcendental critique. With Husserl, for example, we saw that he criticized Kant's claim that the transcendental categories are the condition for intuition, that is, sensibility or experience. In *Logical Investigations*, Husserl claims that Kant 'fail[ed] to appreciate the deep difference between intuition and signification, their possible separation and their usual commixture.'[4] That is, Kant failed to appreciate the pre-logical objectivation of intuition (i.e., the self-givenness of an object to direct intuition) which a signitive act merely intends through such things as language and concepts (i.e., Logos). As a result, Husserl claims that Kant 'fails to distinguish between concepts, as the universal meaning of words, and concepts as a species of authentic universal presentation.'[5] In other words, Husserl argues that what Kant takes to be conditioned (i.e., the givenness of an object to intuition) is presupposed and unwittingly used as the model to explain the conditions (i.e., the signitive concepts, or transcendental categories, that, as Husserl sees it, merely intend or re-present this object).

In Husserl's transcendental phenomenology, consequently, Husserl attempts to reveal the conditions which make possible the self-givenness of an object to intuition, and in Husserl's *Phenomenology of Internal Time-Consciousness* we saw that it was the self-givenness of an absolute consciousness to itself – the paradoxical entity that constitutes its own unity – which is the condition that makes possible the givenness of objects generally, even the objects of perception.[6] Thus the sense data of perception were themselves, as we saw, constituted as givens only on the basis of an absolute consciousness, a consciousness that is already given to itself.[7] Husserl's transcendental phenomenology therefore sought to reveal this fundamental consciousness, and it was precisely in Husserl's phenomenological reduction that he attempted to discern, as a pure residuum, the pure transcendental ego (i.e., absolute conscious-ness) as the self-present condition upon which all objectivity is consti-tuted – that is, the constituted objectivity of the natural attitude. The natural attitude is therefore conditioned by an absolute constituting con-sciousness.

We can now begin to understand more clearly Merleau-Ponty's criti-cism of Husserl, and we can also recognize that this criticism is, in the end, within the tradition of the transcendental critique. That is, Merleau-Ponty claims that Husserl has presupposed the conditioned and has unwittingly used it as the model to explain the conditions. In particular, Husserl's argument for an absolute constituting consciousness presup-poses the natural attitude itself (i.e., what he took to be conditioned). The result of this presupposition, as discussed in chapter IV, is that the phenomenological reduction becomes impossible to complete – that is, it is impossible to reduce the world, or make it coincident with, an abso-lute constituting consciousness. As a result, Husserl was led to claim that we have a primordial faith in this world – that is, *Urdoxa*, or *Weltthe-sis*. The reason for this, Merleau-Ponty argues, is that consciousness is in a world that is already given to it, and this being-in-the-world of con-sciousness makes possible the distinction between self (consciousness, or 'in me') and other (world, or 'outside of me').[8] In other words, it is only because there is already an experience of the world that one can then pose, in reflection, the relationship of one's self or consciousness to this world; or, it is the condition which makes possible the phenomeno-logical reduction. And the failure of this reduction reveals, as we saw, our 'wonder in "the face of the world".' As Merleau-Ponty says, 'the problem of the world, and, to begin with, that of one's own body, con-sists in the fact that *it is all there*.'[9]

Merleau-Ponty's transcendental critique of Husserl thus leads him to claim that there is a fundamental experience of the world which is prior to all thought, and it leads him away from the transcendental deduction of the 'conditions of possibility' for experience, and towards the reve-lation of a fundamental experience: 'Everything changes when a phe-nomenological or existential philosophy assigns itself the task, not of explaining the world or of discovering its "conditions of possibility," but rather of formulating an experience of the world, a *contact* with the world which precedes all thought *about* the world.'[10]

There is thus an original contact or experience of the world, an origi-nal coincidence of self and world, and it is this experience which is prior to, and the basis for, our later being able to differentiate a self from the world, and, consequently, of being able to think *about* the world.[11] But this self, or cogito, which thinks about the world, must be understood to be both wholly subjective and wholly objective; that is, the cogito is transcendental, for Merleau-Ponty, if it is both self and other, or the experiential coincidence of constituting and constituted. Merleau-Ponty will then admit that 'the primary truth is indeed "I think," but only provided that we understand thereby "I belong to myself" while belonging to the world ... [or that] ... Inside and outside are inseparable. The world is wholly inside and I am wholly outside myself.'[12]

And that which experiences the coincidence of inside and outside, constituting and constituted, is, as discussed earlier, the perceiving body; or, the paradox of the perceiving body (i.e., the paradox of perception). In the end, therefore, Merleau-Ponty's transcendental critique leads him to the recognition of paradox, the paradox of the perceiving body, and it is this experienced paradox that is revealed to be the condition prior to all thought. Furthermore, Merleau-Ponty's transcendental critique of Husserl's transcendental phenomenology leads him to call for a phenomenology of phenomenology; and this, ultimately, again entails the revealing of paradox:

> To phenomenology understood as direct description needs to be added a phenomenology of phenomenology. We must return to the cogito in search of a more fundamental Logos than that of objective thought ... At the level of [objective] being it will never be intelligible that the subject should be both *naturans* and *naturatus*, infinite and finite. But if we rediscover time beneath the subject, and if we relate to the paradox of time those of the body, the world, the thing, and others, we shall understand that beyond these there is nothing to understand.[13]

Thus, as Merleau-Ponty turns to analyse that event which made possible the perception of the other as Other, he recognizes that this cannot be done by simply describing phenomena as phenomena. In other words, Merleau-Ponty needs to reveal that event which makes possible the description of phenomena as phenomena; or, as Merleau-Ponty puts it, we need 'a phenomenology of phenomenology.' And as this phenomenology of phenomenology reveals the paradoxical nature of the event which makes possible the perception of phenomena as phenomena, or how a subject 'should be both *naturans* and *naturata*,' we then begin to understand the other paradoxes, for example, the paradox of the other as Other.

2. Psychopathology and the Experience of the World

An initial and fundamental consequence of this paradox, of a cogito that is both *naturans* and *naturatus*, is that there need be no mediation between *that* which is perceived (i.e., sensations) and *what* is perceived (i.e., identifiable objects). In other words, the cogito is not to be understood as that which interprets a meaningless and formless stratum of sensations, or what Husserl calls *hyle*, and then imparts to this stratum a recognizable form, or *morphe*. The cogito is, rather, already in the world of sensations, and these sensations are, in turn, already taken up as meaningful. That is, as a consequence of the paradoxical coincidence of self and other, inside and outside, there is also the coincidence of *hyle* and *morphe*, a coincidence that is simply our fundamental experience and contact with the world: 'There is no *hyle*, no sensation which is not in communication with other sensations or the sensations of other people, and for this very reason there is no *morphe*, no apprehension or apperception, the office of which is to give significance to a matter that has none, and to ensure the *a priori* unity of my experience, and experience shared with others.'[14]

Merleau-Ponty thus appears to agree with Gurwitsch's claim that 'a separation between *hyle* and *morphe* is not even abstractly possible.'[15] However, Gurwitsch rejected, as we saw earlier, Husserl's claim that there is a self-constituting pure ego, 'that paradoxical and contradictory entity.'[16] As a result, Gurwitsch ultimately identified the form or sense of an object with the object itself, as a percept or aspect of this object (i.e., percept theory). This object, Gurwitsch claims, is itself to be understood as a gestalt, as an objective unity and interdependence of parts. Of this position, however, Husserl was not only aware, but also critical. Merleau-Ponty was himself sympathetic to these criticisms. In short, Husserl is critical of the gestalt claim that consciousness, or one's ego, is simply to be understood as an objective gestalt, and as, ultimately, no different from the gestalt of a perceived object. As Gurwitsch puts it, the ego 'is nothing other than the concrete totality of the dispositions and actions it supports, and it may be found nowhere outside these psychic unities.'[17] This is, for Husserl, only another attempt to naturalize consciousness and subjectivity, an attempt Husserl consistently opposed throughout his life.

Merleau-Ponty was well aware of this criticism: 'As Husserl sees it, the very fact that one uses the same term "Gestalt" to designate the unity of consciousness and that of the lamp (i.e., a perceived object) jus-

tifies the conclusion that Gestalt psychology naturalizes consciousness.'[18] Merleau-Ponty, contrary to most gestalt theorists, is sympathetic
to Husserl's attempt to reveal the transcendental foundations for objectivity; however, this attempt reveals, he claims, the paradoxical coincidence of a subject with the world, and it is precisely this paradoxical
coincidence which Gurwitsch rejects. Merleau-Ponty thus agrees with
Husserl's claim that we should not naturalize consciousness, that we
should reveal the transcendental foundations, yet he does not accept
Husserl's move to a transcendental ego that is completely abstracted
from the world. What Merleau-Ponty will attempt to do, therefore, is to
formulate that fundamentally paradoxical experience, that contact with
the world that is neither to be naturalized, as with Gurwitsch, nor
reduced to pure immanence, as with Husserl, but is, rather, to be understood as the middle path between the two: 'There is undeniably something between transcendent nature, naturalism's being in itself, and the
immanence of mind, its acts, and its noema. It is into this interval that
we must try to advance.'[19]

This middle path continues, as it did in *The Structure of Behavior*, to
emphasize the notion of structure. In *The Phenomenology of Perception*,
this structure emerges as the structured horizon of the world. In other
words, the paradoxical coincidence of the subject and the world is constitutive of structure; consequently, as in *The Structure of Behavior*, the
subject cannot be reduced to the world, or be understood as a naturalized consciousness, nor can the world be reduced to the subject, as the
objective correlate of a constituting consciousness. The subject must be
seen as being already situated in the world, and it must be acknowledged that this world is the horizon for all its activities, the horizon
upon which a structure emerges. For example, Merleau-Ponty claims
that the perception of 'the constancy of color is only an abstract component of the constancy of things, which in turn is grounded in the primordial consciousness of the world as the horizon of all our experiences.'[20]
The same is also true of the constancy of forms and sizes, and, in citing
an experiment to illustrate this point, Merleau-Ponty again contrasts
humans and animals:

> The constancy of forms and sizes in perception is therefore not an intellec-
> tual function, but an existential one, which means that it has to be related to
> the pre-logical act by which the subject takes up his place in the world.
> When a human subject is placed at the center of a sphere on which discs of
> equal diameter are fixed, it is noticed that constancy is much more perfect

in the horizontal than in the vertical plane. The huge moon on the horizon contrasted with the very small one at the zenith is merely a particular case of the same law. For apes, on the other hand, vertical movement in trees is as natural as is horizontal movement on the ground for us, with the result that vertical constancy is faultless.[21]

For both humans and apes, therefore, there emerges a general perceptual structure, a structure that reflects their lived experience of the world, that is, their contact with the world. The question, however, is to discern what differentiates humans from animals, and, in *The Phenomenology of Perception*, we find Merleau-Ponty continuing to base this difference on an ability to abstract – that is, the ability to recognize the virtual as virtual. For example, if someone placed a ruler between herself and another person, and if she asked this person to imagine the ruler as part of a line that stretches the entire length of the room, in most cases the person would be able to react appropriately by correctly pointing out the things in the room that were on one side of the line or the other. Some psychiatric patients, however, are unable to do this – they can't say which objects are on which side. The moral that Merleau-Ponty draws from this example is that the patient is unable to do what the normal person can; that is, organize the world according to one's own projects, or, to put it another way, project these projects onto the world as the site of their fulfilment, both actual and virtual. Normal humans are thus capable of an abstract centrifugal movement, a movement whereby one's projects can be projected onto the world as a possibility of this world (i.e., as virtual):

> Concrete movement is centripetal whereas abstract movement is centrifugal. The former occurs in the realm of being or of the actual, the latter on the other hand in that of the virtual or the non-existent; the first adheres to a given background, the second throws out its own background. The normal function which makes abstract movement possible is one of 'projection' whereby the subject of movement keeps in front of him an area of free space in which what does not naturally exist may take on a semblance of existence.[22]

This centrifugal movement, moreover, implies the paradoxical oneness of the subject and the world; or, the paradox of a unity or whole (i.e., the world as the horizon of experience) that is present in each of its parts and aspects. The reason is that, in order for the subject to project 'its own background,' the subject must be able to recognize this projection as a projection (i.e., the virtual as virtual); in other words, it entails the paradox of seeing the virtual (i.e., the unity of one's project) through the actual (i.e., the aspects of the world that are given). The normal person is thus able to identify her projects in the world, or polarize the perceptual field,[23] but she is able at the same time to differentiate this project from what is actually the case (i.e., she recognizes the virtual as virtual). What occurs with the patient, on the other hand, is that his experience reverts to the primary coincidence of self and world, to an experience for which the virtual is not recognized as such; that is, he is unable to abstract:

> What protects the sane man against delirium or hallucination is not his critical powers, but the structure of his space ... What brings about both hallucinations and myths is a shrinkage in the space directly experienced, a rooting of things in our body, the overwhelming proximity of the object, the oneness of man and the world, which is, not indeed abolished, but repressed by everyday perception or by objective thought, and which philosophical consciousness rediscovers.[24]

This quotation, in addition to what we have been saying about paradox, sheds light on Merleau-Ponty's further claim that 'the schizophrenic and the philosopher each knocks himself against the paradoxes of existence ... [and each] ... fails to recapture completely the world ... The schizoprhenic is ruled by his failure which expresses itself in a few enigmatic phrases ... the philosopher's failure leaves behind a furrow of expressive acts which enable us to rediscover our situation.'

The schizophrenic reacts to the paradoxical coincidence of 'man and world' by being unable to abstract, to see the virtual as virtual; or, as Merleau-Ponty claims of Schneider, 'he is "tied" to actuality,' and is unable to put himself into a situation (i.e., project his background, or recognize the virtual as virtual). The philosopher, on the other hand, acts upon this situation by attempting to re-present it in language; that is, he attempts to restore that paradoxical experience which made possible the recognition of the virtual as virtual and, in turn, made language possible. In short, the philosopher knocks himself against the paradox of expressing the inexpressible, of speaking the silence; yet it is nevertheless this task which Merleau-Ponty claims needs to be attempted: 'Our view of man will remain superficial so long as we fail to go back to that origin, so long as we fail to find, beneath the chatter of words, the primordial silence, and as long as we do not describe the action which breaks this silence. The spoken word is a gesture, and its meaning a world.'[25]

We need, therefore, to attempt to understand the advent of paradox, the advent of the infinite within the finite, or, finally, the advent of the world (infinite) within the gesture (finite). And with this attempt always in mind, Merleau-Ponty, as he analyses the disturbances of language as well as psychomotor disturbances, discovers that these disturbances reflect a failure to accommodate the advent of paradox, a failure to put one's self into a situation. In short, they will remain at the level of the silent and paradoxical coincidence of man and world, words and things.[26]

This failure, nevertheless, is still structured; that is, the paradoxical coincidence of man and world is, as was also the case in *The Structure of Behavior*, constitutive of structure. Consequently, the behaviour of the patient, as with the behaviour of animals, is to be seen as signifying a vital structure; in other words, within each behaviour there is expressed the unity or totality of their world, the world (or milieu) that prompts their behaviour, both actual and virtual.[27] The same is true of language, except that language, as an ability to use symbols, requires being able to recognize the virtual as virtual; and it is the paradox of this recognition which motivates the task of expression, the task of saying what it is we see, and of using words to refer to things. But this task will never be completed, or *actualized*, nor will it ever be unambiguous, because language entails seeing the virtual as virtual, not as *actual*. And this failure to make the virtual actual is not an impediment to expression; rather, it is the very opening of the world to being expressed, the event whereby the meaning of a gesture becomes 'the world.' In other words, the meaning of an expression or gesture is conditioned by the fact that our experience of the world exceeds the world as it is actually given. In perception, for example, we perceive a unified object though we are only given a part; consequently, Merleau-Ponty claims that perception itself is already 'primordial expression';[28] and language, as conditioned by this 'paradox of expression,'[29] is in turn 'the excess of what we live over what has already been said.'[30] This excess, or what Merleau-Ponty also refers to as leakage (*échappage*), makes it impossible to go directly to what is said; on the contrary, one must go obliquely, indirectly, for what is not said is as important as what is said. The fissures speak and the voices of silence are taken up; that is, the virtual is taken up as virtual, and this for the reason that perception, as well as all our actions, presupposes the paradoxical coincidence of man and world, infinite and finite, word and thing (i.e., the paradox of expression). And it is this paradoxical coincidence, or the paradox that Merleau-Ponty's critique reveals, which allows Merleau-Ponty to speak of a subject that is always and already situated in the world (the inside that is outside). Thus, we find Merleau-Ponty making frequent use of the facts of psychology, but we also find Merleau-Ponty speaking of the world that this subject expresses or thinks (the outside that is inside) – the world that is the horizon and meaning of all our actions, words, and thoughts. Merleau-Ponty emphasizes each of these aspects, for they reflect what he calls the 'to and fro of existence';[31] they reflect our original and paradoxical contact with the world, a contact that is, in the end, our existence. This existence, moreover, is an existence 'shared with others,'[32] an existence wherein our primordial experience of the world (i.e., the paradoxical coincidence of self and world) is also an experience of the other (i.e., the paradoxical coincidence of self and other). In other words, Merleau-Ponty's transcendental critique concludes that 'transcendental subjectivity *is* intersubjectivity.'

3. The Body-Subject and the Problem of 'the Other'

Merleau-Ponty's discussion of psychological disturbances reveals an important point – namely, the philosopher and the patient each come up against the primordial oneness of self and world, or 'the paradoxes of existence.' The philosopher attempts yet fails to rediscover and express completely this experience of oneness; and the patient's, or schizophrenic's, experience results in a failure to express or communicate. In each instance, however, the philosopher and schizophrenic are confronted with an experience that is not our everyday experience; it is not the experience of the natural attitude. As Merleau-Ponty puts it, 'the oneness of man and the world ... is ... *repressed* by everyday perception or objective thought.'[33] In other words, the experience that makes possible our everyday perception and objective thought – that is, the positings of the natural attitude – is repressed and forgotten by this very thought. In short, the conditions for thought are *repressed* by thought itself.

What is repressed and forgotten is what is essential to the experience of oneness: that is, the *non-positing* nature of this experience. The experience of everyday perception and objective thought is one that posits objects for this experience (i.e., the natural attitude as the thesis, or positing, of the world), whereas the paradoxical coincidence of man and the world which makes this possible is itself non-positing. The reason is that a positing experience entails a distinction between that which posits (i.e., a subject, or 'man') and that which is posited (i.e., an object, or 'world'); that is, positing implies a separation, or a dualism, between an experience and that which is experienced. Therefore, the primordial experience of oneness, as a coincidence which makes this dualism possible, must be non-positing.

The same is true, Merleau-Ponty argues, of our experience of the other: there is an experiential coincidence of self and other that is the condition for the distinction between self and other. This experience is, furthermore, a non-positing experience, or, as Merleau-Ponty interprets the direction Husserl's thought was taking, it is '"intersubjectivity"; that is ... a consciousness which is neither self nor other.'[34] It is this intersubjectivity, as an example of a non-positing consciousness, that is the condition for objectivity, for the positing of objects, egos, and alter egos. In short, Merleau-Ponty argues that the transcendental condition for objectivity is a fundamental paradoxical experience; thus the formulation 'transcendental subjectivity is intersubjectivity.'

These arguments echo, in many ways, Husserl's argument for a non-positing condition for the positing of objects. The noema, for example, was seen to be the neutral and non-positing correlate of consciousness which makes possible the positing of transcendent objects (i.e., the natural attitude). The noema was also interpreted to be the paradoxical coincidence of sense and object, or self and object, and it was the failure to recognize this that led to two contrasting interpretations of the noema. For Husserl, however, the noema is itself grounded in the more fundamental unity and oneness of consciousness. It was the self-constituted unity of consciousness itself that made possible an immanently constituted and objective correlate of consciousness (i.e., the noema). And it was precisely this unity and 'oneness' of consciousness that led to the problem of the other, to the problem of accounting for the constitution of an other that is *already constituted* – that is, an other self-constituted consciousness. This problem, Merleau-Ponty argues, cannot be resolved as long as the fundamental unity and oneness that conditions objectivity is a oneness of an absolute constituting consciousness.

For Merleau-Ponty, his solution to this problem turns on the claim that it is the perceiving body that experiences itself as *already constituted* at the same time that it constitutes. That is, the oneness is not a oneness of consciousness, but a oneness of one's body, the world, and others – a oneness that Merleau-Ponty's transcendental critique reveals to be the paradox of the world, of the *already constituted*: 'The problem of the world, and, to begin with, one's own body, consists in the fact that it is all there.'[35] This revelation, however, is not of a body in the sense of an objective body; that is, the body as a posited or seen object. To do this would generate a regress: that is, every objective positing is justified by a body that must in turn be posited, which likewise entails another body that would perceive this body, and so on *ad infinitum*.[36] For Merleau-Ponty, however, the body is neither posited, in this sense, nor positing; it is, rather, the paradoxical coincidence whereby it is always already posited in every positing, but is itself not to be identified with, as was also the case with the noema, a positing or posited object. The body, therefore, is the non-positing and non-posited condition for positing, or for perceiving an object: 'I observe external objects with my body, I handle them, examine them, walk round them, but my body itself is a thing which I do not observe; in order to be able to do so, I should need the use of a second body which itself would be unobservable.'[37]

The body is thus the always-already-given and -constituted object which makes possible the observation and constitution of objects. The body itself, however, as that which is the non-positing and non-posited condition, is, as a result, never given in the manner of an object; or, as Merleau-Ponty puts it, it is never completely constituted: 'What prevents its [the body's] ever being an object, ever being "completely constituted" is that it is that by which there are objects.'[38] Furthermore, it is this unobserved, non-posited condition that conditions the paradox of perception, the positing of a unity of unobserved aspects through each observed aspect or perspective: 'if objects may never show me more than one of their facets, this is because I am myself in a certain place from which I see them and which I cannot see.'[39] In other words, it is the paradoxical experience of the perceiving body, of being already constituted while constituting, that is the condition for perceiving an already constituted object that is simultaneously open to further perceptions, to further constitutions (recall the 'violence of perception').

The echo of Husserl's argument, therefore, entails Merleau-Ponty's claim that it is the paradoxical unity and identity of the body, just as it was the paradoxical unity of absolute consciousness, for Husserl, that is the condition which makes objectivity possible. Merleau-Ponty also agrees with Husserl that it is the role of the subject to posit objects, or to synthesize and constitute the unity of objects; consequently, Merleau-Ponty will claim that it is the subject that effects 'the paradoxical synthesis of an infinity of perceptual aspects':[40] 'The object is made determinate as an identifiable being only through a whole open series of possible experiences, and exists only for a subject who carries out this identification.'[41] This subject, however, is not, as it was for Husserl, an absolute constituting consciousness, but is, rather, the lived body. But this body as subject nevertheless is, just as it was for Husserl, something that is not to be confused with that which it makes possible – that is, the posited objects or beings of the natural attitude. For this reason, Merleau-Ponty can be seen to agree with Husserl's claim that the subject is completely different from that which it makes possible. This subject is irreducibly different from, and that which is repressed by, the 'everyday perception or objective thought' it makes possible.

But does not this similarity with Husserl also open the door to similar difficulties? For example, on the one hand, Merleau-Ponty claims that the body-subject is that which makes objective determinations possible, but is not to be confused with these objects; on the other hand, the body-subject is that always- and already-given identity or object that makes possible the perceptual and subjective consciousness of objects. In other words, the body-subject is always already situated in the world; it is already *constituted*; and it is also the horizon for all the subject's actions, thoughts, and perceptions – that is, the condition for the *constituting* subject, for effecting the 'infinite synthesis.' This body-subject, however, is, as we have seen Merleau-Ponty argue, to be understood as that which experiences itself as the paradox of being already constituted while constituting; however, as a paradox of the body, it appears that the paradoxical relationship between constituting and constituted is mediated by the identity of the body, by the body-subject that experiences this paradox. Therefore, it seems that the problems which arose in Husserl's thought when the noema was interpreted to be the mediating identity between consciousness and reality might also occur in Merleau-Ponty's thought as a result of interpreting the body-subject to be the mediating identity between constituting and constituted.

The difficulty which emerges is, as with Husserl, the problem of the other. If the body-subject is that identity which mediates the paradoxical relation between a constituting and intending consciousness and the reality or being that is given as constituted for this consciousness, then the problem is to account for the correlation of the two aspects that are mediated by this body-subject. The problem is to explain the correlation between the body as subject, the body as the identity which conditions the positings of a subject, and the body as object, the body as the already-constituted identity that conditions the givenness of posited objects. And the reason explaining such a correlation is difficult is because, as with Husserl, it is the *identity* of the body-subject that mediates their correlation; consequently, the problem is to account for *difference* without reducing it to the identity of the body-subject. In short, the problem is to account for the other as Other, and, as we have shown earlier, there is a tendency in Merleau-Ponty's thought to reduce the otherness of the Other (i.e., difference) to the identity of the body-subject; thus Merleau-Ponty is seen to say things like 'the other's body is a kind of replica of myself, a wandering double which haunts my surroundings more than it appears in them.'[42]

These difficulties in Merleau-Ponty's account of the other have been widely recognized, and have been seen to persist even in Merleau-Ponty's last writings. Claude Lefort, for example, claims that there is a tension in Merleau-Ponty's thought that leaves his account of the other inadequate. This tension, within the context of *The Visible and the Invisible*, is, Lefort argues, between Merleau-Ponty's desire to account for the otherness of the Other (i.e., difference) and his insistence that such an account be made in terms of 'reversibility' – that is, the reversibility of the same 'Flesh' (i.e., identity).[43] We are not in a position to explain this tension with respect to *The Visible and the Invisible* (we will in chapter VII), but we claim that it is already present at the time of *The Phenomenology of Perception*. The tension here, as should be clear, is between Merleau-Ponty's claim that it is the paradoxical coincidence of 'man and the world,' self and other, which is the condition for differentiating between self and other; and Merleau-Ponty's claim that it is the identity of the body-subject that is the condition for objectivity, for the positing identification of self, other, and objects. In other words, the tension is between a fundamental difference (i.e., paradox as differentiating condition, or as 'transcendental contradiction'),[44] and a fundamental identity (i.e., the body-subject). We thus find Merleau-Ponty claiming both that it is the paradoxical nature of perception that characterizes our access to being, or our ability to identify and posit objects, and that it is the identity of the body-subject which makes such an identification possible. In short, the paradox is a paradox of the body.

This last claim, however, is open to a transcendental critique; that is, it appears Merleau-Ponty is unwittingly using what he takes to be conditioned as the model in explaining the conditions. For example, he claims that our access to and identification of beings is conditioned by the paradox of the perceiving body; however, this perceiving body, or body-subject, is, in the end, itself interpreted to be the identity that makes identification possible. The body is always already *identified*, and this in turn makes identification possible. In short, Merleau-Ponty presupposes the paradoxical nature of *identification* (i.e., paradox of perception as *conditioned* by the body-subject) and unwittingly uses it to explain the paradox of the lived body that is its *condition* (i.e., the body-subject as an *identified*, already-given object). The nature of identification is thus used to explain the nature of the already identified (i.e., paradox). Or, to put it another way, Merleau-Ponty presupposes precisely what needs to be explained. We will expand upon this difficulty in much greater detail in the final part of this text. For now, however, I bring it in to demonstrate a consequence of the tension in Merleau-Ponty's thought, a tension between identity and difference that Lefort was correct to point out.

Some might argue, however, that we have misinterpreted Merleau-Ponty's understanding of identity and difference. They might argue, along Heideggerean lines, that there is indeed a fundamental identity that is the condition for objectivity, for the identity of objects; however, they would argue that there is nevertheless a fundamental difference between the conditioning identity and the conditioned identity. In short, they would claim that Merleau-Ponty is simply stating in his own terms the Heideggerean distinction between Being and being; that is, what is important for Merleau-Ponty is not identity, but, rather, the 'Ontological difference.' Furthermore, our claim that Merleau-Ponty's position is susceptible to a transcendental critique, that it presupposes what it intends to explain, is not a damning criticism; it is, to the contrary, merely the recognition of what Heidegger calls the 'hermeneutic circle.' That is, all our investigations simply seek to determine more precisely what is already pre-given; consequently, the investigation into perception is simply an effort to clarify what is always already given to perception – namely, the lived body.[45]

This interpretation, however, although it might be what Merleau-Ponty should say if he were to endorse Heidegger's theory of the 'Ontological difference,' is not what he actually does say. In fact, Merleau-Ponty is critical of Heidegger's notion of the 'Ontological difference.' In his essay 'Phenomenology and the Sciences of Man,' Merleau-Ponty claims that 'Heidegger remained fixed in [his] thesis of a pure and simple opposition between philosophy and the sciences ... between the ontological and the ontic.'[46] For Merleau-Ponty, however, as well as Husserl as read by Merleau-Ponty, this difference is only 'a point of departure,' a difference that itself needs to be accounted for. Furthermore, Merleau-Ponty claims that, to account for this difference, we need to consider the role of paradox, a role that Merleau-Ponty only alludes to in this essay: 'It will not be possible for us here to reflect at length on this paradox.'[47] In other words, to account for the ontological difference, one needs to discuss the paradoxical coincidence of man and the world, self and other, which is the condition that makes possible the difference between philosophy and science, the ontological and the ontic. That is, one needs to account for paradox as that fundamental differentiating condition.

This does not resolve the tension we claim to be present in Merleau-Ponty's thought; rather, it accentuates it. On the one hand, Merleau-Ponty's transcendental critique reveals a fundamental paradox or difference that makes possible the opposition between self and other, self and world, ontological and ontic. For example, a transcendental critique of Heidegger would claim that he presupposes difference (i.e., the ontological difference) when it is precisely this difference that needs to be explained. Consequently, Merleau-Ponty's critique reveals paradox as the differentiating condition which makes this difference possible. On the other hand, Merleau-Ponty's critique reveals the identity and coincidence of self and other, 'man and the world,' and the identity of the body-subject that lives and experiences the paradox.

The question, therefore, is whether that fundamental condition and experience which is repressed by everyday thought, but which is nevertheless the condition of this thought, is to be understood in terms of identity or difference. Merleau-Ponty appears to understand it both ways. For example, he emphasizes the identity and unity of the world, one's body, and others to account for our ability to learn and adapt to new situations; or what I will call the 'domestication' of difference. Merleau-Ponty says, for example, that 'to learn to see colors is to acquire a certain style of seeing, a new use of one's own body; it is to enrich and recast the body image.'[48] It is thus the already-given unity and identity of one's body image which allows for the ability to use this body in new and different ways, to acquire a new style.[49] And a style, for Merleau-Ponty, is simply a deviation from a norm, a difference that emerges on the basis of an already-given identity: 'Style exists (and hence signification) as soon as there are figures and backgrounds, a norm and a deviation';[50] and this norm is simply the identity of the world, and one's body, that is already given: 'Style is what makes all signification possible ... man and signification are sketching themselves against the background of the world through the very operation of style.'[51] This style, furthermore, establishes its own identity, or what Merleau-Ponty calls a 'system of equivalences.' As he puts it, 'the body schema is a lexicon of corporeality in general, a system of equivalences between the inside and the outside which prescribes to one its fulfilment in the other.'[52] Thus, to use an example of Merleau-Ponty's, my handwriting on paper resembles my handwriting on the blackboard, 'although the muscles in each case are not the same.'[53] And finally, just as the body-subject entails the paradoxical identity and coincidence of constituting and constituted, an identity which is the condition for the emergence of difference, or style, so, too, is our original experience of the other one, wherein there is a fundamental identity and coincidence of self and other which is the condition for the emergence of difference, for the difference between self and other: 'With the cogito begins that struggle between consciousnesses, each one of which, as Hegel says, seeks the death of the other. For the struggle ever to begin, and for each consciousness to be capable of suspecting the alien presences which it negates, all must necessarily have some common ground and be mindful of their peaceful coexistence in the world of childhood.'[54]

As Merleau-Ponty turns to reveal this common ground, his method becomes one of revealing difference, or of revealing paradox as the fundamental differentiating condition. For example, in discussing language, Merleau-Ponty claims that 'language is expressive as much through what is between the words as through the words themselves,'[55] or that signs 'do not so much express a meaning as mark a divergence of meaning between itself and other signs.'[56] That is, meaning is not something to be identified with the word or sign itself, but rather is the difference between it and other words. It is this difference, furthermore, that is repressed by everyday language, by the language that has, through domestication, become one where the meaning is identified with the word. But, in order for language to speak, there must be, Merleau-Ponty argues, a fundamental difference at the heart of expression, a fundamental paradox; and it is precisely this difference and paradox which make it possible for one to say something new with an already-given stock of words and meanings.[57] Therefore, if something is truly said, it will be seen as different, as disorienting: 'if the book really teaches me something, if the other person is really another, at a certain stage I must be surprised, disoriented.'[58] Thus, not only does really saying something entail a disorienting difference (i.e., wonder in the face of the 'paradoxical world'), but, if the other is truly other, then it must be equally as disorienting and different. This emphasis upon difference even characterizes Merleau-Ponty's understanding of anthropology, and, in particular, ethnology: 'Ethnology is not a specialty defined by a particular object, "primitive societies." It is a way of thinking, the way which imposes itself when the object is "different," and requires us to transform ourselves ... [but once this transformation is done, one] ... has regained possession of that untamed region of himself, unincorporated in his own culture.'[59]

In other words, to regain possession of that 'untamed region,' one must adapt to that which is different, to that which has not been domesticated (i.e., that which is 'unincorporated in his own culture'); or, one must, as Merleau-Ponty claims philosophy attempts to do, rediscover that paradoxical experience of oneness that is 'repressed by everyday perception or objective thought.' In short, the proper task of philosophy is to untame one's self by restoring that fundamental paradoxical experience, the experience which is the differentiating condition for the dualisms that characterize the natural attitude (i.e., domesticated experience).[60]

But are we not confusing the goal with the means for rediscovering this goal? That is, is not the fundamental condition the already-given identity of the body, world, and others, and the method of 'untaming' simply the best way to peel away the layers of sedimented knowledge that repress this original condition? On the one hand, yes, but we must bear in mind that this original condition is never given, is never 'completely constituted,' and it is only by revealing differences that this condition is restored, if only inadequately. In other words, the fundamental identity can only be rediscovered as difference; or, to put it another way, the fundamental origin and condition can be known only, paradoxically, in the originated and conditioned. It is this paradox that results in the impossibility of a complete rediscovery of the originating identity and coincidence. We are, in effect, condemned to difference and ambiguity: 'The founding term, or originator – time, the unreflective, the fact, language, perception – is primary in the sense that the originated is presented as a determinate or explicit form of the originator, which prevents the latter from reabsorbing the former, and yet the originator is not simply derived from it, since it is through the originated that the originator is made manifest ... This ambiguity cannot be resolved.'[61]

In response to Lefort's claim that there is a tension in Merleau-Ponty's thought, Merleau-Ponty might claim that yes, there is a fundamental paradox and ambiguity which cannot be resolved; consequently, if there is a tension, it is not simply a tension in Merleau-Ponty's thinking, but rather a tension and ambiguity that is human existence.

Although this might be Merleau-Ponty's response, it is still not an adequate response to Lefort's further claim that Merleau-Ponty actually emphasizes a fundamental identity at the expense of adequately accounting for difference – that is, the other as Other. What Merleau-Ponty needs to do, therefore, is to show how the other can emerge as Other, and as an other that is essentially ambiguous, without reducing this other to the identity of the self – that is, the body-subject. It is perhaps recognition of this need that motivated Merleau-Ponty, during the period between *The Phenomenology of Perception* and his last writings, *The Visible and the Invisible*, to devote much of his efforts to clarifying the position of the subject with respect to others, and to others in the context of history and politics, a history that is essentially ambiguous. Therefore, before we turn to the debate that surrounds Lefort's criticism of Merleau-Ponty's theory of the other as presented in *The Visible and the Invisible*, it will be helpful to discuss briefly some of the important themes that were later to emerge in Merleau-Ponty's last writings.

VI. The Social Self

1. The Paradox of Limitation and Access

A theme that will remain constant throughout the period between the publication of *The Phenomenology of Perception* and Merleau-Ponty's work on *The Visible and the Invisible* is that of paradox. For example, Merleau-Ponty will continue to claim that the fundamental identity and condition of thought is revealed only through difference, through the conditioned; or, as he also puts it, the originator is manifest only in the originated. And it was this paradox that led us, in chapter V, to say that we are condemned to difference and ambiguity. It seems we should also say, following Merleau-Ponty's claim that the infinite is paradoxically presented through the finite, that we are condemned to finitude. Thus it appears we should agree with Ricoeur's claim that Merleau-Ponty's philosophy is 'entirely in the service of a philosophy of finitude.'[1] On the one hand, yes, we are condemned to finitude; however, this finitude is, paradoxically, our access to the infinite. Consequently, we will not claim, as Ricoeur did, that this philosophy of finitude is unable to account for 'the devotion to universality and to truth,'[2] a devotion that Ricoeur claims is essential to Husserl's phenomenology. We claim, rather, that, for Merleau-Ponty, our access to truth and universality is paradoxically accomplished only through the finite and particular.

This latter paradox we can call the 'paradox of limitation and access'; that is, our access to universal truths and essences is made possible, paradoxically, by that which limits our access to the universal. Merleau-Ponty presents this paradox in 'Phenomenology and the Sciences of Man,' an essay that is a transcription from a course he taught at the Sorbonne in 1950–1: 'We must ... become aware of this paradox – that we never free ourselves from the particular except by taking over a situation that is all at once, and inseparably, both limitation and access to the universal.'[3]

Merleau-Ponty then goes on in this same essay to say that Husserl himself, with his notion of *Urdoxa*, had this same insight: Husserl's 'most profound reflection consists in rediscovering a basic faith, or opinion [*Urdoxa*] – that is, a reason which is already incorporated in sensible phenomena.'[4] In other words, Merleau-Ponty claims that Husserl's notion of *Urdoxa* reflects an insight into the unity which makes possible the distinction between *that* which is perceived (i.e., sensations, or *hyle*) and *what* is perceived (i.e., identifiable form of an object, or *morphe*). It was this unity, or the coincidence of *that* and *what*, which we found to be an unresolved difficulty in Husserl's phenomenology. For Merleau-Ponty, however, this unity is precisely the paradoxical unity and coincidence of 'man and the world,' self and other, and this paradoxical coincidence makes possible the distinction between *that* which is experienced (i.e., intended) and *what* is experienced (or intended): 'The insight into essences rests simply on the fact that in our experience we can distinguish *the fact that* we are living through something from *what it is* we are living through in this fact.'[5]

We thus return to our earlier problem of explaining the correlation between *what* is intended by signitive acts, and *that* which is given to intuitive acts. This correlation never found adequate expression, and in the end this surfaced in the failure to account for the other as Other. The problem thus became one of explaining how *what* is intended or constituted by consciousness could be *that* which *is not* constituted by consciousness, and thus be given to consciousness as Other. In short, the problem that remains unresolved is the problem of transcendence, and, therefore, to account for the other requires, as Merleau-Ponty claims, resolving this problem: 'The existential modality of the social is at one with all problems of transcendence ... [that is,] how the presence to myself ... is at the same time depresentation and throws me outside myself.'[6] And Merleau-Ponty's solution, as we have seen, entails the claim that there is a fundamentally paradoxical union and coincidence of self and other, 'man and the world,' *hyle* and *morphe*; and it is this paradox that makes possible the distinction between self and other, *hyle* and *morphe*, and, most important, immanence and transcendence. As a result of this paradox, therefore, 'the presence to myself' *is* 'depresentation and throws me outside myself.' This is clearly the case, as we have shown, with respect to the paradox of perception: 'there is a paradox of immanence and transcendence in perception. Immanence, because the perceived object cannot be foreign to him who perceives; transcendence, because it always contains something more than what is actually given.'[7]

This paradox of perception, however, is in turn conditioned by the identity of the body-subject (as we argued in the previous chapter); consequently, in so far as the paradox is grounded in the identity of the body-subject – is a paradox of this body – then the difficulty of accounting for the other, and therefore the problem of transcendence, will remain. The other will always be just the replica or analogue of the body-subject, and thus the problem Merleau-Ponty recognized in Husserl surfaces again in his own thought.

By the time of *The Visible and the Invisible*, however, Merleau-Ponty no longer refers to the paradox of the body-subject, or what he calls the 'paradox of man,' and refers, instead, to a 'paradox of Being': 'it is indeed a paradox of Being, not a paradox of man, that we are dealing with here.'[8] As a result, in approaching the problems of transcendence, the emphasis is not on the self-presence of the body-subject, and the paradox of this body-subject which is the condition for transcendence (i.e., depresentation, or difference); the emphasis is, rather, on the self-presence of Being, or what Merleau-Ponty calls the 'reversibility of the Flesh,' which, as a paradox of Being, is the condition for transcendence. There is thus a fundamental shift (or turning) in Merleau-Ponty's thought: rather than understand the access to being and others on the basis of a body-subject, Merleau-Ponty understands the body-subject on the basis of Being, and a Being that is always other to itself (i.e., 'wild Being,' or the 'paradox of Being'). With this shift, Merleau-Ponty can be seen to resolve the difficulties that resulted when he reduced the other to the identity of the body-subject.

Whether or not Merleau-Ponty did in fact resolve these problems will be discussed in the next chapter; however, the important point to note is that the role of paradox is more general in his later writings – a paradox of Being, not a paradox of man. It is this increased generality which one can see taking shape in Merleau-Ponty's writings during the period after *The Phenomenology of Perception*. For example, rather than continuing his emphasis on the role of the body-subject, Merleau-Ponty's emphasis is increasingly on the social self, on that self that is self-present only in a social setting, or in a world that is shared and perceived by others. It is true that Merleau-Ponty made these points in *The Phenomenology of Perception*, and also that there was, up until the end, a continuing emphasis upon the perceiving body. Despite this, however, Merleau-Ponty discusses paradox not simply as the paradox of the body-subject that is constitutive of structure, and which structuralizes perception, language, and thought; he turns more to a discussion of the paradoxes of art, language, and culture, and will argue that these paradoxes are constitutive of structure in a much more general manner than allowed for by the analysis of the body-subject. That is, art, language, and culture cannot be reduced to the identity of the body-subject.

This last claim should not be surprising. We find Merleau-Ponty saying something quite similar in *The Structure of Behavior*: 'there is the body as mass of chemical components in interaction [i.e., physical structure], the body as dialectic of living being and its biological milieu [i.e., vital structure], and the body as dialectic of social subject and his group [i.e., symbolic structure] ... Each of these degrees is soul with respect to the preceding one, body with respect to the following one.'[9]

In other words, each of these structures is of increasing generality, or, to use Merleau-Ponty's term, they 'integrate the lower structures.' Consequently, to say that the paradoxes of art, language, and culture are more general, or that they cannot be reduced to the body-subject, is simply to say, as Merleau-Ponty did in *The Structure of Behavior*, that they integrate the lower structures (e.g., the body-subject). However, the highest level of integration, the symbolic structure, is itself ultimately grounded in the paradox of perception. As a result, perception, as 'primordial expression' (i.e., symbolic structure), is conditioned by the paradox of the perceiving body, and thus it is the identity of the body-subject which emerges, as we have argued, as the condition for art, language, and culture (i.e., symbolic structures). But as Merleau-Ponty's thought develops, the emphasis is upon the paradox that 'encroaches' upon the body-subject, or the paradox that cannot be reduced to the paradox of the body-subject. In short, we will see an emerging transition from the paradox of man to the paradox of Being.

2. Art: Reflections on Cézanne

The shift in Merleau-Ponty's thought that we want to elaborate is particularly evident in Merleau-Ponty's writings on art. These writings, and especially those concerned with Cézanne, provide unique bookends to his philosophy. From Merleau-Ponty's early essay 'Cézanne's Doubt' (1945), to the last work he ever saw published, 'Eye and Mind' (1961), he continued to call upon art to bolster his discussions of perception. And with the emphasis upon the experience of the painter, and the problems of expression that confront the painter, these discussions throw into relief the turn that Merleau-Ponty took from a paradox of man to a paradox of Being.

In 'Cézanne's Doubt,' Merleau-Ponty claims that Cézanne refused simply to represent the world as perceived in everyday perception; that is, his painting does not try to re-present a world of identifiable objects with clear boundaries, or, to use Merleau-Ponty's metaphor, he does not paint 'the envelope of things.' For Cézanne, the problem is, as it was for Merleau-Ponty, to reveal those conditions which make possible our everyday perception – that is, the conditions that are 'repressed' by this everyday perception. Thus, 'Cézanne's painting suspends these habits of thought and reveals the base of inhuman nature upon which man has installed himself.'[10] Cézanne's painting reveals, as did Merleau-Ponty's phenomenological reduction, the fact that the world is always already there as the horizon upon which our knowledge and perceptions develop.

The result of this effort, according to Merleau-Ponty, is that Cézanne's paintings reveal paradox. Cézanne is confronted with the task of painting an object both as an infinite sum of perspectives and as given only from a finite perspective. Cézanne thus discovers that, although objects of everyday perception are given from one perspective, these objects, as real, entail more than what is actually given. What is real transcends appearance (i.e., their actual perspective). Merleau-Ponty therefore claims that 'his [Cézanne's] painting was paradoxical: he was pursuing reality without giving up the sensuous surface.'[11] Thus, Cezanne's use of distorted perspective, or the multiple perspectives of the same object on the same canvas, are not intended to distort reality, but, rather, to express this reality more accurately.

Cézanne's paradoxical painting is, as Merleau-Ponty interprets it here, representative of the paradox of perception, and, as a result, his painting is simply a manifestation of the more fundamental paradox of the perceiving body (i.e., the body-subject). We therefore find Merleau-Ponty, in The Phenomenology of Perception, comparing an analysis of Cézanne's painting with the analysis of the body: 'The body is to be compared, not to a physical object, but rather to a work of art ... Any analysis of Cézanne's work, if I have not seen his pictures, leaves me with a choice between several possible Cézannes, and it is the sight of the pictures which provides me with the only existing Cézanne, and therein the analyses find their full meaning.'[12]

In other words, to understand Cézanne, to gain access to the style or essence of Cézanne, one needs to actually see a work of Cézanne's. There is a paradox of limitation and access with respect to any analysis of Cézanne's work: we access the essence or style of his work only by seeing the finite and limited manifestations of this work. The only access to the universal is through the particular – that is, we are condemned to finitude. However, we do, paradoxically, access this universal, and the paradox of this access is simply another consequence of the paradox of perception. And this paradox of perception, furthermore, is founded upon the paradox of the body-subject, and it is for this reason that we find Merleau-Ponty comparing the body to a work of art. Art is therefore used as an example to clarify what Merleau-Ponty wants to say about the body.

At the time of *The Visible and the Invisible*, however, Merleau-Ponty's understanding of art is quite different. In 'Eye and Mind,' for example, what is perceived, and therefore put down on a canvas, is not understood with respect to a paradox of the body; rather, the perceived and the perceiving body (body-subject) are each seen to be manifestations of the same Being. Merleau-Ponty states that 'the visible world and the world of my motor projects are each total parts of the same Being.'[13] This same Being, furthermore, is not simply the objective correlate of a body-subject – in other words, it is not that which is given to the subject that effects the paradoxical infinite synthesis. The body-subject, and the world that this subject perceives, are each made of the same stuff, the same flesh, and for this reason the perceived world will at times encroach upon the subject, or awaken an echo in the subject: '"Nature is on the inside," says Cézanne. Quality, light, color, depth, which are there before us, are there only because they awaken an echo in our body and because the body welcomes them.'[14] In short, the body-subject is not the fundamental condition that makes possible the access to being, to the perceived; it is Being that is fundamental, and the body-subject and the perceived are each aspects of this Being.

This change is also reflected in Merleau-Ponty's understanding of paradox. It is not the paradox of perception which characterizes the body-subject's access to being and reality, but it is the paradox of Being that makes possible the relationship of a perceiving being to a perceived being. Furthermore, this paradox of Being is also the paradoxical coincidence of seeing and seen, the coincidence that is the differentiating condition which makes possible the difference between seeing and seen, and it is the coincidence painters will at times experience when they feel that the painted is painting itself through them: 'There really is inspiration and expiration of Being, action and passion so slightly discernible that it becomes impossible to distinguish between what sees and what is seen, what paints and what is painted.'[15]

This paradox, or what Merleau-Ponty also calls a 'dehiscence of Being,'[16] makes vision possible as the result of a necessary invisibility; in other words, there is a separation or gap (the French word is *écart*) at the very heart of Being between the visible and the invisible, a presence that is absence; and it is this paradox of Being which makes the paradoxes of perception, art, and expression possible. Consequently, as the artist delves into the conditions for perception, he finds himself confronted with the effort to express that 'inarticulate cry';[17] and it is this 'inarticulate cry,' or the invisibility that the artist attempts to make visible, which opens the field and horizon of all painting: 'If no painting comes to be *the* painting, if no work is ever absolutely completed and done with, still each creation changes, alters, enlightens, deepens, confirms, exalts, re-creates, or creates in advance all others.'[18]

The emphasis is thus clearly upon the paradox of Being, and it is this paradox which emerges as the condition for the paradox of the perceiving subject. We can also see, in some of the writings prior to 'Eye and Mind,' an understanding of language and culture that anticipates this position.

3. Language

Merleau-Ponty, Wittgenstein, and the 'Private Language' Argument

At the time of writing *The Phenomenology of Perception*, Merleau-Ponty understands language, as he did with art, to be conditioned by the body's paradoxical relation to, and inherence in, a world and a situation. And it is only within the context of this always-already-given situation that language emerges. Furthermore, this situation is also that which conditions the meaning of a word, the meaning being originally this word's use within a given situation: 'As for the meaning of a word, I learn it as I learn to use a tool, by seeing it used in the context of a certain situation.'[19] Only later are we able to abstract the meaning of a word from an actual situation (i.e., see the virtual *as* virtual).

A consequence of this is that Merleau-Ponty can be seen to have, *à la* Wittgenstein, a version of the 'private language' argument. That is, Merleau-Ponty argues against the claim that the meaning of a word is something in the head, something private; or, put another way, that the meaning of a word is something other than human activity. The meanings of the words of a language, Merleau-Ponty argues, as does Wittgenstein, is nothing but a form of activity in a situation – language is a 'form of life,' as Wittgenstein calls it. Merleau-Ponty is clear on this point: 'Thought is no internal thing, and does not exist independently of the world and of words. What misleads us in this connection, and causes us to believe in a thought which exists for itself prior to expression, is thought already constituted and expressed, which we can silently recall to ourselves, and through which we acquire the illusion of an inner life.'[20]

To clarify this point with respect to Wittgenstein's 'private language' argument, we will turn to a discussion of Wittgenstein's famous rule-following paradox: 'This was our paradox: no course of action could be determined by a rule, because every course of action can be made out to accord with the rule.'[21] That is, we will examine Wittgenstein's claim that no course of action is determined by a rule which 'exists prior to' this action. Furthermore, we will discuss Kripke's claim that 'Wittgensteinian scepticism, resulting from the paradox, is the most radical and original sceptical problem that philosophy has seen to date.'[22]

The sceptical problem that arises here concerns the independence of rules with respect to actions. For example, when I was a child learning the rules of addition, the teacher set forth several examples. She explained ordination by counting on her fingers, or by counting the objects in the room; however, when I understood ordination, I did not simply memorize the numbers or learn to count up only to a certain finite number of things. I learned to count any number of things, to an infinite sum. How, one may ask, did I learn to do this when the teacher simply counted a finite number of objects in the room? And, when I count, who is to say that I am doing it right? Is there a rule that I am following, and, if so, do I consciously follow it? And who is to say, to follow Kripke, that I am following the plus rule and not the quus rule? That is, Kripke claims that, upon seeing a mathematical problem such as 68 + 57, those who understand the meaning of 'plus' will produce the sum 125. They grasp the 'plus' rule and can apply it to the given problem, and if the teacher were standing over those students, she might tell them that they have got it and simply have to go on in the same manner. But what is this same manner? What if, for the sake of the argument, these students had never before added numbers that were greater than or equal to 57? Consequently, even though it may be the case that they have followed the plus rule in the past, the problem here concerns the justification of this rule in the future. Let us suppose that someone tells us that 68 + 57 = 5. One would probably call such a person insane; however, although it appears we meant plus in the past, we might actually have meant quus, where quus is 'x ± y = x + y iff x, y < 57; otherwise the answer is 5.' And since this person has never followed the plus rule in a situation where x or y was not less than 57, who is to say that he didn't mean quus in the past, and now that he has a problem where x and y are equal to and greater than 57, what is the justification for answering 125 rather than 5?

In order to refute the sceptic, it seems that one would need to point to some fact in one's past usage which justifies one's present usage as well as any future use of the plus rule. But, with the sceptical paradox, the problem is not one of knowing whether 68 plus 57 is 125 or not. If I meant plus, then I also meant 125. The problem is, rather, in justifying whether what is meant is plus or quus; and it is by claiming that there is a fact in the head, a rule which exists prior to an action, which has been used, Wittgenstein claims, in order to resolve this sceptical problem. Wittgenstein, however, accepts the sceptic's claim that there are no such rules, that there is no ultimate grounding or rule from which our actions follow. What grounds language, he claims, is simply 'an ungrounded way of acting,'[23] and this ungrounded way of acting expresses, as it does for Merleau-Ponty, relationships to the world that, although they are not objectively precise, bear a family resemblance to each other, a regularity and constancy which makes language communicable. This is an essential component of Wittgenstein's paradox, for, just as there is no rule followed in calculating, talking, and acting, each calculation, word, and action can be made to accord with a rule and thus be seen to have a certain regularity. If things were quite different and there were no characteristic expression for joy, pain, or fear; if rule became exception and exception rule; or if they happened with equal frequency – 'this would make normal language-games lose their point.'[24] It is thus a fact that mathematicians rarely quarrel over the results of a calculation; it is a fact that, when I tell my friend how wonderfully blue the sky is, I assume he sees the same colour as I do and would have used the same word to describe it. In addition, the importance of this regularity is integral to Wittgenstein's concept of 'forms of life,' and this is why Kripke says, 'The regularity must be taken as a brute fact. So too for Wittgenstein "what has to be accepted, the given, is forms of life".'[25]

This form of life reflects simply the way we do things, our ungrounded way of acting, and, as such, is the given that cannot be justified. For example, in learning the plus rule, we acquired a way of acting, a form of life, and, although this rule may be vague or lacking in ultimate justifications (i.e., the sceptical paradox), it is nevertheless the case that we do act, and, as members of a community of people who do arithmetic, we act with a certain regularity. It is thus 'wrong-headed,' Wittgenstein claims, and unnecessary to call 'meaning a mental activity; unless, that is, one is setting out to produce confusion.'[26] We acquire the meaning of a word when we learn to use it in the context of certain situations, or by acquiring a regularity to our active use of words, and it is this regularity which makes us a member of the community – that is, a social self. Wittgenstein therefore claims that 'we got to know the nature of *calculating* by learning to calculate ... the rule is not needed. Nothing is lacking. We do calculate according to a rule, and that is enough.'[27] In other words, there is no justification for our language-games. We use language with a certain regularity, and that is it; we can't go back any further to any pre-existing rules or meanings that will justify and account for this regularity, and any philosophical attempt to establish such a foundation is doomed. Wittgenstein thus claims that 'in the end when one is doing philosophy one gets to a point where one would like just to emit an inarticulate sound.'[28] There is an end, therefore, to the justification process, but this end is an ungrounded and inarticulate form of life, or, as Wittgenstein describes 'form of life,' it is 'something animal'[29] – a form of animal activity. 'Giving grounds, however, justifying the evidence, comes to an end; but the end is not certain propositions' striking us as immediately true, that is, it is not a kind of seeing on our part; it is our acting, which lies at the bottom of the language-game.'[30]

There is thus a clear parallel between Wittgenstein's and Merleau-Ponty's understanding of language. They each take the meaning of a word to be its use in a given situation, and they each claim that, as a result, the meaning of a word is not to be identified with something private, with some rule in the mind which accounts for the regularity with which we use these words. For Wittgenstein and Merleau-Ponty, therefore, the mind is nothing but a form of activity, an activity that is always already in the world and in a situation. The mind is not prior to language – it is, Merleau-Ponty argues, nothing but the active use of language: 'All language is mind. It is a verbal melody which presupposes an intellectual vigilance. But the mind that governs language is not mind for itself; it is paradoxically a mind that possesses itself only by losing itself in language.'[31]

Despite these parallels, however, the moral that each draws from these discussions is quite different. Wittgenstein's discussion of the paradox of rule-following leads him to claim that 'meaning' is an ungrounded activity, but it is nevertheless an ungrounded social activity. That is, it is a form of life or regularity that one shares with a community, and it is this regularity that is the condition for being a member of this community, a member who 'understands' this 'meaning.' Merleau-Ponty, on the other hand, claims that the paradox of mind and language, that mind 'possesses itself only by losing itself in language,' is conditioned by the paradox of the body, and, as was the case with art, this paradox of language and mind only clarifies this more fundamental condition: 'It has always been observed that speech or gesture transfigure the body, but no more was said on the subject than that they develop or disclose another power, that of thought or soul. The fact was overlooked that, in order to express it, the body must in the last analysis become the thought or intention that it signifies for us.'[32]

In the end, therefore, Merleau-Ponty does not make the move to the social self that Wittgenstein does; rather he continues to conclude that the body-subject is the fundamental condition for language. Shortly after the publication of *The Phenomenology of Perception*, however, Merleau-Ponty's thought was inspired by the work of Ferdinand de Saussure (in the academic year 1948–9 Merleau-Ponty taught a course on Saussure at the Sorbonne), and this influence becomes evident as we see Merleau-Ponty making moves towards a notion of the social self.

The Influence of Saussure

The most evident disparity between Merleau-Ponty's and Saussure's views on language concerns the relationship between language and the body. Merleau-Ponty, as we saw, claims that language is, in the end, conditioned by the body-subject's paradoxical relationship to the world. Saussure, to the contrary, argues that language is not tied to, or conditioned by, the body-subject. Saussure claims that even fashion, which seems to be free of limitations, is in fact limited by the needs of fit, needs 'dictated by the human body'; a 'language, to the contrary, is in no way limited in its choice of means.'[33] In other words, the 'signal is unmotivated: that is to say arbitrary in relation to its signification, with which it has no natural connexion in reality.'[34] That the signal, or sign, is arbitrary will have important consequences for Saussure's theory of language (i.e., *langue*). In particular, by understanding the sign to be arbitrary – for example, *chapeau*, hat, and *Hut* are only arbitrarily related to that which they signify – we can see why Saussure claims that 'Language (versus Speech) is a system which admits no other order than its own.'[35] That is, language is independent of both the individuals who speak the language (i.e., parole), and the concepts or objects that are referred to by this language. In short, Saussure will claim that language is an independent and self-contained *system*, or, as it is more commonly called, *structure*.

Saussure's understanding of structure can be seen to have strong affinities with Merleau-Ponty's. For example, we saw that, in *The Structure of Behavior*, there is a paradox which is constitutive of structure, a paradox whereby the *structure* of behaviour could be reduced neither to physiological relations nor to intellectualist ideas. Similarly, for Saussure, there is a paradox that is constitutive of the structure of language, a paradox whereby the structure of language can be reduced neither to the thoughts that the sound-patterns materialize through signs nor to the relationship between these different signs (i.e., words): 'The paradoxical part of it is this. On the one hand, the concept [signified] appears to be just the counterpart of a sound pattern [signifier], as one constituent part of a linguistic sign. On the other hand, this linguistic sign itself, as the link uniting two constituent elements [i.e., signifier-signified], likewise has counterparts. These are the other signs in the language.'[36]

In other words, language functions as an intermediary between thought and sound,[37] but, in order to do so, language entails a 'paradoxical principle'[38] wherein the signs of a language are both dissimilar and similar; that is, dissimilar to that which is signified, but similar in so far as they are related to the other signs of the *same* language. To put this yet another way, a word is *self*-contained and meaningful only in so far as it is related to the *other* words of the language.

To clarify this, Saussure gives the example of money. A five-franc coin has value (read: meaning) if it can be exchanged for something *dissimilar*, a newspaper, for example. At the same time, the value of this coin can be exchanged for or compared with something similar, a one-franc coin, for example. The value of this coin is thus dependent upon its relationship to the other coins in the same system (i.e., the franc), and can also be related to other *similar* systems – for example, the dollar. There is thus a simultaneous dissimilarity and similarity that is the condition for the value of the coin. The same is also true for the meaning of a word. The *structure* of language, as Saussure understands it, is such that there is, at the heart of identifiable signs and meanings, difference; or, *the para-*

dox of language is that identity is difference. Saussure is explicit on this point: 'In the language itself, there are only differences. Even more important than that is the fact that, although in general a difference presupposes positive terms between which the difference holds, in a language there are only differences, and no positive terms.'[39]

There is thus an important parallel between Merleau-Ponty's and Saussure's understanding of structure: they each emphasize the role of paradox as constitutive of structure. There is an important difference, however, between Saussure and Merleau-Ponty on this point. On the one hand, Saussure discusses the paradox that is constitutive of language, and of a language that is self-contained and independent of the body, including the speech and gestures of this body. On the other hand, Merleau-Ponty, although recognizing Saussure's distinction between speech and language, will claim, in *The Phenomenology of Perception*, that the paradox of language is ultimately conditioned by the paradox of the body-subject. In effect, Merleau-Ponty claims that language is simply sedimented or domesticated speech, the 'repository and residue of acts of *speech*.'[40] In other words, Merleau-Ponty claims that language is the 'repository' for identifiable words and expressions, and these identifications are, in the end, conditioned by the differentiating activity of the body-subject, or the paradox of the lived body (i.e., paradox as differentiating condition). After *The Phenomenology of Perception*, however, and, in particular, after Merleau-Ponty's 1948–9 course on Saussure, Merleau-Ponty begins to emphasize the differences that are intrinsic to language itself. Rather than language being the identity conditioned by difference (i.e., the body-subject), language is itself understood to be a difference that conditions identity (i.e., meaning). We thus find Merleau-Ponty claiming, in very Saussurean terms, that signs do 'not so much express a meaning as mark a divergence of meaning between itself and other signs';[41] and, later in this same essay, he claims that 'meaning appears only at the intersection of and as it were in the interval between words.'[42] And in *Consciousness and the Acquisition of Language*, a transcription from a course he taught the year after his course on Saussure, we find him virtually stating Saussure's position: 'What makes a word refer is not a resemblance between word and referent, nor the internal character of either. Rather, it is the relationship between the word "sun" and the totality of all English words; it is the manner in which it differentiates itself from them. The word only has meaning through the whole institution of language.'[43]

It is precisely this 'institution of language,' or what Saussure called the 'system of language that is independent of subjects that speak,' that begins to emerge in Merleau-Ponty's thought as an institution or structure that cannot be reduced to the structure of the body-subject. Thus, the paradox that is constitutive of the structure of language – Saussure's 'paradoxical principle' – is a paradox that is not derivative from the paradox of the lived body. In fact, by the time of *The Visible and the Invisible*, the paradox of language will reflect not the paradox of the body-subject, but a paradox of Being. This claim, furthermore, will follow Merleau-Ponty's Saussurean critique of his earlier position. For example, Merleau-Ponty argues that, if the term 'consciousness' (or subject) is to be meaningful, it will be so on the basis of the differences between itself and all other words in the language. The identifiable meaning of this word is possible only as a result of difference; consequently, in *The Visible and the Invisible*, Merleau-Ponty argues that his earlier work presupposed the identity and meaning of the subject (i.e., the body-subject as we have been discussing it), and that 'to make the reduction, to return to immanence and to the consciousness of ... it is necessary to have words.'[44] In other words, one must have the identity of words in order to reveal, through the phenomenological reduction, the identity of the subject as pure immanence. For this reason, Merleau-Ponty states that there is a 'mythology of a self-consciousness to which the word "consciousness" would refer – There are only differences between significations.'[45] In short, what Merleau-Ponty, in *The Phenomenology of Perception*, takes to be conditioned – namely, the *identifiable* words of language – is presupposed and used to explain the conditions – namely, the *identity* of the body-subject. Merleau-Ponty is therefore, in *The Visible and the Invisible*, submitting his earlier position to, as we have discussed it earlier, a transcendental critique.

It is as a result of this transcendental critique that Merleau-Ponty turns, not to a discussion of the paradox of the body-subject, but to the paradox of Being; or, since a philosophy of the subject (what Merleau-Ponty calls a 'philosophy of "consciousness"')[46] presupposes the identifications of language, Merleau-Ponty will turn to an explication of a fundamental difference or paradox that is the condition for language itself, and this is precisely the difference, or *écart*, of what Merleau-Ponty calls 'brute' or 'wild' Being.[47] As a result, Merleau-Ponty claims that the metaphysical consciousness–objective distinction (i.e., self–world) is itself conditioned by Being, that 'it is an event of the order of brute or wild being which, ontologically, is primary.'[48] The body-subject is thus not the primary condition for the disclosure and perception of beings;

rather, Merleau-Ponty claims that the Self is to be understood as a 'correlative encroachment of "thing" and "world".'[49] It is the relationship of Being to itself which conditions the horizonal disclosure of a *world* of perceived *things*. Language itself, furthermore, is in turn conditioned by this relationship of Being, by the 'reversibility' or 'chiasm' of Being, and as such there is an encroachment of Being in language such that, as with art and perception, it is not a subject that speaks (i.e., a body-subject who uses language as a tool), but Being that speaks itself, or that conditions its own expression: 'It is not we who perceive, it is the thing that perceives itself yonder – it is not we who speak, it is the truth that speaks itself at the depths of speech – Becoming-nature of man which is the becoming-man of nature – The world is a field, and as such is always open.'[50]

In other words, the brute or wild Being is the condition which makes speech and language possible; however, this wild Being for ever transcends all articulations, is the silence which is never spoken and the invisibility that is never made visible; but this is not a failure or impediment to speech and language – it is, rather, that condition which leaves expression 'always open.' The first word, as with the first artwork, breaks the silence and begins the task of expression, a task that is never completed, but is always just beginning.

We can now see that there were anticipations of the turn Merleau-Ponty's philosophy took in *The Visible and the Invisible*. In particular, the influence of Saussure on Merleau-Ponty's thought was instrumental in laying the groundwork for the transcendental critique that Merleau-Ponty would direct towards his earlier work. Saussure's thought, however, was to have a major influence upon French thought in general. For example, the tradition of structuralism can trace its roots directly to the thought of Saussure, and Lévi-Strauss's structural anthropology is an acknowledged development of many of Saussure's concepts. The developments in structural anthropology, however, were also present to some degree in Merleau-Ponty's thought, and from the publication of *The Phenomenology of Perception* to his final writings and notes, there is a continued interest and discussion of culture and history. This discussion, moreover, also reflects the turn in Merleau-Ponty's thought that we are attempting to clarify.

4. Culture: Lévi-Strauss and the Social Self

In Merleau-Ponty's early work on culture and history, *Humanism and*

Terror (1947), he continued to emphasize the paradoxical role of the body-subject; or the paradoxical coincidence of 'man and the world,' self and other. It is as a result of this paradox, and, in particular, the paradox of being the exterior one presents to others, that conditions the tragedies and violence of history. For example, in the Moscow trials of the late thirties, Bukharin and others were brought up on charges of counter-revolutionary activity, yet they themselves believed that they were fighting for the cause of the revolution, a revolution they believe failed with Stalin. In Merleau-Ponty's interpretation of this event, he argues that neither should Bukharin be faulted for failing to go along with the established revolutionary party (i.e., Stalin), nor should the Stalinists be completely faulted for convicting and executing Bukharin; rather, this situation is a consequence of the paradoxical coincidence of 'man and the world,' or, in this case, the individual and history: 'the true nature of tragedy appears once *the same man* has understood both that he cannot disavow the objective pattern of his actions, that he is what he is for others in the context of history, and yet that the motive of his actions constitutes a man's worth as he himself experiences it.'[51]

Violence is thus an essential possibility which results from this paradox, a possibility that occurs when the 'objective pattern' of one's intentions ends up, in the eyes of others, being contrary to these intentions. This is, furthermore, a variation on the theme of the 'violence of perception' – that is, where what we perceive from one perspective as a paradoxical synthesis and unity may be, on further inspection, shattered and destroyed. What I perceived to be my friend approaching turned out, when they got closer, to be a total stranger. In short, the violence of history is understood on the basis of the paradox and violence of perception, and thus on the paradox of the body-subject – that is, '*the same man.*'

Implicit within this conflict between the individual and history, between one's intentions and their 'objective pattern,' is, for Merleau-Ponty, the struggle between individuals, and, subsequently, between classes. In effect, in *Humanism and Terror*, Merleau-Ponty carries forward the analysis, discussed earlier, that with the cogito begins the struggle between consciousnesses, between self and other.[52] This struggle, as was the case in *The Phenomenology of Perception*, finds its source in the paradox of the body-subject:

But consciousness can do nothing without its body and can only act upon others by acting on their bodies. It can only reduce them to slavery by making nature an appendix of its body, by appropriating nature to itself and establishing in nature its instruments of power. Thus history is essentially a struggle – the struggle of the master and the slave, the struggle between the classes – and this is a necessity of the human condition; because of the fundamental paradox that man is an indivisible consciousness no one is able to affirm himself except by reducing the others to objects.[53]

When we discussed the struggle between consciousnesses with reference to *The Phenomenology of Perception*, we saw that underlying this was a paradoxical experience of self and other, or what Merleau-Ponty called 'their peaceful coexistence in the world of childhood.' And it is this fundamental intersubjective experience that makes possible the emergence of the cogito and its attendant struggles (i.e., paradox as differentiating condition). Similarly, with respect to the struggle between the classes, Merleau-Ponty claims that there is an underlying intersubjectivity, a paradoxical coincidence of self and other; and it is this coincidence and peaceful coexistence which is the meaning Merleau-Ponty gives to Marx's conception of the proletariat: 'The proletariat is no sum of wills each choosing the Revolution on their own behalf, nor yet an objective force like gravity or universal attraction; it is the sole authentic intersubjectivity because it alone lives simultaneously the separation and union of individuals.'[54]

The Marxist revolutionary is therefore someone who attempts to restore this original coincidence, this peaceful coexistence; and it is the repression of this 'authentic intersubjectivity' that the revolution is intended to overcome. In other words, Marxists, as Merleau-Ponty interprets and supports Marxism, are much like the phenomenologist in that they attempt to restore that fundamental paradoxical experience – that is, the paradoxical coincidence of 'man and the world,' self and other.

After the publication of *The Phenomenology of Perception*, and, in particular, after Merleau-Ponty's course on Saussure, the emphasis is less on the paradox of the body-subject, the body-subject as the condition both for class struggle and for successful proletarian revolution; rather, the emphasis is increasingly on the culture itself as a structure which encroaches upon and envelopes the body-subject. Therefore, just as Merleau-Ponty's Saussurean analysis of language led him to see language, not as the domestication of differences, and thus as the repository of identity, but, rather, as a fundamental system of differences in its own right, so, too, does Merleau-Ponty begin to see culture in this light.

For this reason, Merleau-Ponty endorses Lévi-Strauss's structural anthropology, and he also recognizes the affinity between Saussure and Lévi-Strauss:

> When Saussure used to say that linguistic signs are diacritical – that they function only through their differences ... he was making us see the unity which lies beneath a language's explicit signification, a systematization which is achieved in a language before its conceptual principle is known. For social anthropology, society is composed of systems of this type: systems of kinship and direct consanguinity; systems of art, myth and ritual.[55]

As a result, and this exemplifies the encroachment of the structure of culture on the subject, Merleau-Ponty claims that 'the subjects living in a society do not necessarily know about the principle of exchange which governs them, any more than the speaking subject needs to go through a linguistic analysis of his language in order to speak ... Rather than their having got it [i.e., structure], it has, if we may put it this way, "got them".'[56]

In other words, in the same way that language (*langue*) transcends and conditions the instances of speech (*parole*), so, too, does culture transcend and condition social facts. To understand another culture, therefore, it is not enough simply to gather the facts of this culture (this is, in effect, Lévi-Strauss's criticism of Franz Boas). One must comprehend the system of differences that conditions, or structuralizes, these facts. What is important is thus not the facts, nor the words, but the structure of differences that is always between the words, between the facts, and is that which gives them meaning and value. It is for this reason that Merleau-Ponty calls for the untaming of that sensibility which has been incorporated into one's own culture, into the identity and structure of this culture. And this untaming is an ethnology when it is a 'way of thinking which imposes itself when the object is "different," and requires us to transform (i.e., untame) ourselves.'[57] In short, the culture as structure, as a system of differences that cannot be reduced to the identity of either 'things or ideas,'[58] imposes (i.e., encroaches) itself as 'different,' and to understand this culture one must not try to reduce it either to one's own culture or to the identity of things and ideas. One must, rather, as Merleau-Ponty says elsewhere, 'learn from the facts and *enter into them*.'[59] One must experience the structure that is the condition for these facts.

This experience of the structure of culture is not, however, conditioned by the paradox of the body-subject; the experiential coincidence of man and the world, self and other – that is, that peaceful coexistence. It is rather an experience wherein that which is conditioned by the subject (body-subject) and that which is conditioned by culture become indiscernible. It is, analogous to the experience of the artist and the speaker, an experience where one does not know whether culture is a product of man, or whether man is a product of culture. In short, it is an experience conditioned by the 'paradox of Being, not a paradox of man.'[60] And it is this paradox of Being – the visible that is invisible, 'the leaving of oneself [that is] a retiring into oneself, and vice versa'[61] – that makes the untaming of the ethnologist possible. In other words, it is the fundamental difference and separation (*écart*) of wild Being which makes possible the ethnologist's experience of a *different* culture. Ethnology, therefore, as was the case with art and language, is in the end derivative of Being: 'Psychology, logic, ethnology are rival dogmatisms that destroy one another; philosophy alone, precisely because it aims at the total domain of Being, renders them compatible by relativizing them. The regions of knowledge, left to themselves, are in conflict and contradiction.'[62]

This total domain of Being is not to be confused with the being of the body-subject that, through the paradox of perception, gains access to being; rather Being is that which is always already there, or what Merleau-Ponty calls 'pure transcendence,'[63] and which makes this act of perception possible. Merleau-Ponty thus claims that 'what is proper to the perceived: to be already there, to not be through the act of perception, to be the reason for that act, and not the reverse.'[64]

With this quote we see perhaps Merleau-Ponty's clearest formulation and recognition of the turn, or reversal, his thought took: it is not the paradoxical nature of the body-subject which is the access to being; it is the paradox of Being which is the access of being – that is, a perceiving being – to itself – that is, the perceived being.

The question remains, however, whether this reversal is able to resolve the difficulties we saw in Merleau-Ponty's account of the other. Does Merleau-Ponty's discussion of wild Being, and the fundamental difference, separation (*écart*), and paradox of this Being, avoid the consequence of reducing the other as Other – as difference – to identity? Claude Lefort claims that Merleau-Ponty does not resolve this difficulty; M.C. Dillon claims that he does. Therefore, to get a better grasp on Merleau-Ponty's efforts to account for the other as Other, we will turn to a discussion of this debate. In the end, this discussion will reveal

Merleau-Ponty's continuing struggle with the problem of transcendence, a problem poststructuralists such as Foucault, Deleuze, and Derrida have abandoned. The next chapter begins to sketch some of the reasons why they are no longer concerned with this problem.

VII. Untaming the Flesh

1. Introduction: Flesh as Differentiating Condition

In his unfinished and posthumously published book, *The Visible and the Invisible*, Merleau-Ponty was unfortunately not able to address adequately many aspects of the ontological position he was working through. Merleau-Ponty anticipated writing long sections on Nature and Logos (the Logos of Being), but, when he died, he left behind only some notes which merely hint at what he might have said. However, he was able to express with some thoroughness a number of notions that allow us to understand more clearly the turn his thought took from his earlier phenomenological position. In particular, these notions elucidate the sense in which it is not the paradoxical nature of the body-subject which conditions the access to being, but the paradox of Being which conditions the access of being – that is, a perceiving being – to itself – that is, perceived being. And it is this access of Being to itself which Merleau-Ponty's notion of 'reversibility' is meant to express. In addition, the notion of 'flesh' (*la chair*) is intended to express that which is reversed – that is, the reversibility of *the flesh*. It is therefore the reversibility of the flesh which *is* the access of this flesh – the flesh of the perceiving body – to itself – the flesh of the world.

There is, however, an apparent equivocation in Merleau-Ponty's use of the term 'flesh.' On the one hand, the reversibility of the flesh is understood to be a reversibility that is never completed, that is in a state of non-coincidence, and, as such, is only an *'identity* in principle.'[1] The access of the flesh to itself is always unfinished, is always left open, and it is the fundamental gap or separation (*écart*) of wild Being which is the condition both for reversibility and for the perpetual incompletion of this reversibility. According to this understanding of the flesh, the flesh is fundamentally divergent, or entails a separation or difference that is always already there, a difference that cannot be reduced to identity and coincidence. Merleau-Ponty thus argues, and against Sartre specifically, that 'this separation (*écart*) which, in first approximation, forms meaning, is not a no I affect myself with, a lack which constitutes a lack by the upsurge of an end which I give myself – it is a natural negativity, a first institution, always already there.'[2]

In other words, there is a fundamental difference or divergence that is the condition for identity, and this a further development of the Saussurean claim that the system of differences makes meaning possible. And it is this interpretation of the flesh that accounts for M.C. Dillon's claim that 'flesh must be understood as primordially dehiscent.'[3] That is, as dehiscent the flesh entails a fundamental separation and split from which identity arises, just as the 'dehiscence' of a seed gives rise to a plant.

On the other hand, the flesh is also interpreted to be that identity which fills this fundamental separation and divergence (*écart*): 'this divergence is not a void, [but] it is filled precisely by the flesh as the place of emergence of a vision.'[4] As we will elaborate below, it is the identity and sameness of the flesh which make vision possible. It is because the flesh of one's body is *the same* as the flesh of the world that there is the possibility of vision, for a vision that is characterized by reversibility. And it is this interpretation of the flesh which leads Claude Lefort to stress the identity of the flesh prior to its return to itself in the reversibility of vision. Lefort thus emphasizes quotes such as these in Merleau-Ponty's late writings:

> The body is an exemplar sensible, which offers to him who inhabits it and senses it the wherewithal *to sense everything that resembles himself* on the outside, such that, caught up in the tissue of things, it draws it entirely to itself, incorporates it, and, with the same movement, communicates to the things upon which it closes over *that identity without superposition*, that difference without contradiction, that divergence between the within and the without that constitutes its natal secret.[5]

Or again, in 'Eye and Mind,' Merleau-Ponty quotes Klee:

> 'Some days I felt that the trees were looking at me, were speaking to me' ... [and Merleau-Ponty concludes from this that] ... There really is inspiration

and expiration of Being, action and passion so slightly discernible that it becomes impossible to distinguish between what sees and what is seen, what paints and what is painted.'[6]

Lefort, however, also recognizes the tendency in Merleau-Ponty's writings to emphasize the fundamental divergence and separation. In short, the equivocation in the use of the term 'flesh' appears, in Merleau-Ponty's thought, as Lefort interprets him, to result in a tension in which 'what was first announced in terms of overlapping, homogeneity, and reversibility [i.e., flesh as identity, as the same] seems later to be qualified in terms of segregation, fission, alterity [i.e., flesh as difference].'[7] Lefort nevertheless emphasizes the identity and sameness of the 'flesh,' and consequently interprets reversibility as a *symmetrical* relationship between seer and seen – that is, the flesh of the world and the flesh of the body equally see and are seen (e.g., painter seen by the trees). Lefort thus situates reversibility with Merleau-Ponty's 'first announced ... terms of overlapping and homogeneity.' Dillon, on the other hand, because he emphasizes the 'primordially dehiscent' nature of the flesh, is led to understand reversibility as an *asymmetrical* relationship between seer and seen. Therefore, despite what Merleau-Ponty says in 'Eye and Mind' (Dillon claims that the implications of symmetry in this essay were an 'oversight' on Merleau-Ponty's part), one is not perceived by the trees in the same way that one perceives the trees. There is a fundamental divergence and separation between the flesh of the world and the flesh of the body.

Merleau-Ponty, however, can be seen to want to affirm both the symmetrical and the asymmetrical positions regarding reversibility. In a late note, for example, Merleau-Ponty claims that 'the things touch me as I touch them and touch myself: flesh of the world – distinct from my flesh: the double inscription of outside and inside.'[8] In other words, Lefort seems to be right in claiming that there is a symmetry of the flesh, that 'the things touch me as I touch them,' but Dillon is right to argue for a fundamental difference between the flesh of the world and the flesh of the body. There is, in short, a paradox of identity and difference which Merleau-Ponty's thought seems to be contending with: that is, there is a fundamental difference that is simultaneously a fundamental identity (Dillon, as we will discuss later, refers to this as an 'identity-within-difference').

The paradox that emerges here is analogous to Merleau-Ponty's early understanding of paradox – that is, paradox is constitutive of an irreducible structure. In short, it allows Merleau-Ponty to take the 'middle path.' On the one hand, by not reducing the flesh to a pure and simple identity, Merleau-Ponty should be able to circumvent the earlier difficulties of accounting for the other as Other (as different). On the other hand, by not reducing the flesh to an absolute difference or disjunction, Merleau-Ponty is able to avoid, as Dillon correctly points out, a mind/body dualism which Merleau-Ponty argues results in solipsism and scepticism. Merleau-Ponty cites Sartre's distinction between the being-in-itself and being-for-itself as an example.[9] The flesh should be understood, therefore, neither as identity, nor as non-identity, non-coincidence, or difference, if difference is understood as a difference between positive terms (recall our discussion of Saussure), but should be understood as paradox, as the differentiating condition which makes possible the distinction between identity and difference, coincidence and non-coincidence; and, as paradox, the flesh is a fundamental dis-unity, the non-identifiable and unknowable condition for identification and knowledge. This is the sense in which we understand Merleau-Ponty's intention to

start from this: there is not identity, nor non-identity, or non-coincidence, there is inside and outside turning about one another.

My central 'nothingness' [alluding to Sartre] is like the point of the stroboscopic spiral which is who knows where, which is 'nobody.'[10]

In other words, the flesh is not identity or non-identity, but is a 'chiasm,' a paradoxical reversibility which makes possible the distinction between perceiver and perceived, identity and difference. The flesh is thus, analogous to our earlier discussion of the noema, that differentiating condition which is not to be identified with that which is differentiated (flesh as boundary). The flesh, or the central nothingness, is thus much like the point over which a top spins: it is not the pointed end of the top, or the point of ground or earth which pushes against the downward thrust of the top's point, but it is the point which is neither spinning nor not spinning. It is the point where the balance achieves a static spin of movement – in other words, a non-moving movement. And it is this non-moving movement, or flesh as paradox and differentiating condition, which makes possible the distinction between rest and motion, or, by analogy, identity and difference.

We argue that it is this implicit paradox which is at the heart of the debate between Lefort and Dillon. We claim that Merleau-Ponty can and should be seen to emphasize the flesh as identity and the flesh as difference, and reversibility as symmetrical and asymmetrical, not because the flesh is both of these, but because it is the paradoxical condition which makes the distinction possible. However, the failure to recognize this paradox has resulted in two contrasting interpretations. In short, Lefort claims that the identity of flesh is prior to difference (e.g., the other), and Dillon claims that flesh is the difference prior to identity.

To further clarify these positions, and to begin elaborating the sense in which we take paradox to be the differentiating condition, we shall discuss Dillon's and Lefort's evaluation of Merleau-Ponty's account of the other. This will in turn shed light on the reason Lefort and Dillon have such opposed views regarding the relationship of Merleau-Ponty's thought to the transcendental tradition.

2. Lefort: Flesh Is Immanence

With Lefort's stress upon the flesh as that which stays the same throughout the reversibility process, it is not surprising that he takes reversibility to be symmetrical. I and the world each see and are seen because we are made of the same stuff – flesh. Or, as Merleau-Ponty defines 'chiasm': 'every relation with being is simultaneously a taking and a being taken, the hold is held, it is inscribed in *the same being* that it takes hold of.'[11] And it is precisely this being 'inscribed in the same being,' the same flesh, which is the condition, Lefort claims, for vision.

To justify this interpretation, Lefort cites the several places where the flesh is described in terms of a genesis, or, as Lefort describes it, 'as a movement of self-begetting.'[12] For example, Merleau-Ponty analogizes the genesis of vision to 'the current making of an embryo [into] a newborn infant, of a visible [into] a seer, and of a body [into] a mind, or at least a flesh.'[13] That is, the dual relationship of flesh to itself, of the hold that is held, the touching that is touched, is analogous to the dual relationship of genetic material to itself (i.e., sperm and egg), and of the process which leads to the birth of an infant. The infant, as with vision, is born of this type of relationship. For this reason, we find Merleau-Ponty stating in the working notes that 'Nature is at the first day ... do a psychoanalysis of Nature: it is the flesh, the mother.'[14] Vision is thus the result of the relationship of flesh to itself, of the self-constituted unity and identity of the flesh – that is, the reversibility of the *same* flesh. The flesh is 'at the first day'; it is 'the mother' of all vision.

There is a parallel here between Lefort's interpretation of the flesh and our earlier interpretation of Husserl's theory of time-consciousness. In particular, we saw that it was the self-constituted unity of time-consciousness the self-genesis of time-consciousness, so to speak, that was the condition which made possible the consciousness, of objective time. In other words, it was the *immanently* self-constituted unity of time-consciousness which makes possible, or is the mother of, the consciousness of *transcendent* unities. Similarly, Lefort claims that, for Merleau-Ponty, it is the self-genesis of flesh, or the intrinsic identity of the flesh with itself, which makes possible all vision. It is the mother of all vision. Lefort will then stress such statements as this by Merleau-Ponty: 'there is a fundamental narcissism of all vision.'[15] In short, all vision is at bottom a relationship of flesh to it*self*, and it is this narcissism which Lefort takes to be Merleau-Ponty's understanding of reversibility as symmetrical.

Lefort can therefore be seen to argue for a continuing effort on Merleau-Ponty's part to carry forward Husserl's transcendental project – that is, the project of revealing the fundamental identity which is the condition for objectivity, and for the differentiations of the natural attitude. Analogously, the flesh is, for Merleau-Ponty, that fundamental identity which is the condition for vision, and for the objective differentiations of this vision; or, in Merleau-Ponty's terminology, his project is to reveal the 'wild,' 'vertical' being that is the condition for the domesticated 'horizontal' being of everyday perception.[16] This project, furthermore, continues the task that Merleau-Ponty set for himself in *The Phenomenology of Perception:* the task of restoring an experience of the world prior to our everyday experience of the world (i.e., the phenomenological reduction which restores the 'wonder in the face of the world'   that philosophy must examine the experience of the world 'before it [the world] is a thing one speaks of and which is taken for granted, before it has been reduced to a set of manageable disposable significations.'[17] In short, rather than presupposing the givenness of the world, Merleau-Ponty takes as his problem, as he did in *The Phenomenology of Perception*, the very advent of this world to one who perceives, reflects upon, and experiences this world. Merleau-Ponty is continuing, therefore, to further explicate Husserl's notion of Urdoxa, or that fundamental belief and opinion which is prior to, and makes possible, all positing consciousnesses. Consequently, Merleau-Ponty is interested in revealing the conditions which make possible the distinction between *what* is being experienced – *what* is objectively meant, intended, or experienced – and the fact *that* there is an experience. Merleau-Ponty is explicit on this point: 'We do not establish ourselves in a universe – on the contrary we ask that the distinction between the that and the what, between the essence and the conditions of existence, be reconsidered by referring to the experience of the world that precedes that distinction.'

This experience, in the end, is the experience of reversibility, the relationship of flesh to itself – 'the narcissism of all vision.' However, it is this interpretation of the symmetrical reversibility and narcissism of flesh, or the relationship of the flesh to itself as the condition for all objectivity, which Lefort claims leaves Merleau-Ponty's account of the other inadequate. For example, Merleau-Ponty claims that 'the flesh is a mirror phenomenon and the mirror is an extension of my relation with my body.'[18] This relation is that of touching oneself, or seeing oneself. And it is this mirror phenomenon, or the recognition of one's self, that is the condition for recognizing others. Merleau-Ponty thus says, along these lines, that 'the reason why I have evidence of the other man's being there when I shake his hand is that his hand is substituted for my left hand, and my body annexes the body of another person in that sort of reflection [i.e., reversibility] it is paradoxically the seat of.'[19]

The reversibility of the flesh, the identity of the flesh with itself (i.e., the touching–touched, sentient–sensible relation), is the basis upon which one comes to recognize the other; however, Lefort claims that this does not account for the other as Other, as transcendent and different. The other is, in the end, simply reduced to the identity of the flesh, to the binary relationship of reversibility. And since this relationship of reversibility is a relation of the same flesh, and a relationship that is the mother of all vision, including a vision of the other, Lefort concludes that Merleau-Ponty is unable to account for the other as Other: 'I could not help noting that the identification between flesh and mother enlightens Merleau-Ponty's description of the relation sentient–sensible within the body as well as between the body and the outside. This relation always corresponds to the pattern of a dual relation. So what in general is not taken into account is the other, the third one, the representative of otherness.'[20]

In the end, therefore, Merleau-Ponty's transcendental project reveals the identity of the flesh as the condition for otherness, for difference. The other is simply an extension of the self-genesis of the flesh: in short, the other is an extension of the self. So, Merleau-Ponty, according to Lefort, is unable to resolve the difficulties present in Husserl's account of the other. They each reduce the other to being an extension of the self, and thus are unable to account for the other as Other, as difference and transcendence. Lefort will then conclude by asking rhetorically 'whether the world that Merleau-Ponty attempted to explore was not an already tamed world rather than that wild experience which he hoped to give expression.'[21]

Lefort's interpretation of the flesh, however, stresses the role of flesh as the same, as the self-identity which is the mother of all difference; but he fails to take into consideration Merleau-Ponty's emphasis upon paradox, upon that *irreducible difference* which is the differentiating condition for the identifications of everyday perception. Lefort recognizes Merleau-Ponty's use of the term 'paradox' to describe the coincidence of the flesh of the body with the flesh of the world (i.e., his later version of the paradoxical coincidence of 'man and the world'), but he emphasizes the coincidence and identity that is paradoxical, not the paradox that conditions this coincidence and identity. In short, Lefort has not interpreted the flesh as paradoxa, as that differentiating condition which is not to be identified with identity or difference, difference being understood as between identifiable terms. The flesh is, we claim, that which makes such distinctions possible; or, to put it another way, it is paradoxically identity and difference. Therefore, by not recognizing this paradox, Lefort is confronted with an either/or: either the flesh is that fundamental identity which is the condition that makes difference possible, or the flesh is the fundamental difference that makes identity possible. Lefort opts for the first; Dillon, as we will see, opts for the second.

3. Dillon: Flesh Is Transcendence

In Dillon's interpretation of Merleau-Ponty, Merleau-Ponty would indeed be unable to account for the transcendence of the other if this account were to be made on the basis of the reversibility of the same flesh. However, Dillon claims that this is not Merleau-Ponty's position. In fact, in the working notes to *The Visible and the Invisible*, Merleau-Ponty calls for the recognition of the third term Lefort claimed was lacking, for the transcendence that cannot be reduced to the dual relationship of sentient–sensible, subject–object. This term is precisely the separation and divergence (*écart*) which makes this relationship possible. In other words, the self-presence of the flesh through reversibility is not, Dillon claims, a presence of coincidence and identity; rather, it is a presence which entails absence, or a presence through divergence and separation; and it is this divergence that is more fundamental than coincidence. Merleau-Ponty is explicit on this point:

... the for-itself ... as an incontestable, but derived characteristic: it is the culmination of separation (*écart*) in differentiation – self-presence is presence to a differentiated world.

... To be conscious = to have a figure on a ground – one cannot go back any further.

... Self-presence that is an absence from oneself, a contact with self through the divergence (*écart*) with regard to self – The figure on a ground, the simplest '*Etwas*.'[22]

This separation and divergence, furthermore, is the third term Lefort called for, a third term Merleau-Ponty recognizes:

... the figure-ground distinction introduces a third term between the 'subject' and the 'object.' It is that separation (*écart*) first of all that is the perceptual meaning.[23]

On the basis of statements such as these, Dillon will emphasize the fundamental difference and divergence that is the condition for identity – the difference within which identity will emerge. And it is exactly this emergence of identity within difference that is Merleau-Ponty's very definition of transcendence: 'Transcendence is identity within difference.'[24] That is, transcendence is the fundamental separation and divergence that is 'always already there.'[25] This difference and divergence is not, as Dillon claims Lefort argues, an extension of the body or the flesh as self-identity, but it is a difference that transcends this self and which must be adapted to – thus 'the contact with self through divergence,' through 'encroachment.' Even an object, for example, is not fundamentally an identity, as it was with Husserl's notion of an 'object in general,' but difference. The identity of an object emerges only on the horizon of difference, on the basis of the figure–ground distinction; and it is this difference, as we saw, which is all Merleau-Ponty takes consciousness to be (i.e., 'to have a figure on a ground – one cannot go back any further'). Consequently, Merleau-Ponty claims that 'transcendence is identity within difference,' and therefore a transcendent object is at first difference, and only later identity: 'We have to pass from the thing (spatial or temporal) as identity, to the thing (spatial or temporal) as difference, that is, as transcendence, that is, as always "behind," beyond, far-off.'[26]

It is this fundamental difference and divergence that motivates Dillon's claim that the 'flesh must be understood as primordially dehiscent.'[27] Reversibility, therefore, is not a doubling of the same, but a doubling of difference; and Dillon will subsequently argue that not only do I and the trees not perceive each other in the same way, but neither do I perceive myself in the same way that others perceive me. In short, Dillon claims that, despite Merleau-Ponty's apparent claims to the contrary (see our earlier quote), 'shaking hands with the other is not the same as shaking hands with oneself.'[28] In other words, the reversibility of the flesh is fundamentally asymmetrical, or, it is a self-presence through divergence. And it is only on the basis of this asymmetry, and within the field and horizon of difference, that the problem of the *identity* of the other emerges. Dillon will thus claim that when 'the differentiation between self and other is thematized, it will be a grounded differentiation, a differentiation grounded in the fission of the flesh and not simply a fiat of consciousness.'[29]

The problem of the other, as well as the problem of transcendence, is only a problem, Dillon argues, for a philosophy that attempts to understand the other on the basis of a transcendental subjectivity, a transcendental ego or self. This was reflected in the conclusions that were drawn from an analysis of childhood consciousness – that is, Merleau-Ponty's discussion of the 'peaceful coexistence [between self and other] in childhood.' The conclusion that there is a coincidence of self and other in childhood follows, for Dillon, from the assumption that there is neither a reflection upon, nor an awareness of, an identifiable and distinct *self*. Dillon thus claims that 'only within the standpoint of the philosophy of transcendental consciousness can one make the inference from (a) lack of conscious differentiation to (b) lack of differentiation altogether.'[30] Dillon will counter this position by claiming it is simply a fact 'that the infant cannot live its mother's flesh ... its mouth recognizes the transcendence of Mother right from the start.'[31] There is not, in other words, identity and symmetry from the start, but difference and asymmetry: in short, transcendence.

With this understanding of the flesh, Dillon turns to an analysis of Merleau-Ponty's efforts to resolve his earlier difficulties in accounting for the transcendence of the other. This difficulty, we saw, stemmed from the fact that it was on the basis of the identity of the body-subject that the other appears. The other, consequently, was reduced to this identity, or to the self. Dillon claims that Merleau-Ponty was aware that 'the problem of organization is not solved by shifting the agency of constitution from transcendental ego to lived body.'[32] In other words, the conditions for the experience of the world were seen to be determined by the immanent nature of the subject, and it is this subject that constitutes or synthesizes this world. Note, for example, Merleau-Ponty's claim that the paradox of the body-subject entailed the 'infinite synthesis' of perceptual aspects through one aspect, and that it was this synthesis which made possible the experience (i.e., perception) of an object. The problem, we saw, was to account for the experience of the other as Other, as another constituting and synthesizing subject. This could not be done adequately, and, in the end, the other came to be understood as a projection of immanence by immanence, and not as transcendence.

In recognition of this problem, Dillon claims that Merleau-Ponty abandons the transcendental project; that is, the task of revealing those subjective conditions which make objective everyday experience possible. In particular, Dillon claims that Merleau-Ponty abandons the project of accounting for transcendence on the basis of an immanent subjectivity. On the one hand, Merleau-Ponty does seem to be abandoning this project. He claims that 'the problems posed in Ph.P. [*The Phenomenology of Perception*] are insoluble because I start there from the "consciousness"–"object" distinction';[33] or, as he also puts it, he retained in his early work 'the philosophy of "consciousness".'[34] As a result, Dillon claims the flesh is to be understood as transcendence, as identity-within-difference, and consequently the flesh is associated with, or identified with, the unity of the world. The asymmetry of reversibility, the fundamental dehiscence of flesh, is a difference grounded in the world: 'we (the trees and I) are both flesh of a unitary world.'[35] The flesh *is* transcendence, and as such it is grounded in the transcendent unity of the world. On the other hand, Lefort seems to be correct in claiming that Merleau-Ponty, in *The Visible and the Invisible*, is still continuing to operate within the parameters of the transcendental project. Even Dillon, for example, cites with approval Merleau-Ponty's claim that 'I am always on the same side of my body,'[36] and concludes from this that 'the anonymity of the body is infected with the germ of mineness.'[37] In other words, Dillon admits that, for Merleau-Ponty, there continues to be the recognition of an irreducible subjectivity, a 'germ of mineness,' and he further argues that this essential 'mineness' is a fundamental reason for the asymmetry of reversibility – that is, why the other doesn't perceive me in the same way that I perceive myself. Dillon therefore seems unjustified in claiming that Merleau-Ponty abandons the transcendental project,[38] and thus Lefort seems to be justified in identifying the flesh with the self-constituted unity of the subject; or, in other words, in claiming that the flesh *is* immanence, and as such is grounded in the unity of the self.

We thus have a sharp contrast with respect to the interpretations of the notion 'flesh.' On the one hand, Lefort identifies the flesh with *immanence*. The flesh is the self-constituted unity of the self. With this interpretation, however, Lefort does not give adequate credit to Merleau-Ponty's effort to account for the transcendence of the other. On the other hand, Dillon identifies the flesh with *transcendence*. The flesh is the transcendent unity of the world. This interpretation, as we saw, does not recognize Merleau-Ponty's continuing adherence to the transcendental project, to the task of revealing the subjective conditions of objectivity (i.e., the natural, everyday attitude). At the heart of these contrasting interpretations is the failure to recognize the flesh as 'paradoxa'; that is, the flesh as the differentiating condition which is to be identified neither with immanence nor with transcendence. They fail to see that the flesh is neither a fundamental identity and coincidence, nor a fundamental difference and divergence. As a consequence of this failure, there emerges an unnecessary either/or: either there is a fundamental identity which is the transcendental condition, and we are left unable to account for difference (Lefort), or difference is fundamental and we are left having to abandon the transcendental project, the project of deducing *identifiable* subjective conditions (Dillon). What we want to claim, however, is that if the flesh is interpreted as paradoxa, then it is not to be identified with immanence or transcendence, identity or difference, but it is the transcendental condition which makes these identifications possible.

4. Flesh and Paradoxa

We first introduced the term 'paradoxa' when discussing Husserl's theory of the perceptual noema. In this context, we argued that the noema is to be identified neither with a posited sense (i.e., concept theory) nor with a posited object (i.e., percept theory), but it is, rather, the condition which makes this positing possible. In other words, the perceptual noema as paradoxa is the differentiating condition which allows for the positing of sense, or concepts, and the positing of objects, or percepts. The perceptual noema, in short, is the condition which makes possible the irreducible difference *between* sense and object, intending acts and intuitive acts. The perceptual noema is not a difference between two already identified and posited terms – for example, sense and object – but it is a difference without positive terms, and the difference which makes possible the difference *between* positive terms. This is the sense in which we understand paradoxa as the differentiating condition.

Our analyses of Husserl were led to this notion of paradoxa because of Husserl's own efforts to establish the conditions which make possible the relationship between two irreducibly different types of acts (i.e., signitive and intuitive), and two irreducibly different types of knowledge (i.e., inductive and intuitive). For example, Husserl accepts the Platonic claim that there is an irreducible difference between an ideal objective truth (knowledge) and a contingent subjective truth (opinion), but he did not accept Plato's claim that these ideal objective truths pre-exist their being intuited and known by subjects – what Husserl called 'Platonic Realism.' Husserl's project, therefore, was to show the relationship between these objective truths and the subjects who know and intuit them, and this, then, emerged as the problem of fulfilment, or the problem of explaining how a subject comes to have intuitively *fulfilled* and objective knowledge.

Husserl was unable, as we saw, to account for fulfilment. Each fulfilling act was, as an act, in turn determined by a sense which is in need of fulfilment; and so on *ad infinitum*. There thus emerged an epistemological infinite regress in Husserl's account of fulfilment as set forth in *Logical Investigations;* however, in *The Phenomenology of Internal Time-Consciousness*, Husserl claimed that this regress is, in the end, grounded in a self-constituted absolute consciousness – that is, a consciousness where sense and object, intending and intended, do coincide, or are fulfilled. It is this consciousness which is therefore the condition which makes possible the difference between intending and intuitive acts. This absolute consciousness is, in other words, the differentiating condition – that is, paradoxa.

It was this understanding of an absolute consciousness as developed in *The Phenomenology of Internal Time-Consciousness* which paved the way for Husserl's later development of the concept 'noema.' However, the emphasis in these later works changed, as Ricoeur and others are correct to point out. With the concept of the 'noema,' Husserl is not simply trying to account for the relationship between an intending act and an intuitive act of consciousness, but, rather, for the relationship between consciousness and the reality intended through and by consciousness. In short, the problem becomes one of accounting for transcendence. And, as we discussed Husserl's theory of the perceptual noema, we claimed that the perceptual noema is to be understood as that which makes possible the relationship between the sense *immanent* to consciousness and the object which *transcends* this consciousness. In other words, the perceptual noema was interpreted to be the differentiating condition which makes possible the irreducible difference *between* a posited sense and a posited object – that is, as paradoxa. And it was the failure to recognize this that resulted in two contrasting interpretations: Gurwitsch identified the perceptual noema as a posited object, as a percept; and Føllesdal identified it with a posited sense, as a concept.

The noema, however, was itself ultimately grounded in the unity of an absolute constituting consciousness, the pure transcendental ego; consequently, the problem of transcendence becomes, in Husserl's later works, the problem of the other, the problem of accounting for the transcendence of the other (note especially the Fifth Cartesian Meditation). It is precisely in relation to this problem that Merleau-Ponty carries forward Husserl's thought. In particular, by arguing for the paradoxical nature of structure, Merleau-Ponty attempts to chart a middle path between idealism and naturalism, intellectualism and realism. This path attempts to resolve Husserl's difficulties in accounting for the transcendence of the other, a difficulty that will remain, Merleau-Ponty argues, as long as the other is understood on the basis of an absolute constituting consciousness. Merleau-Ponty will thus argue for the paradoxical coincidence of consciousness and object, 'man and the world,' self and other, and claims that this is a coincidence lived by the body-subject. It is therefore the lived body that becomes, in Merleau-Ponty's thought, the fundamental differentiating condition (paradoxa).

This account has its own problems, however. If the other is understood on the basis of the identity of the body-subject, then the other is ultimately reduced to the identity of this body, or of this self. Thus the other emerges only as a 'double' of oneself, as a visible analogue to oneself, but not as a transcendent self that cannot be reduced to the identity of oneself. In short, Merleau-Ponty was unable to account for the *difference* of the other.

After his contact with the work of Saussure, however, Merleau-Ponty made great strides in his ability to account for the difference and transcendence of the other. In Saussure's writings, Merleau-Ponty recognized the importance of what Saussure calls the 'system of differences'; that is, a system of differences that cannot be reduced to a set of differences *between* positive terms, but is, rather, a system of differences which makes the differentiation between positive terms possible. Merleau-Ponty later adopts this Saussurean notion and argues for a differentiating condition which makes possible the difference between self and other, consciousness and object – put another way, Merleau-Ponty develops an understanding of what we call 'paradoxa.' And it is this understanding of a differentiating condition which led to Merleau-

Ponty's transcendental critique of his position in *The Phenomenology of Perception*. In *The Visible and the Invisible*, for example, Merleau-Ponty claimed that his 'philosophy of consciousness' had presupposed the conditioned – that is, the *identifiable* words of language – and used this to explain the conditions – namely, the *identity* of the body-subject. Merleau-Ponty then turns, in *The Visible and the Invisible*, to an analysis of that difference and divergence (*écart*) that is 'always already there'; the difference that makes possible the distinction between identifiable words, subjects, objects, and so on.

It is as a differentiating condition that we understand Merleau-Ponty's notion of the 'flesh.' In other words, the flesh, as with Husserl's notion of the perceptual noema, is understood as paradoxa. Furthermore, Merleau-Ponty's notion of the flesh is intended to demonstrate the conditions which make possible the relationship between immanence and transcendence; or, to put it another way, the flesh is the differentiating condition which makes possible the irreducible difference *between* immanence and transcendence. As paradoxa, however, the flesh is neither to be identified with immanence or transcendence, yet Lefort and Dillon, by not understanding flesh as paradoxa, do precisely that: Lefort identifies the flesh with *immanence*, and Dillon identifies it with *transcendence*.

But Merleau-Ponty's notion of the flesh, however, is in turn grounded in the fundamental unity of Being. In other words, the flesh is, as Merleau-Ponty puts it, an element, style, or manner of Being: 'The flesh is not matter, is not mind, is not substance. To designate it, we should need the old term "element" in the sense it was used to speak of water, air, earth, and fire, that is, in the sense of a general thing ... The flesh is in this sense an "element" of Being.'[39]

Despite the differences between Lefort and Dillon, therefore, they each seem to be correct to stress the fact that the flesh is the flesh of a unity, whether it be the unity and coincidence of immanent subjectivity as Lefort interprets it, or the unity of the transcendent world as Dillon interprets it (e.g., 'we are both flesh of a unitary world'). The flesh is thus grounded or rooted in the unity of Being, and thus, when Merleau-Ponty does discuss paradox in *The Visible and the Invisible*, it is not paradox as a differentiating condition (i.e., as paradoxa), but paradox rooted in Being – 'a paradox *of* Being.' Flesh and paradox is therefore simply the manner or style of this 'one sole Being,' and it is this Being which is the condition for the paradox of this Being, for paradox as the differentiating condition (i.e., paradoxa).

This last claim is susceptible to the same transcendental critique that both Husserl and Merleau-Ponty took with respect to their predecessors. In particular, Merleau-Ponty argues for the claim that identity is conditioned by difference, by the separation and divergence (*écart*) of wild Being, but he then claims that this is a divergence and difference of the 'same Being,' of the 'one sole Being' – that is, a 'paradox of Being.' Paradox and difference are thus ultimately conditioned by the identity and unity of Being, and thus the conditioned – identity – is used to explain the conditions – Being. Thus, Merleau-Ponty continues to be susceptible to the same critique that he himself made of his earlier work, and, as Lefort is correct to say, he has therefore not adequately accounted for difference, or transcendence. Difference is, in the end, reduced to a difference of Being, a difference rooted in the identity of Being; consequently, Lefort was also not unjustified in asking rhetorically whether 'the world that Merleau-Ponty attempted to explore was not an already tamed world rather than that wild experience which he hoped to give expression.'[40]

What will an untaming of this tamed world entail? How will the transcendental critique of Merleau-Ponty's last writings result in an untaming of the flesh? That is, how will this be a restoration of flesh as difference, as the differentiating condition which makes identity possible; and will this be a flesh that is not derivative of identity, or a tamed flesh that is the flesh of a unitary world, the flesh of the same Being – that is, the flesh of identity? To answer these questions, we enter upon the terrain of 'post-structuralism'; most especially, we encounter the writings of Foucault, Deleuze, and Derrida. And in these writings we find that they carry forward this transcendental critique, or what is more commonly known as the 'critique of metaphysics.'

An initial consequence of this critique will be that the poststructuralists will no longer be concerned with the problem of transcendence. In fact, Foucault claims that, for him, the 'essential task was to free the history of thought from its subjection to transcendence ... freed from that circle of the lost origin.'[41] In other words, the transcendental critique of metaphysics is a critique of reducing difference to identity – for example, Merleau-Ponty's notion of flesh and paradox as grounded in the identity of the same Being. As a result, the poststructuralists are not concerned with accounting for difference – that is, transcendence – and with establishing the *identifiable* conditions that are the origin of difference (e.g., transcendence as conditioned by immanence), or the proper boundaries of difference (e.g., Kant's categories); rather, they are concerned with accounting for identity, for the conditions which allow for certain identities to emerge as the norm, as the proper limits, values, boundaries, and so on. These conditions, furthermore, are understood by the poststructuralists to be *non-identifiable*, or a pure difference and paradox that is the differentiating condition which allows for the possibility of identity. Thus, in Foucault's work, he speaks of power as that non-identifiable condition which is seen only through its effects, but yet is the historical condition wherein norms, values, and standards are made possible; Derrida speaks of 'différance' as that fundamental *difference* which continually *defers* the return to an *identifiable*, self-identical origin (e.g., absolute consciousness; body-subject); and Deleuze speaks of paradox as the differentiating condition which makes identity possible, and all thought which always and only thinks in terms of identity.

To further clarify this critique and its consequences, I turn now to the final part of this essay. In particular, I will compare and contrast the work of Merleau-Ponty and Deleuze. This will be especially illuminating, for they each place a strong emphasis upon paradox; however, a marked contrast emerges in their respective understandings of paradox, and this contrast reflects Deleuze's transcendental critique of Merleau-Ponty and the tradition of metaphysics and transcendental philosophy of which he believes Merleau-Ponty is a part. In the end, rather than difference being grounded and rooted in the identity of Being, as Merleau-Ponty argues, we will explore Deleuze's claim that identity is conditioned by a fundamental difference, by a difference or paradox that continually subverts identity. In short, we will see how the poststructuralists, and, in particular, Deleuze, continue to develop and expand upon the theme of a pure differentiating condition; or, to put it another way, we will expand upon the theme of paradoxa as a concept which arose as a response to the problem of difference.

PART THREE

The Poststructuralist Turn

VIII. Cinema Paradoxa

As we have seen, Merleau-Ponty ultimately turns towards an ontological grounding of paradox. That is, he argues that the paradox is a paradox of Being, a characteristic or trait of Being. It is this grounding of the paradox in Being that emerges as a pre-established harmony, as the return of Being to itself, or as the leaving of oneself that is a return to oneself. It is therefore not paradox, but the identity of Being, which conditions the absence that is presence, the leaving that is a return, and the visible that is invisible. In other words, paradox is understood only as a description of the manner of Being itself – its style.

This grounding of paradox in Being, or the transcendental critique that reveals identity as the condition prior to difference, resulted in two contrasting interpretations. On the one hand, Lefort emphasizes the identity of the flesh as that fundamental element which fills the fundamental separation (*écart*) at the heart of Being, and claims that Merleau-Ponty is subsequently unable to account for the difference and transcendence of the other. Dillon, on the other hand, emphasizes the identity of Being as wild Being, as separation and divergence (*écart*). Dillon thus claims that, if it is the fundamental separation or differentiation of wild Being that is foundational, then it is wrong to pursue the *identity* of some transcendental condition; and therefore he abandons Merleau-Ponty's transcendentalism. Dillon's position, however, seems to needlessly abandon a crucial aspect of Merleau-Ponty's thought; therefore, in attempting to counter what we believe to be a source of confusion in Dillon and Lefort, we shall not maintain the assumption that a transcendental critique must deduce the identity of something. Rather we claim that Merleau-Ponty's transcendental critique reveals the constitutive role of paradox as a fundamental differentiating condition – that is, as the difference which conditions identity. There are many indications in Merleau-Ponty's thought that this was the direction he was moving in; however, in the end, paradox emerges, not as the fundamental transcendental condition, but as something itself conditioned by the identity of something even more basic – namely, Being. It is this last move which leads Lefort and Dillon to their contrasting interpretations and criticisms of Merleau-Ponty: either identity is the transcendental condition, and we are left unable to account for difference; or difference is, and we are left having to abandon the transcendental method, the method of deducing *identifiable* conditions. However, by not making the move to grounding paradox on identity, we will indeed be disagreeing with many of Merleau-Ponty's explicit claims; nevertheless, by pushing Merleau-Ponty's understanding of paradox farther than he did himself, I believe we are simply following through on the unthought element in his philosophy, and thus we are thinking through Merleau-Ponty much in the same way that he thought through Husserl. Furthermore, this carrying forward of Merleau-Ponty is also something we will find having already been done in the works of Gilles Deleuze; that is, Deleuze does claim that the fundamental transcendental condition is paradox, and with this move he sets forth a 'philosophy of difference.'

In carrying forward Merleau-Ponty's notion of paradox, and in comparing the results here with Deleuze, we will (1) compare Merleau-Ponty's understanding of paradox with Deleuze's and show that Deleuze reverses Merleau-Ponty's formulation. Furthermore, this reversal reflects (2) Deleuze's critique of Merleau-Ponty's transcendental method of deducing identifiable conditions (e.g., Being), whereby paradox itself is understood as conditioned. This critique will be seen to be the same as both Merleau-Ponty's criticisms of Husserl and Husserl's criticisms of Kant: that is, Deleuze would argue that Merleau-Ponty has presupposed that which he hopes to explain by taking the conditioned – paradox – as the model in explaining the conditions, for example, the paradox of Being. It is this critique which leads to Deleuze's reversal of the transcendental tradition whereby the fundamental and non-identifiable difference of paradox itself is deduced as the fundamental transcendental condition. And, finally, (3) we will sketch the consequence of this reversal as it applies to Deleuze's theory of perception, a theory that is set forth in his writings on cinema.

1. Paradox

The term 'paradox' appears many times throughout Merleau-Ponty's writings. He speaks of the paradox of perception, expression, freedom, and Being; and, in all these cases, it is not clear whether there is or should be a consistent pattern to his many uses of the term. Despite these ambiguities, however, the term does appear to be used in generally two different, yet related, senses.

The first sense is what I call the 'paradox of infinite series.' This is the paradox whereby an infinite series of parts or aspects is synthesized through a single part or aspect. For example, in perceiving an object, we perceive this object from a single perspective, and, although we are presented only with a single aspect of this object, we nevertheless perceive this object as a self-contained unity, as the unity of an infinite number of possible perspectives or aspects. Merleau-Ponty thus claims that 'perception is here understood as a reference to a whole which can be grasped, in principle, only through certain of its parts or aspects ... Perception is thus paradoxical.'[1] In addition, Merleau-Ponty defines being and reality as an infinite series of possibilities: 'The real,' he claims, 'lends itself to unending exploration; it is inexhaustible.'[2] A house, for example, 'is not the house seen from nowhere, but the house seen from everywhere. The completed object is translucent being shot through from all sides by *an infinite number of present scrutinies* ...'[3] And it is the paradoxical synthesis of this infinite series in perception that opens us up to being: 'the perception of a thing opens me up to being by realizing the paradoxical synthesis of an infinity of perceptual aspects.'[4] The paradox of infinite series thus characterizes for Merleau-Ponty the relationship between a perceiving subject and being (or reality).

The second sense of paradox, I call the 'paradox of identity and difference.' This paradox is initially used in describing the relationship of one subject to an-other. For example, if the other is to be truly other, if the other is to be an ego that cannot be reduced to my own, then the other must be understood as fundamentally different from me; however, if it is only through one's own experience that one comes to recognize the other, then the other is dependent upon my coming to identify him as such. The problem is thus to account for difference without reducing it to the identity of one's own experience (i.e., the transcendental ego, in the case of Husserl). This problem will remain intractable, Merleau-Ponty argues, as long as the other person is dependent upon one's own constituting consciousness;[5] however, the problem is resolved if there is an experience that is paradoxically both constituting and constituted, an experience that is self (identity) and other (difference). This is precisely what Merleau-Ponty claims to be the experience of the body: 'This subject which experiences itself as constituted at the moment it functions as constituting is my body.'[6] In particular, this is the experience of the body as a perceiving body, as a body perceptually related to a world of identifiable things (i.e., beings, realities'), and thus the paradox of identity and difference ties in to the paradox of infinite series.

By the time of *The Visible and the Invisible*, the paradox of identity and difference plays a more central role. In this work, Merleau-Ponty claims that, at the heart of Being, there is a fundamental separation or difference (*écart*), a difference that is simultaneously overcome by the identity of this same Being – that is, by the identity of the Flesh. In other words, the paradox of identity and difference is not simply a description of a subject's relation to another subject; rather, it is, as Merleau-Ponty stresses, 'a paradox of Being, not a paradox of man that we are dealing with here.'[7] We therefore have, following from the fundamental difference at the heart of Being, a difference that refuses to be identified: 'Start from this: there is not identity, nor non-identity, or non-coincidence, there is inside and outside turning about one another.'[8] And this continual turning-about that results from the fundamental separation at the heart of Being is nevertheless a turning-about of the *same* Being in that it is the paradoxical identity and difference of Being (i.e., 'a paradox of Being'). It is for this reason that Merleau-Ponty says the difference or separation is not a void or a vacuum, but 'is filled precisely by the flesh as the place of emergence of vision.' Or, to put it another way, it is the identity of Being (or flesh) that is always turning-about itself, that is always divergent and different from itself, which conditions perception when this Being returns to itself,[9] when the difference is paradoxically an identity; and thus the paradox of identity and difference ties in again with the paradox of infinite series (i.e., perception).

To summarize, the paradox of infinite series entails the synthesis of an infinite number of parts and aspects through a single part or aspect; and the paradox of identity and difference entails a fundamental difference (i.e., separation, divergence, *écart*) that is simultaneously a fundamental identity. In both cases, moreover, these paradoxes characterize either a relationship to being or a relationship of Being. Thus, for Merleau-Ponty, the term 'paradox' is simply the manner in which he understands either an infinite synthesis of *being* or the fundamental difference of *Being* that is simultaneously the identity of *Being*; and the paradox arises when either the unity of being comes into contradiction with the conditions for being given this unity (i.e., perspectival perception) or the fundamental difference at the heart of Being comes into contradiction with the identity that emerges when this Being returns to itself as vision (i.e., perception again). In each case, however, it is with respect to Being that paradox emerges as a trait or characteristic of this Being, and thus these paradoxes ultimately find their source in Being – they are *rooted* in Being. This is the sense in which we take Merleau-Ponty to understand paradox as something which is itself conditioned: conditioned by Being. And it is also at this point where we find Deleuze disagreeing most markedly. In fact, one could say that Deleuze, although concerned with both the paradox of infinite series and the paradox of identity and difference, reverses Merleau-Ponty's understanding of paradox. This reversal emphasizes the proliferation of differences, not the synthesis of differences; and it emphasizes a fundamental difference, not a fundamental identity. Thus, rather than formulate the paradox of infinite series as 'the synthesis of an infinite number of parts and aspects through a single part or aspect,' Deleuze would say that, 'within a single part or aspect, there is an infinite proliferation of parts and aspects'; and rather than say that there is a 'fundamental difference that is simultaneously a fundamental identity,' Deleuze would say that there is a 'fundamental identity that is simultaneously a fundamental difference.' In doing this, Deleuze discusses these paradoxes, not with respect to Being, but with respect to time.

With reference to a discussion of time, a Deleuzean formulation of the paradox of infinite series would run as follows: within a present moment there is an infinite division of this moment into past and future. In other words, each present moment is simultaneously displaced by what Deleuze calls a 'paradoxical instance,' an 'instance which is endlessly displaced and absent from its own place,'[10] and is 'at once past and future.'[11] It is this paradoxical instance which generates within any present moment an infinite series of pasts and futures: 'a future and past divide the present at every instant [i.e., paradoxical instance] and subdivide it ad infinitum into past and future, in both directions at once.'[12]

Deleuze uses the Stoic term *Aion* to refer to this infinite series at the heart of every present, and it is opposed to an understanding of time whereby the present moment is the whole or unity which delimits a past and future. In other words, it is to be contrasted with a time that is measured relative to a present moment, or what Deleuze refers to as *Chronos*, or chronological time. Merleau-Ponty can be seen to adopt this latter view of time in that the flesh, the flesh of my body and the flesh of the world, 'is not only one perceived among others, it is the measurant of all';[13] and, when developing this theme with respect to time, he later adds that 'it is a question of finding in the present, the flesh of the world (and not in the past), an "ever new" and always the same.'[14] Deleuze, on the contrary, understands the present in terms of a 'paradoxical instance' which places the present into disequilibrium with itself, which is at once past and future – never the same – and is what Deleuze calls *Aion*.

This theory of *Aion* leads to the formulation of the paradox of identity and difference: every moment, as an identifiable unity or whole, and as the measure of chronological time, is simultaneously an enduring interval, an interval which is the difference between a past and a future – a non-chronological intermezzo, or *Aion*. To put it in the terms discussed above, every fundamental identity (i.e., moment of chronological time) is simultaneously a fundamental difference (i.e., a paradoxical instance or *Aion*). Consequently, each present moment harbours, as a result of the paradoxical instance, two sides of an interval (i.e., the infinite series of pasts and futures) that are in disequilibrium with each other.[15] Within a chronological series of moments, therefore, the 'paradox is to introduce an interval in the moment itself';[16] or, as we have formulated the paradox, the unity of the moment is simultaneously a disjunction (i.e., the difference that is the interval).

Since Deleuze states these paradoxes in terms of fundamental features about time, it is not surprising to find that he and Merleau-Ponty each have dramatically different formulations of the paradoxes of 'infinite series' and 'identity and difference.' Whereas Merleau-Ponty's paradoxes are rooted in a relationship to Being, for Deleuze they are described as relationships of time; however, it would be wrong to say that Deleuze's paradoxes are rooted in time in the same way that Merleau-Ponty's are rooted in Being. On the contrary, the roots of Deleuze's paradoxes are perpetually displaced from themselves, and thus refuse to be 'totalized' into a single root: Being. This totalizable rooting Deleuze describes as the 'arborescent model,' that is, a system of roots and relations all connected to a single trunk (read: Being). Deleuze proposes, to the contrary, a 'rhizomatic model': a system of roots and relations that are not totalized, or totalizable. Thus, rather than a single tree which grows towards the sky with deep roots in the earth, we have here the image of ivy spreading in all directions over a 'smooth surface.'

For this reason, we find Deleuze's writings replete with terms and metaphors that refer to surfaces: 'smooth surfaces,' 'planes of consistency,' 'plateaus,' and so on.

To clarify these points further, and to continue the contrast of Deleuze's thought with Merleau-Ponty's, we shall continue to discuss Deleuze's notion of paradox and focus upon his reversal: that is, his emphasis on a non-totalizable proliferation of difference rather than the synthesis of differences (infinite series) that Merleau-Ponty proposes. To do this, we will turn to Deleuze's and Merleau-Ponty's writings on cinema, for it is within these writings that the differences we are trying to bring out become most evident. In particular, Deleuze explicitly refers to Merleau-Ponty's theory of perception in order to clarify what we have called his 'reversal.' It is also within these writings that Deleuze sets forth the arguments for the claim that it is a non-totalizable and paradoxical instance which is the fundamental transcendental condition of all thought and perception. Cinema itself will be seen to be conditioned by this paradoxical instance, and thus Deleuze will claim that the essence of cinema is precisely 'the "impower of thought" ... the inexistence of a whole which could be thought.'[17] Cinema will therefore be the example we shall use in our ongoing attempt to carry Merleau-Ponty's transcendental critique to the point of deducing paradox itself as the fundamental transcendental condition, the condition for all thought, perception, and language.

2. Cinema

The Mind–Body Problem

One reason for Deleuze's interest in cinema is that it sheds light on the Cartesian mind–body problem. If the mind, following Descartes, is 'a thinking and unextended thing,' the problem, then, is in explaining the relationship between the mind and an extended, unthinking body. How can the *movements* of these extended bodies produce *images*, such as in perception, and how can a non-extended mental *image* produce *movements*, such as in voluntary action? In other words, we are confronted again with the problem of difference: that is, how can mind and body be irreducibly different yet nevertheless related to each other? In order to resolve this problem, one can try to overcome the duality of mind and body, movement and image, by showing that there is a fundamental mind–body relationship, a relationship which is made possible by an essential conjunction and link of mind and body (e.g., Descartes's pineal gland), movement and image, consciousness and thing, a conjunction that allows for the possibility of perception and voluntary action. In cinema, Deleuze claims there is just this sort of conjunction; for example, there is the movement of the reel, the rapid succession of individual frames (twenty-four per second), and there is the cinematographic image, the image of a continuous and fluid movement on the screen. However, in cinema there is not first a movement which then gives rise to an image, nor is there an image independent of any movement, an image whereby movement is something abstract that gets added to the image. In cinema the movement and the image are simultaneous, and cinema 'immediately gives us a movement-image.'[18] Cinema thus entails a fundamental conjunction of movement and image, a movement-image, and this is precisely what sparks Deleuze's philosophical interest in cinema, for he believes that the movement-image places cinema solidly within the philosophical debate surrounding the mind–body problem; or, it can be seen as a response to the problem of difference. To demonstrate this, we will contrast Merleau-Ponty's and Bergson's treatment of the mind–body problem, and then discuss the consequences these theories have with respect to cinema. This will also help our overall goal of contrasting Deleuze's and Merleau-Ponty's thought, because Deleuze actually sides with Bergson and will use many of Bergson's concepts to discuss cinema.

The mind–body problem is, for Merleau-Ponty, only a problem if we fail to see that, from the start, consciousness is already in things, that consciousness or mind grasps itself only by losing itself in the world. This is also true, for example, of the relationship between mind and language: 'the mind that governs language is not mind for itself; it is paradoxically a mind that possesses itself only by losing itself in language.'[19] In other words, the problem of consciousness, world, language, and the relationship between them arises only when we forget that everything is already there, that consciousness is always and only in the world. The problem for Merleau-Ponty, therefore, is to restore this fact of a world and body that are always already there, always already constituted: 'The problem of the world, and, to begin with, that of one's own body, consists in the fact that it is all there.'[20] It is wrong therefore to claim that the world, and one's body, are constituted by an absolute consciousness; rather, we are to understand the human situation as one where constituting and constituted are ambiguously interrelated and involved, wrapped up within the very existence of the body. That is, the body is neither simply a constituted, extended, and unthinking thing, nor is the mind simply an unextended, constituting, and thinking thing; on the contrary, as bodily subjectivity we are forever between concrete being and psyche in a 'movement to and fro of existence which at one time allows itself to take corporeal form and at others moves towards personal acts.'[21] We are thus neither pure for-itself (*res cogitans*) nor pure in-itself (*res extensa*), but are always between the two in an ambiguous to and fro Merleau-Ponty calls 'existence.'[22] It is only the failure to account for this ambiguous existence, that to-and-fro conjunction of mind and body, which leads one to pose as problematic the relationship between mind and body. Furthermore, since this bodily existence is understood to be 'our anchorage in a world,'[23] and if the world is also 'the horizon of all our experiences,'[24] then we find that for Merleau-Ponty, our ambiguous existence is the condition not only for the formulation of the mind–body problem, but of all possible experience, including the experience of cinema. Cinema is therefore to be understood as something which is made possible by a body that is one's anchorage to the world: this, as we will now see, is precisely the manner in which Merleau-Ponty interprets cinema.

In *The Phenomenology of Perception*, when discussing perception as an act which is anchored within an infinite horizon of possible acts, a horizon or world that is always 'already there,' Merleau-Ponty criticizes the cinematographic image as an impoverished perception. And it is impoverished precisely because it is not anchored to the world as the body is, and thus the horizon of the camera is not that of the body. In fact, Merleau-Ponty claims that 'the screen has no horizons.'[25] The cinematographic image frames only a fraction of the horizon that is given in natural perception, and, as the shots cut from scene to scene, person to person, the horizon ends at the borders of each new frame. The infinitely open horizon of natural perception is thus glimpsed at only through the finite window of the camera's shutter; and it is just this finitude, this bordering of natural perception, which leads Merleau-Ponty to say that the film has no horizon, or that it is an impoverished perception.

Although each frame of a film is not, in itself, a horizonal world with an infinite number of possibilities, the frames are related among themselves, according to Merleau-Ponty, much in the way that the notes of a melody are related to one another. In other words, Merleau-Ponty understands the film as a gestalt, as a structural interdependency of all the parts (i.e., frames).[26] For example, even though each frame or shot can be used in a variety of different ways, as the Russian film-makers have shown in developing the use of montage, the effect of each frame depends upon its structural role in the film as a whole (i.e., its gestalt).[27] That is, there is no horizonal presence within a film, the ambiguous presence of a horizon of possible objects of perception; rather, the film is to be understood as itself an object within the horizon of natural perception, and thus it has only a secondary and derivative horizon. We might, for example, while watching a film, want to see something that is off-camera – a woman who is heard screaming – but the suspense or expectancy that might arise here is due precisely to the felt contrast between the horizonal nature of natural perception and the lack of horizons characteristic of the frame or shot.

This contrast was used effectively by D.W. Griffith in his use of cross-cutting. For example, the camera frames a woman in distress, screaming and under attack, and then the film cuts to the hero on his horse coming to rescue her; the film then cuts back to the woman, this time in increasing danger, and then back to the hero on his horse, now much closer; and the cross-cutting quickens in order to build the suspenseful anticipation of the final rescue scene. What we have then is a skilful structuring of shots which are intended to instil this feeling of suspense and expectancy in the viewer; however, it is as an object within the horizon of natural perception, that is, as a skilfully structured and directed film, which prompts this sense of expectancy, anticipation, possibility, and even ambiguity (e.g., will he rescue her in time?). The film itself, nevertheless, is not this horizon, but just an object that appears on the horizon of natural perception, and it is only in appealing to this natural horizon that the film is able to achieve its desired effects (e.g., suspense, illusion, laughter[28]). We must therefore get clearer on the relationship between the film and the natural horizon of perception.

In *The Phenomenology of Perception*, and immediately following the claim that the screen has no horizons, Merleau-Ponty speaks of the horizon of natural perception: 'I direct my gaze upon a sector of the landscape, which comes to life and is disclosed, while the other objects recede into the periphery and become dormant while, however, not ceasing to be there.'[29] In other words, as a body anchored in the world, the horizon of this world is always there, and thus, even if I turn my back or attention from something, it is always still there, and I have just to redirect my gaze to bring it back. In a film, however, what we see is dependent upon what is given in the frame or shot itself, and the suspense, ambiguities, and horizons are opened up only when this shot is seen in relation to the other shots and frames of the film. In other words, whereas the horizon of possibilities is *intrinsic* to natural perception, to a bodily perception anchored to the world, this horizon of possibilities is *extrinsic* to the frame. The horizon is dependent upon the frame's relationship to other frames (e.g., Griffith's cross-cutting) – that is, the external relations of these frames. And it is only when a film is literally put together well that one feels a world opening before one, a world where something new is being said and shown; however, this 'putting together' is a possibility only of the world that is always already there, the world that is the ground and horizon of all our wonders, all our thoughts; the world that is the silence which precedes all speech. It is this world which is the model the film tries to copy, the original wonder the film tries to restore, the silence the film tries to speak. Therein lies film's power, but also its secondary and derivative status.

There is a positive side, however, to this limited and derivative nature of cinema. Since the horizon of natural perception is reduced to the framings of the cinematographic image, this horizonless perception has the consequence of being less ambiguous, less unclear. If the horizon of possibilities is greatly reduced, so, too, is the openness and ambiguity which characterizes natural perception. As Merleau-Ponty argues in an essay on film, 'the perceived form is never perfect in real life ... it always has blurs, smudges, and superfluous matter ... Cinematographic drama is ... [however] ... finer-grained than real-life dramas: it takes place in a world that is more exact than the real world.'[30] Furthermore, this 'more exact' world of cinema is also an excellent vehicle for demonstrating the relationship of a human subject with the world; or, to put it another way, cinema presents a 'more exact' picture of the relation between mind and body, self and world, and thus is helpful in confronting the mind–body problem. Merleau-Ponty is explicit on this point:

> Phenomenological or existential philosophy is largely an expression of surprise at this inherence of the self in the world and in others, a description of this paradox and permeation, and an attempt to make us *see* the bond between subject and world, between subject and others, rather than to *explain* it as the classical philosophies did by resorting to absolute spirit. Well cinema is particularly suited to make manifest the union of mind and body, mind and world, and the expression of one in the other.[31]

Cinema's more exact nature thus leads to a less ambiguous and more precise way of revealing the relationships of human subjects and the world; that is, cinema is an excellent manner of description, in the manner of phenomenological description. Phenomenology and cinema are thus both attempting to describe the paradoxical union of a subject and the world, mind and body, self and other; and, to the extent that Merleau-Ponty finds cinema doing this, he recognizes and respects the pertinence of cinema to philosophical issues (e.g., mind–body). Merleau-Ponty's interest in cinema is thus motivated by reasons very similar to those which sparked Deleuze's interest, that is, the usefulness of cinema in approaching the philosophical issue of mind–body. However, their understanding of the nature of cinema itself, and the conclusions they draw therefrom, could not be more different.

Deleuze's Transcendental Critique

When Deleuze turns to a critique of Merleau-Ponty's position on cinema, he claims that Merleau-Ponty was not mistaken to say that the screen has no horizon, that it gives only a partial glimpse of the world. Rather, he erred in not recognizing that this is also true of the body itself as it perceives the world. Deleuze quotes Bergson in claiming that, as a perceiving body, 'we take snapshots, as it were, of passing reality ... Perception, intellection, language so proceed in general.'[32] In other words, Deleuze, as he interprets Bergson, claims that the perceiving body is to be understood in the manner of a camera, and that Merleau-Ponty's criticisms of cinema are thus equally as valid to a theory of the perceiving body. Furthermore, whereas Merleau-Ponty claims cinema to be an impoverished perception because the frame lacks horizons as a result of an unanchored camera – that is, the cuts, shots, and framings could be put together in a way that runs counter to the anchored perception of the body – Deleuze claims, on the other hand, that it is precisely this lack of horizons within the frame, and the unanchored nature of the camera, that best characterize Bergson's theory of perception.

A clear contrast emerges here. On the one hand, Merleau-Ponty claims it is the body as anchored to the world that is the condition for the film, and the standard by which the success of a film is measured. In other words, *natural perception is the condition for the framings of the camera*. On the other hand, Bergson claims that the framing of the camera, or what he calls the 'photograph,' 'is already taken, already developed in the very heart of things and at all the points of space.'[33] This claim reflects Bergson's more general claim that there is only a difference of degree 'between *being* and *being consciously* perceived.'[34] For Bergson consciously perceiving something, or natural perception in Merleau-Ponty's sense, is only a special case of a perception that is already present within things, and what characterizes this latter perception is that it is simply a relationship between images,[35] for example, the relationship between the body and the world. However, Bergson believes the relationship between body and world, or consciously perceiving, differs only in degree from the relationships that exist in the world generally, a world that he describes to be the relationship of each image acting 'through every one of its points upon all the points of all other images.'[36] Bergson thus understands being perceived to be simply a relationship between images, or, to put it in scientific terms, every thing (every image) is related to everything else (every other image) equally on the basis of external relations of cause and effect (i.e., Natural Law). It is thus as a special case of this type of perception that Bergson understands natural perception. In particular, he understands natural perception 'to be a kind of photographic view of things, taken from a fixed point by that special apparatus which is called an organ of perception.'[37] Natural perception, in Merleau-Ponty's sense, is thus a subtraction from the perception that is already taken at the very heart of things, and it occurs when perception gets anchored to a 'fixed point' (i.e., the 'organ of perception') which is merely the 'black screen on which the image could be shown.'[38] The relationships between images are now no longer equal, but are placed in relation to a privileged image – that is, the body. The body, however, is simply that which stops or anchors a perception which is always already there; consequently, we can see that, for Bergson, *it is the frame, the already taken photograph, that is the condition for natural perception.*

This contrast reflects, for Deleuze, a tendency on the part of phenomenology, a tendency Bergson opposes, to adhere to the traditional philosophical position regarding the the subject (i.e., mind or spirit). Deleuze claims that phenomenology is continuing

in the philosophical tradition which placed light on the side of spirit and made consciousness a beam of light which drew things out of their native darkness ... but, instead of making light an internal light, it simply opened it on to the exterior, rather as if the intentionality of consciousness was the ray of an electric lamp ('all consciousness is consciousness *of* something'). For Bergson, it is completely the opposite. Things are luminous by themselves without anything illuminating them: all consciousness is something, it is indistinguishable from the thing, that is from the image of light ... As for our consciousness of fact, it will merely be the opacity without which light 'is always propagated without its source ever having been revealed.'[39]

For Merleau-Ponty the light is centred on or anchored to a subject in the world, and it is this subject that shines its light on a world that is always already there ('wonder at the world'). It is this anchored light which is the condition for the framings of the camera – that is, an unanchored perception. For Bergson, and for Deleuze as he develops Bergson's thesis, the light itself is what is always already there, and the anchored perception is merely an opacity ('the black screen') which stops this light. It is therefore an unanchored light, an unanchored perception, which is understood by Deleuze, following Bergson, to be the condition for natural perception, for perception that is anchored to a 'fixed point.'

To more adequately understand this opposition, and to show Deleuze's motivation for taking a Bergsonian stand against phenomenology, we need to recognize that it is not simply a matter of disagreeing with the philosophical tradition concerning the subject; rather, this opposition reflects his more general opposition to, and reversal of, what he takes to be traditional transcendental philosophy and metaphysics. This tradition, Deleuze claims, presents us with a false dilemma, an unnecessary either/or: 'What is common to metaphysics and transcendental philosophy is, above all, this alternative which they both impose on us: *either* an undifferentiated ground, a groundlessness, formless nonbeing, or an abyss without differences and without properties; *or* a supremely individuated Being and an intensely personalized Form.'[40]

On the one hand, traditional metaphysics claims that the descriptive properties, categories, and predicates of a *thing* are derived from the individuality of infinite Being. Therefore, either they (e.g., man, horse, pug-nosed) are only limited realities in that their reality is conditioned by this pure and infinite Being, or, if they are not so conditioned, then they express nothing real, and are consequently relegated to 'non-being or to the bottomless abyss.'[41] To the extent that Merleau-Ponty claims the world is the infinite horizon of human experience (i.e., 'the real is infinite and inexhaustible'), and the horizon of horizons (i.e., the fundamental condition for experience), it is clear that he, too, is doing what Deleuze claims to be traditional metaphysics. And thus, Merleau-Ponty would also agree with Heidegger's claim that there is the world, and outside that, nothing – the metaphysician's either/or.

On the other hand, traditional transcendental philosophy claims that all differences, properties, predicates, and categories are derived from the form of the individual finite subject. In other words, these differences are conditioned by that which a subject can know: that is, the limits of knowledge. Anything that is not so conditioned transgresses the limits of knowledge and is thus relegated to non-being, or to the abyss; and it is the determination of these finite limits which characterizes Kant's transcendental critique. Merleau-Ponty, in so far as his transcendental critique reveals the pre-existence of the world as the always-given condition of human perception, knowledge, and experience, is also continuing in the transcendental tradition, even if he ultimately leaves it behind for a metaphysics of the world that is 'always there.' Nevertheless, Merleau-Ponty would continue to claim that either what we know is conditioned by our existence in the world, or it is in the abyss of the unknowable – the transcendental either/or.

In both cases, Deleuze claims that these properties, and so on, or what he calls 'singularities,' become imprisoned singularities. That is, either all singularities are centred upon a privileged singularity – that is, either the pure individuated Being (e.g., God), or the pure finite form of the human subject – or they are nothing at all; they are mere phantoms. These privileged properties, or the fundamental conditions from which the other properties are derived, remain forever the same. Each privileged property is therefore a fundamental identity which is the condition that preconceives all possible differences, and either difference is conditioned by this fundamental identity (e.g., the immutability of God, the pure forms of human knowledge), or there are no differences at all, just a pure undifferentiated abyss. It is precisely this last either/or which Deleuze's reversal of traditional transcendental philosophy and metaphysics is meant to supplant.

In order to avoid the either/or we have been discussing, Deleuze will not claim either that there are no differences, only an undifferentiated abyss, or that all differences are related either to the forms of human knowledge or to the identity of Being. Deleuze, on the contrary, wants to account for difference in itself, a difference that is not defined in terms of identity. In doing this, he believes he is simply carrying forward Kant's critique (and Nietzsche's project) of delimiting the transcendental conditions of thought, or the unconscious motivations of thought. To this extent, therefore, Deleuze's reversal is not done *ex nihilo*, and Deleuze would argue that his project is simply a thinking through of the tradition in order to reveal its proper conditions and motivations. For this reason Foucault has said that Deleuze's method is 'rigorously Freudian';[42] that is, he analyses the marginal discourses of philosophy, the comments or statements made in passing, the discourses that have slipped (i.e., Freudian 'slips') through the mesh of tradition, and he does this in order to show that these discourses reveal the repressions, omissions, and unconscious motivations at work in philosophy. And it is precisely a fundamental difference, or paradox, which Deleuze claims is the 'passion and pathos of philosophy,' or the unconscious motivation Deleuze's analysis attempts to bring out. For example, in his essay 'Plato and the Simulacrum,' Deleuze argues that Plato's discussion of the simulacrum reveals the fundamental difference which is the motivation for the Platonic distinction between essence and appearance, model and copy. In short, in this essay he argues that paradox and difference is the condition and motivation of thought, a condition that philosophy repeatedly domesticates by claiming some identity is the condition for difference. To reverse the tradition, therefore, Deleuze begins with a reversal of Platonism.

This reversal, however, is not a simple inversion of the relationship between essence and appearance; rather, it is the extraction of the condition which motivates this relationship. Deleuze argues that this motivating condition is the fundamental difference, falsity, and dissimilarity of the simulacrum. To show this, Deleuze focuses upon the *Sophist* and Plato's distinction between εικον (*eikon*) – a likeness or good copy – and φαντασμα (phantasma or simulacrum) – a mere semblance or bad copy. This distinction characterizes the attempt to track down the sophist, to show that the sophist's knowledge is a mere semblance, or simulacrum, of knowledge, whereas Socrates would be seen to bear a likeness of knowledge. The sophist's knowledge is therefore unfounded and false, and Socrates' knowledge is well founded – it has a grain of truth. That is, a good copy (εικον) is good because it adequately resembles a model. The good copy or knowledge can trace its lineage to a model or Idea. The bad copy (φαντασμα), on the other hand, is fundamentally dissimilar to the model, and harbours an intrinsic difference and falsity; as a result, a knowledge that is a mere semblance, a simulacrum, could claim that something is both hot and cold (Philebus 24a–d), old and young (Parmenides 154–5), so to avoid such consequences, Plato disenfranchises the bad copy and argues for the primacy of the good copy, for the primacy of the relationship of resemblance between the model and the copy.

The reversal of Platonism will not be, therefore, the inversion of the supremacy of essence over appearance, but the reversal of the primacy of the model–copy relationship over the simulacrum. What is reversed is the claim that the simulacrum is conditioned by the model–copy relationship. It is this relationship, Deleuze argues, which is conditioned by the simulacrum (i.e., paradoxa as differentiating condition). The seeds of this reversal, furthermore, were sown by Plato himself. For example, at the end of the *Sophist*, after attempting to track down and separate the sophist (simulacrum) from the philosopher (*eikon*), the stranger claims that the sophist is 'one who in private and with brief speeches compels his interlocutor to contradict himself' (268b). In other words, the sophist does precisely what Socrates himself does, and for this reason Seth Benardete, in his commentary on the *Sophist*, claims that 'Socrates and the sophist are indistinguishable in appearance.'[43] That is, the good copy (*eikon*) is indistinguishable in appearance from the bad copy, from the simulacrum, and thus the supremacy of the *eikon* is put into doubt by the simulacrum: that is, the superiority of the philosopher over the sophist becomes questionable (is subverted) when they are seen to be indistinguishable from each other. The irreducible difference between the philosopher and the sophist, the *eikon* and the simulacrum, thus entails a fundamental relationship wherein the two sides are indistinguishable. In short, we are confronted with the problem of difference, and it is precisely this problem which motivates the Platonic move to mimesis, to the superiority of *eikon* on the basis of its resemblance to an Idea or model. That is, to remove the doubts about the superiority of the philosopher, doubts which arose because 'Socrates and the sophist are indistinguishable in *appearance*,' Plato claims that the philosopher's appearance bears a resemblance to an Idea or form, to a fundamental *reality*, whereas the sophist harbours a fundamental dissimilarity and falsity, a fundamental non-reality (i.e., simulacrum). But it was precisely this fundamental difference (simulacrum) which motivated the move to its disenfranchisement (e.g., the banishment of the poets in the *Republic*) when it subverted the superiority and irreducible difference (i.e., sophist as irreducibly different from the philosopher) of the *eikon*. To put it another way, Plato's writings can be seen to develop as a response to the problem of difference. It is therefore within Plato's writings themselves that one sees the possibility of its reversal, for the positing of a fundamental difference which is the condition and motivation of the model–copy relationship. As Deleuze argues, again in reference to the *Sophist*, 'Plato discovers, in the flash of an instant, that the simulacrum is not simply a false copy, but that it places in question the very notions of copy and model ... Was it not Plato himself who pointed out the direction for the reversal of Platonism.'[44]

In Deleuze's writings on cinema, there is also revealed to be a fundamental difference or paradox that is its motivating condition. Before we turn to this, however, it is important here to refer again to Merleau-

Ponty, for he is also critical of traditional transcendental philosophy, and this critique in turn argues for a fundamental paradox. Furthermore, just as Deleuze claims a truly radical transcendental philosophy should reveal a fundamental paradox that is the 'pathos and passion of philosophy,' that is 'not contradictory ... [but] ... rather allows us to be present at the genesis of contradiction,'[45] so, too, does Merleau-Ponty claim that a truly radical transcendental philosophy (a.k.a. a radical phenomenological reduction) should reveal that the 'world is strange and paradoxical.' Let us further examine Merleau-Ponty's understanding of paradox.

Merleau-Ponty Revisited

The fundamental difference between phenomenology and traditional transcendental philosophy, as Merleau-Ponty sees it, is that phenomenology is 'a study of the *advent* of being to consciousness, instead of presuming its possibility as given in advance. It is striking how transcendental philosophies of the classical type never question the possibility of effecting the complete disclosure which they always assume done somewhere.'[46]

It is precisely this effecting of a complete disclosure which, as we have seen, Merleau-Ponty describes as paradoxical. For example, a perceived object is completely disclosed from a single perspective (paradox of infinite series), and a subject finds himself only by losing himself in a world, by being a subject already and always in the world (paradox of identity and difference). Merleau-Ponty therefore claims that a truly radical transcendental philosophy needs to take its own presumptions as the problem, its presumption of a pre-given or preconceived being or subject.[47] It is thus the very disclosure of a being or a subject that is the problem for Merleau-Ponty, and the manner of this disclosure is, as we have seen, fundamentally paradoxical. A properly aligned transcendental philosophy will therefore confront paradox, or reveal that the disclosure of being is at heart paradoxical, and it was the avoidance of the paradoxical nature of this disclosure which led transcendental philosophies to presuppose that which was to be disclosed. Merleau-Ponty, on the other hand, rather than presupposing this condition, and rather than assuming that the conditioned disclosure of being is already done somewhere, recognizes that it is the paradoxical nature of this disclosure which is precisely the problem, or, we could say, that paradox is 'the passion and pathos of philosophy.'

Merleau-Ponty's understanding of paradox, however, is, as men-

tioned earlier, tied to a relationship between *beings*: that is, the disclosure of *being* through the *being* of the perceiving subject. The ground and
condition for the disclosure of being is itself an example of this being,
and this is why we claimed earlier that Merleau-Ponty's notion of paradox is rooted in being: that is, the paradox expresses a relationship of
being (perceiver–perceived). In the end, therefore, that which is to be
explained – a disclosed and perceived *being* – is itself the model used to
explain the ground and condition of this disclosure, that is, a perceiving
being. This presupposition is not a fault of a truly radical transcendental
philosophy, however, nor a fault of phenomenology and the phenomenological reduction; rather, it is the fundamental paradox proper to
them both: that is, we know the conditions only in the conditioned.[48]
And it is this paradox which is philosophy's fundamental problem: 'The
problem of the world, and, to begin with, that of one's own body, consists in the fact that it is all there.'[49] In other words, the transcendental
condition is the world and body which are already there, already given.
The world and one's body are the very model of givenness itself, and
transcendental philosophies can only restore, or copy, this primordial
model, this 'wonder at the world.' This is also true of cinema, as we saw,
where it is the paradoxical inherence of a subject in a world which is
proper movie material, and it is this relationship which cinema, if successful, is able to copy and describe.

We can begin to see more clearly Merleau-Ponty's reason for arguing
that paradox is rooted in being, in the relationship between a perceived
being and the bodily, perspectival perceiving of this being. In short, the
paradox expresses the manner in which the perceiving being and the
perceived being are related, and the transcendental condition, as we
saw, is simply the paradoxical inherence of a perceiving subject in a
body that is anchored to a world that is its already given infinite horizon. It is this move which led us to claim earlier that Merleau-Ponty
goes beyond transcendental philosophy to metaphysics (and, in his last
writings, this becomes an explicit move to ontology). It is thus the
already-given unity of a world, the world as the horizon for the totality
of all our actions, thoughts, perceptions, that is the ground for the occurrence of the paradox, for the paradoxical inherence of a subject in this
world. Thus either the paradox is conditioned by being, by the horizon
of the world, or it is nothing: the metaphysician's either/or. And
Merleau-Ponty's paradox is a metaphysical paradox (or a 'paradox of
Being,' as he says in *The Visible and the Invisible*), a paradox conditioned
by the givenness and unity of the world: it is rooted in being.

It is this understanding of paradox, or Merleau-Ponty's traditional metaphysics, which Deleuze reverses: therefore, it is the givenness and unity of the world which is conditioned by paradox, not vice versa. That is, the perceiver–perceived relation is not a paradox conditioned by the givenness of the world; rather, the perceiver–perceived relation is itself conditioned by paradox, or by paradoxa as the non-identifiable differentiating condition (e.g., paradoxical instance or *Aion*) which makes the distinction between perceiver and perceived possible. It is thus not the primordial unity and givenness of the world which allows for the possibility of perception; it is the primordial dis-unity and difference of paradox which allows for the possibility of perception. As a result, for Deleuze cinema is not, as it was for Merleau-Ponty, secondary to the conditions of natural perception; to the contrary, and following Bergson, natural perception is what is secondary to the conditions exemplified by cinema. That is, cinema is not to be faulted if its images are not anchored to a perceiving body (i.e., a central privileged image) – it is cinema's advantage. Thus, although the camera may catch (i.e., photograph and frame) only glimpses of the world, brief exposures to the movements and changes of this world, and since these movements and changes are not related to the fixed point of the body, then the camera is not constrained or tied to the world as the body is, and is therefore better able to frame these movements and changes, better able to follow their course (e.g., through cutting and montage). The cinematographic image therefore charts the territory between natural, subjective perception and the purely objective perception that Bergson discusses, or it gives an accounting of the relationship between idealism and realism (i.e., a response to the problem of difference). That is, the cinematographic image or frame can be neither purely subjective, in that the frame is not directly anchored to a perceiving body (i.e., Merleau-Ponty's criticism), nor purely objective, because the frame is nevertheless only a passing glimpse of the world. The frame is to be understood, rather, as the differentiating condition for subjective (Merleau-Ponty) and objective perception (Bergson). The frame is thus the boundary which differentiates a subjective perception and an objective perception, but is not to be identified with either side. Consequently, just as the noema was understood to be the boundary or differentiating condition between subjective meaning (concept theory) and objective meaning (percept theory), so, too, is the frame to be understood as the differentiating condition for perception – the boundary between perceiver and perceived. As Deleuze argues, 'if cinema goes beyond perception, it is in the sense that it reaches the genetic element of all possible perception, that is, the point which changes, and which makes perception change, the differential of perception itself.'[50] In other words, the frame is precisely the fundamental difference which is the condition and motivation of cinema; the fundamental difference which entails, for Deleuze, the reversal of traditional transcendental philosophy and metaphysics. The frame is paradoxa.

We are now able, by continuing to take cinema as an example, to understand the reason for Deleuze's reversal of Merleau-Ponty's formulation of paradox (i.e., the paradox of 'infinite series' and 'identity and difference').

Peirce's Categories

The model–copy relationship is crucial to Merleau-Ponty's understanding of paradox. In fact, it is the paradoxical nature of the model–copy relationship itself (i.e., condition–conditioned) that is the proper task of philosophy to reveal. And what Merleau-Ponty's phenomenological reduction reveals is that the ground and condition for the disclosure of being, for the perception of beings, is itself an example of this being – that is, the perceiving body – and it is fundamentally similar to the being which is disclosed. In other words, the condition resembles that which is conditioned, and hence we can see Merleau-Ponty's kinship to Plato. Deleuze, on the other hand, would claim that Merleau-Ponty has used the conditioned – that is, the identifications of everyday perception – as the model to explain the conditions – in other words, the identity of the body (*The Phenomenology of Perception*) or Being (*The Visible and the Invisible*); and although Merleau-Ponty recognizes the paradoxical nature of this relationship, this paradox is, in the end, conditioned by a fundamental identity. In short, analogous to Merleau-Ponty's transcendental critique of his predecessors, or even of his own earlier position, Deleuze would claim that Merleau-Ponty has presupposed what he takes to be conditioned – namely, paradox – and has used it to explain the fundamental conditions – that is, the paradox of Being. Difference and paradox are thus understood on the basis of identity, and this Deleuze claims is a fundamental feature of traditional metaphysics and transcendental philosophy. Consequently, when Deleuze turns to discuss perception, he argues that the transcendental condition of perception is not to be understood in terms of the model–copy relationship; rather, the transcendental condition is paradox and implies a fundamental difference and dissimilarity which subverts the model–copy relation of resemblance. As Ronald Bogue is correct to point out, 'Deleuze accepts the necessity of a transcendental foundation of the relation of consciousness to its objects, but he refuses to model the ground on that which it founds.'[51] In other words, Deleuze's reversal of Merleau-Ponty follows his reversal of the transcendental tradition in philosophy (e.g., Plato): that is, rather than the condition and conditioned being related on the basis of that which is the same, or similar – for example, the immutability of God, the pure forms of human knowledge, or the world as the horizon of horizons – Deleuze relates them on the basis of paradox, or on what Deleuze calls 'a paradoxical instance which is endlessly displaced and absent from its own place.' Therefore, although Merleau-Ponty is critical of the transcendental tradition in philosophy, and although he even argues for a fundamental paradox, he nevertheless is committed to the model–copy relationship of similarity (i.e., the similarity of the perceiving being as condition to the perceived being as conditioned). And even though Merleau-Ponty does ultimately argue that this relationship of similarity is itself grounded in the infinite horizon of the world, there is nevertheless a relationship of similarity between the condition which remains the same (i.e., the world) and the conditioned which is derived therefrom (i.e., the paradoxical perceiver–perceived relation, or what we have called Merleau-Ponty's 'metaphysical paradox'). Consequently, Deleuze maintains that Merleau-Ponty's philosophy continues to operate with the assumptions of traditional metaphysics and transcendental philosophy, and, by reversing this tradition, Deleuze gives up these assumptions.

Deleuze's writings on cinema develop the consequences of this reversal, and this can be seen as he sets forth a theory of perception: that is, the frame is not conditioned by some model relationship (natural perception), nor is it the model that remains the same for all the conditioned elements that are derived from it. The frame is, rather, a point absent from its own place, a point that changes; or, as the analysis in his cinema books develops it, a fundamental difference or interval – the interval of movement. And it is this interval, this fundamental difference, which Deleuze argues is the condition for perception.

Within the context of cinema, the interval of movement that is the condition for cinema seems clear: it is the interval between frames, or the interval between the frames on a moving reel of film, that is the condition for the cinematographic movement-image – that is, for the projection of continuous movement on the screen. The cinematographic movement-image is thus made possible by the difference between two frames.[52] And if we consider the fact that each frame is in itself a photographic image, or an already-taken picture, then we can further elaborate Bergson's theory of perception. That is, just as the cinematographic image is made possible by the difference between two images (i.e., frames), so, too, is natural perception made possible by the difference between the body (i.e., the 'organ of perception') and the world. Put another way, there is a beginning and ending point of perception, as Husserl himself argued.[53] For Bergson, however, the beginning point is the action of the real as 'the aggregate of images' which acts 'through every one of its parts on all the points of all other images.'[54] In short, the beginning point of perception is simply the cause–effect interactions of the universe as understood by natural science, but which is discussed here in terms of images.[55] Bergson also refers to this as 'objective perception,' or as the perception and picture that are already present at the very heart of things – that is, as a result of the relation *between different* images. The ending point of perception is the reaction of a body to the action of the real. In other words, it is the 'aggregate of images ... [as] ... referred to the eventual action of one particular image, my body.'[56] Perception is thus understood here as the relation of the real to the possible reactions of the subject, and between the action of the real and the reaction of the subject there is, as Bergson puts it, a 'zone of indetermination.' The reaction to the real is not determined in advance, is not related to the real in the same way that the images of the real are related to each other. And with a greater 'zone of indetermination,' the number of possible reactions to the real will likewise increase, or there will be a higher capability with respect to what Bergson calls 'sensori-motor processes.'[57] In other words, the more the subject is able to react to the real, the more this subject is able to perceive. In the end, therefore, perception begins with what is real, with the action of images upon each other, and only later does it become, for Bergson, subjective perception – that is, a result of the relation *between* the subject (i.e., the sensori-motor processes of the body) and this reality. We thus begin with the perceived, with the picture taken at the heart of things, and only later do we end with the perception of the perceived, or with the perceived as referred to a 'fixed point.'

Deleuze adopts Bergson's theory of perception. In fact, he restates Bergson's claim that perception is primarily and initially objective perception: 'perception is strictly identical to every image, insofar as every image acts and reacts on all others.'[58] Yet this objective perception entails the relation between different images; in other words, even the perception that is present at the very heart of things entails a fundamental difference and interval – that is, the difference between each of the interacting images of the aggregate. Deleuze defines this interval as a 'perception-image,' and it is that which makes objective and subjective perception possible. In the first instance, the perception-image is the condition for the relation between different images (i.e., objective perception); and in the second it is the condition for the relation between these same images and the privileged image of the body (i.e., subjective perception). That is, for Deleuze the perception-image is the fundamental differentiating condition which allows for the possibility of objective and subjective perception, and thus we can begin to see how he does not base his theory of perception on a fundamental identity, but, rather, on a fundamental difference.

In returning to our discussion of cinema, we see that, just as objective and subjective perception were made possible by the fundamental difference of the perception-image, so, too, as we have also seen, is the cinematographic movement-image made possible by the difference between two frames. But, in watching a film, we aren't aware of this difference. We don't perceive or experience the difference between frames. We perceive and experience a continuous unity of movement. As a result, there is a tendency to argue for the supremacy of the movement-image over the perception-image. That is, rather than being understood to be conditioned by a fundamental difference, the movement-image is interpreted to be the condition for difference. Difference is understood to be simply the interval moved, the distance covered, or the measure of this movement, and the perception-image is not seen to be that which makes this possible. Furthermore, this understanding of the perception-image as conditioned by the unity and identity of the movement-image leads to what Deleuze calls the 'deduction of the action-, affection-, and relation-images.' The perception-image is thus seen to function 'like a degree zero in the deduction which is carried out as a function of the movement-image.'[59] In other words, as a pure difference or interval, the perception-image is the condition for the possibility of differentiating between various parts of the movement-image, but is not to be identified with that which it differentiates (recall our earlier discussion of the noema); however, if the perception-image is taken to be conditioned by the movement-image, then there is a tendency to identify it with that which is differentiated. And that which is differentiated (i.e., affection-, action-, relation-images) corresponds, Deleuze claims, to Peirce's categories – 'firstness,' 'secondness,' 'thirdness.'

The affection-image is the result of the perception-image being identified with the possible and virtual reactions of the subject, or with the virtual movements of this subject. The affection-image is thus that which corresponds to the 'zone of indetermination,' to the realm of actions that are not determined in advance. The affection-image therefore expresses, not the actual actions and reactions of the images of the aggregate – that is, the real, but the virtual actions and reactions to the real – that is, the possible. And this is where we see the affection-image corresponding to Peirce's category of 'firstness,' for firstness also expresses the realm of the possible: 'Firstness ... is to be understood as the category of the possible.'[60] For example, the colour red as affection-image, as firstness, is the pure condition of possibility for saying that some thing, a second, is red. Peirce thus claims that, as firstness, red is 'the mode of being redness, before anything in the universe was yet red,'[61] and therefore these affections 'have capacities in themselves which may or may not ever be actualized, although we can know nothing of such possibilities [except] insofar as they are actualized.'[62] This independence of the possible from its actualization, from being referred to a *second*, is precisely the motivation for Peirce's use and definition of the term 'firstness': it is 'the mode of being of that which is such as it is, positively and without reference to anything else.'[63]

The action-image is the result of the perception-image being identified with the actions and reactions of the real, with the movements of the real. The action-image thus entails the relationship between images, or the action of an image 'through every one of its points upon all the points of all other images.' The action-image therefore does express the actual actions and reactions of the aggregate of images, and as such each image implies a second – namely, the second upon which it either acts or reacts. This corresponds to Peirce's category of 'secondness': it 'is the mode of being which is such as it is, with respect to a second but regardless of any third.'[64] For example, if redness in the mode firstness is that which is possible, a pure possibility which is such as it is 'without reference to anything else,' then redness in the mode secondness is that which is actual, or the actualization of this possibility whereby one can say or know that 'this,' a second, 'is red.'

And finally, the relation-image is the result of the perception-image being identified with the unity that links the possible to the actual, or the subject to the world. The perception-image thus returns to the movement-image itself, to the movement-image of which the perception-image was the derivative and secondary function. Consequently, the relation-image will express the 'closure of the deduction.'[65] In other words, for Bergson natural perception, as we saw, is conditioned by the difference between the body, the 'organ of perception,' and the world and reality this body responds to; however, for the body to respond to the world, or for the possible to be related to the actual, they must be related and connected at some level. Bergson claims this connection and link between the possible and the actual is the 'sensori-motor process.'[66] The sensori-motor process of the subject links their possible actions to the real actions of the world, or, as Bergson puts it, it links virtual activity to real activity.[67] Therefore, despite the irreducible difference between firstness and secondness, possible and actual, subject and world, idealism and realism, they are nevertheless fundamentally related at the level of sensori-motor processes; and thus we can see that Bergson's theory emerges as a response to the problem of difference.

Within the context of cinema, it is the movement-image, or the continuous unity of movement we see on the screen, which relates and links the frames of the film. The movement-image relates the beginning frame to the ending frame, or the first frame to the second frame, and so on, and it expresses the unity which links these frames. And thus the perception-image's closure of the deduction entails expressing the unity which accounts for the previously deduced categories – that is, affection and action images, firstness and secondness. Or, to follow Peirce again, the closure of the deduction exemplifies the category of thirdness which 'is the mode of being of that which is such as it is, in bringing a second and third into relation to each other.'[68] In short, thirdness, or the relation-image, establishes the connection between firstness and secondness, subject and object, by being the law[69] which accounts for this relationship. In essence, therefore, Peirce's category of thirdness is also a response to the problem of difference.

Returning to Bergson, Peirce's category of thirdness is that which relates the possible activity of the subject to the real activity of the world. However, since Bergson claims that it is the sensori-motor processes which account for this relationship, then it would be more accurate to say that thirdness expresses the law of these sensori-motor processes themselves – that is, it is the lawful unity or gestalt of these processes. But with this claim we find ourselves, as Deleuze has noted,[70] stating in different terms the position of Merleau-Ponty.

In *The Phenomenology of Perception*, Merleau-Ponty recognizes Bergson's use of the term 'sensori-motor process' as a way of 'seeking to involve consciousness in the world';[71] that is, to link the activities of a subject (virtual activity) to the activities of the world (real activity). However, Merleau-Ponty argues that the distinction Bergson makes between sensation (i.e., virtual activity or affection-image)[72] and movement (i.e., real activity or action-image) is analogous to the distinction between for-itself and in-itself. Similarly, just as the for-itself/in-itself distinction does not adequately account for the involvement of consciousness in the world, for something that is both for and in itself (paradox of 'identity and difference'), so, too, does Bergson's distinction fail to give such an account. Merleau-Ponty will then claim that Bergson's attempt to give such an account by way of sensori-motor processes ultimately reduces the involvement of a subject in the world to the functionings of a sensori-motor present, to a condensed and undifferentiated present. Merleau-Ponty argues that such a compression of time 'never reaches the unique movement whereby the three dimensions of time are constituted, and one cannot see why duration is squeezed into a present, or why consciousness becomes involved in a body and a world.'[73] What is needed, as we have seen Merleau-Ponty argue, is a relational whole or unity which is the condition for distinguishing between consciousness and the world. In short, what is needed is a prior unity, a Peircean thirdness, which is the structured and lawful horizon (i.e., gestalt) that is the condition for the involvement of consciousness in the world and with others. And it is this already-given unity and horizon which it is the proper task of cinema, as well as phenomenology, to restore and describe; and a film, if successful, takes this unity as its model and emerges as a whole or gestalt, as an object wherein every scene, every frame, is an expression of this unity, of this gestalt. As Merleau-Ponty puts it: 'a film is not a sum total of images but a temporal *gestalt*.'[74]

At this point similarities appear between Deleuze and Merleau-Ponty's theories of perception. On the one hand, Merleau-Ponty claims that, in order to account adequately for the involvement of a subject in a world, one needs to recognize the primacy of perception. That is, Merleau-Ponty argues that in perceiving, the perceiving subject is paradoxically in the world (i.e., the paradox of infinite series), and in a world that is the already-given horizon and condition for the subject's involvement in this world. Deleuze also claims that, in order to account for the involvement of a subject in a world, one needs to consider the primacy of the perception-image – that is, the degree zero in the deductions of affection, action, and relational unity. When this perception-image was interpreted to be derivative from the movement-image, however, we saw that it entailed accounting for a fundamental link between a subject and a world – for example, the sensori-motor link between an actual and a possible movement. This sensori-motor link in turn required a relational unity or whole as that which conditioned it, and thus the analysis of the movement-image by way of the perception-image returned to this movement-image as the 'closure of the deduction.' In other words, in analysing the movement-image, Deleuze discusses the sensori-motor conditions of perception (Bergson), but to account for this sensori-motor condition he needed to return to the relational unity of the movement-image itself (i.e., Peirce's thirdness); something Bergson did not do. Deleuze therefore brings in the horizonal conditions for the sensori-motor links, and it is the theory of these conditions, this already given unity and horizon, which is also Merleau-Ponty's position.

This relational unity is, in the end, not only the condition for explaining the sensori-motor links, but the condition for relating a subject to a world, an action to a situation; or, in a phrase, this relational unity, as a sensori-motor whole or gestalt, is the condition for the unity of the plot, for the continuity of narrative. In other words, as Merleau-Ponty argued, this gestalt is the condition for a film which copies and restores it, for the film which 'is not a sum total of images but a temporal *gestalt.*' Thus the unity of plot and narration, and the connections between the narrative as heard and the narrative as seen on the screen, are, in the end, grounded in the sensori-motor whole or gestalt. As Deleuze states this same point: 'the movement-image gives rise to a sensori-motor whole which grounds narration in the image.'[75]

In summary, therefore, to establish a connection within the interval of the perception-image, to bridge the fundamental difference of this interval, Bergson needed to bring in the sensori-motor conditions of perception (Merleau-Ponty, as we have seen, brings in the paradox of infinite series to relate the perceiver to the perceived). Nevertheless, if one is also going to account for this sensori-motor link, then one needs to account for the unity of the movement-image itself, for the relational unity or whole which is the condition for the sensori-motor links. In Merleau-Ponty we saw that it is the identity and unity of the world as gestalt, or structure, which is the condition for the relationship of a subject to a world. In essence, the relational whole and gestalt which is the condition for the sensori-motor links is also the condition for the 'assimilation of the cinematographic image to an utterance,'[76] a subject to a world, a meaning to a word, and a situation to an action: that is, it is the condition for a narrative film.

It is therefore with respect to narrative film that Merleau-Ponty and

Deleuze can be said to agree. For Merleau-Ponty the already-given unity of the world and one's body is the condition for a film that mirrors this unity, this gestalt; and for Deleuze it is the relational unity (thirdness) of the movement-image that is the condition for the unity of the film and its narrative. They each claim, therefore, that it is a prior unity and whole which is the condition for the unity of a film, for a film that can re-create this whole. Furthermore, in *Cinema 1*, Deleuze describes the development of film as an attempt to re-create this relational unity of the movement-image, and his analysis of cinema recapitulates our analysis of the emergence of the relation-image out of the movement-image. In this next section, I will briefly discuss Deleuze's analysis of film as it relates to the issues and terms we have been discussing; however, in the subsequent section we will see that Deleuze ultimately believes that the *cinema of identity* (i.e., the identity of the movement-image as the condition for the fundamental difference of the perception-image, and hence for the deductions that ultimately return to the movement image: affection → action → relational unity) gives way to the *cinema of difference*. That is, cinema will confront its conditions of possibility, its fundamental motivation, and rather than this being a relational unity and identity, it is a fundamental paradox and dis-unity, a fundamental difference that is perpetually displaced and absent from itself; a difference that forever prevents the possibility of unity, of something being wholly present: This condition will be revealed to be paradox, 'the impower of thought ... the inexistence of a whole which could be thought.' The result of this confrontation is that there will occur in cinema a fundamental reversal, a reversal that exemplifies precisely Deleuze's reversal of traditional transcendental philosophy and metaphysics. It also exemplifies Deleuze's reversal of Merleau-Ponty's formulation of the paradox of 'infinite series' and 'identity and difference' – the reversal that was the initial motivation and theme of this essay.

At the Movies

Deleuze adopted Bergson's term 'image,' as we discussed, to account for that which is halfway between idealism and realism, for that which is their differentiating condition. In short, the use of the term 'image' is a response to the problem of difference. As a result, the movement-image is to be identified neither with the movement of things, nor with the movement of ideas – that is, the stream of consciousness. It is to be understood, rather, as the condition which makes these distinctions possible. Similarly, with respect to cinema, the camera, since it is not directly anchored to a perceiving body (*à la* Merleau-Ponty), is, Deleuze argues, 'eminently capable of' presenting the movement-image. For example, as attached to a moving body the camera can extract its movement, its perspective, and free this movement from the body, or the camera can extract a body's movement and present this movement independently of this body, on a screen or television set. The camera therefore presents a movement-image that is not to be identified with the thing that moves, yet it allows for the possibility of seeing what it is like to be that thing which moves. For example, a camera can extract the movements of a bicycle, a plane, an automobile speeding down a mountain road, a roller-coaster, a football player (e.g., the WLAF's helmet-cam), or even a monkey (e.g., the monkey-cam as seen on *Late Show with David Letterman*); and the viewer at home or in the theatre can experience the novelty, thrill, or humour of such movements. On the other hand, as directed to bodies themselves, the camera can present a movement and mobility which is independent of moving bodies. The camera can present a movement-image that is not the movement of a body, but is rather a mobile and unanchored perception. For example, the wandering camera in Renoir's *Rules of the Game* moves past a character, through the garden, and back to the character again; and the camera in King Vidor's *The Crowd* wanders through the crowd, moving past and among the massed bodies.

Implicit within this ability of the camera to extract movement from bodies, or to present movement-images, is a twofold distinction. On the one hand, when the camera is attached to a body, the images are put in relation to a central or privileged *frame* of reference (e.g., car, bicycle, monkey); on the other hand, when the camera is moving among the bodies it is directed towards, it places these objects in relation to each other, and rather than referring to a privileged or central frame of reference (i.e., a body), the mobile perception of the camera decentres the bodies and extracts the mobility which puts them in relation to one another. In other words, within the cinematographic movement-image there is an implicit difference between an objective perception – that is, the movement of the camera puts each body in relation to all the others – and a subjective perception – that is, the movements are put into relation with a central or privileged frame of reference. The cinematographic movement-image thus implies the perception-image; that is, it entails the possibility of distinguishing between a perceiver and a perceived, or between a subjective and an objective perception. Thus, as

Deleuze summarizes this distinction, he claims that 'a subjective perception is one in which the images vary in relation to a central and privileged image [e.g., the body for Merleau-Ponty]; an objective perception
is one where, as in things, all the images vary in relation to one another,
on all their facets and in all their parts [e.g., Bergson].'[77] In cinematic
practice, for example, Antonioni's obsessive framing – his shots which
extend well beyond their expected duration – have the effect of 'making
the camera felt,' of putting the images in relation to the central 'felt'
image of the camera (i.e., a subjective perception). On the other hand, in
Dupont's *Vaudeville*, the camera puts this privileged centre into movement and has the effect of decentring this movement, or of creating an
objective perception. For example, in the scene where the camera takes
on the perspective of the trapeze-artist, the swaying movement leads the
trapeze-artist to see 'the crowd and the ceiling, one in the other, as a
shower of sparks and a whirlpool of floating spots.'[78] In other words,
this perception is no longer a perception of bodies, or even a perception
anchored to a body, but, as unanchored, it is a perception without
boundaries or distances, without prejudice or bias, and it is precisely
this which Deleuze claims is definitive of objectivity. In summary, then,
the perception-image at the heart of the cinematographic movement-
image allows for the possibility of relating either to the subject (subjective perception) or the object (objective perception); and yet, as the differentiating condition, the perception-image is not to be identified with
either side. However, as we have argued, there is a tendency to identify
the perception-image with either side, and it is this which leads to the
deduction of the affection- and action-images.

The affection-image, as discussed above, was seen to be the result of
the perception-image being identified with the virtual and possible
activity of the subject. As such, the affection-image corresponded to
Peirce's 'firstness' category – that is, it is a pure possibility independent
of its actualization, independent of a second. An example of the affection-image in cinema is the use of the close-up. Ingmar Bergmann, for
example, in his film *Persona*, uses the close-up of the face to disconnect
the subjects from their background, their situation, and their unique
persona-lity and behaviour (i.e., actions, or action-images). The close-up
reveals a face that is the possibility for being actualized in a personality,
for being in a situation where this person can act and relate to others.
The close-up of the face thus reveals the possibility of being an acting
individual, and as the condition for this the face is non-individuated
and disconnected: it is 'such as it is, positively and without reference to

anything else.' In *Persona*, this occurs in the scene where a close-up of two faces merge into one, where the two characters become a face that is not to be identified with either, but is nevertheless the condition for their identification, the *possibility* of being actualized in two different personalities. The affection-image is thus the result of the camera's being directed to a subject, to a centred frame of reference, and the close-up of this subject shows this subject as a 'zone of indetermination,' as a pole of virtual or *possible* activity.

If the affection-image is the category of the Possible (i.e., virtual activity), then the action-image is the category of the Real (i.e., real activity). Since the affection-image is understood to be that which is what it is 'without reference to anything else,' and if it is the possibility for such a reference, then the action-image is to be understood as the actualization of this reference. In cinema, the action-image is the relationship of an objective perception to a subjective perception (i.e., firstness); or, as Deleuze argues, it is the relationship between an action and a situation. In other words, the action-image emerges as the relationship between a situation (i.e., an objective and real situation) and an action which transforms this situation and actualizes another (i.e., the actualization of virtual activity). This relationship entails, as we saw, a sensori-motor link. That is, just as there was a sensori-motor link between virtual and real activity, so, too, is there a link which connects a given situation (i.e., real activity) to the possible action or response to this situation (i.e., virtual activity), a link which in turn connects the action to the new situation this action brings about. This sensori-motor link is thus, and this is true of the action-image in general, a link between two sides: for example, virtual–real activity, subject–object, situation–action.

One of the many examples from cinema Deleuze uses to describe the action-image is the documentary. The documentary attempts to describe and present real situations; however, Deleuze points out that there are two ways of doing this. One can begin with a given milieu and situation, both cultural and environmental, and from there explain the behaviours and actions that result from such a situation. Deleuze cites Flaherty's *Nanook of the North* as an example of this approach. One can also begin with the actions and behaviours themselves, and from there deduce the milieu and situation which follows upon such actions. Deleuze cites Grierson's and Rotha's documentaries as an example of this approach (most docu-dramas are of this type as well).

The first approach thus begins with the situation and environment at hand, and the actions are simply that which transforms this initial situation into another (Deleuze calls this the 'SAS' approach – that is, 'situation–action–new situation'). A typical Clint Eastwood movie, for example, finds the Eastwood character riding into a town or situation that his actions transform; and, at the end of the film, he is riding off, leaving behind this new situation.

The second approach begins with an action, and greatly different situations can result from a nearly indiscernible difference in action. This is best seen in burlesque films. In *Chaplin*, for example, there is a scene where Charlie is seen from behind shaking, apparently distraught after his wife has left him, but when he turns around we find he is simply shaking his martini. During a battle scene in *Soldier at Arms*, Charlie is seen scoring a point for each shot he fires, and when a return shot nearly hits him, he subtracts a point. In *Monsieur Verdoux*, the behaviour of the Verdoux who cares for his disabled wife is virtually indistinguishable from that of Verdoux the murderer. And in *The Great Dictator*, the Hitler character, with his small moustache, is nearly indistinguishable from the tramp, and in fact Chaplin plays both roles and fully capitalizes on this similarity. In these examples, a very small difference in action results in largely opposed situations – that is, crying–celebrating, fighting–playing, kind-hearted–murderous, Hitler–tramp.

In this relationship between an action and a situation, or in the action-image as that which relates the two sides of a movement-image (i.e., objective and subjective), we have seen that one account of this relationship is that it is made possible by the sensori-motor link. However, without an adequate account of this sensori-motor link itself, it is difficult to see how perception, or the perception-image, actually accounts for the relationship between the affection- and action-images, between an action and a situation (i.e., we are confronted with the problem of difference). Consequently, what was needed was a prior unity and whole which is the condition for the sensori-motor link. This whole was argued to be the relational unity of the movement-image itself, the whole from which the deductions of affection and action began. It is this relational unity which emerged as the third image deduced from the movement-image – that is, the relation-image – and it completed the deduction, for it returns to the movement-image as the whole or unity of the parts of this image (i.e., its objective and subjective parts). In other words, the relation-image returns to the movement-image as the whole, or third, which is independent of its parts, independent of its affection (firstness) and action (secondness); or, it is what Peirce called 'thirdness' and what Merleau-Ponty called 'gestalt.' In short, the relation-image is the law or structure of the sensori-motor links – it is the structure of behaviour.

The relation-image is most clearly presented in cinema in the films of Hitchcock. What this entails is that neither the actions nor the situations are what is crucial; it is, rather, a third which is independent of these two terms – that is, the relations, gestalt, or thirdness. Thus, in Hitchcock, what is important is not who committed the crime, or the situation which led to the crime, but 'the set of relations in which the action and the one who did it are caught.'[79] For example, *Strangers on a Train* is not simply about a crime that gets committed, but a crime that gets exchanged, that gets put into a logical relation with another. And, in *Rear Window*, the actions and situations are revealed through a third which puts them into relation – that is, the camera and the window – and it is this which explains, for example, why the Jimmy Stewart character has a broken leg (photos of a racing car; a broken camera). In Hitchcock's films, therefore, it is not enough to explain the sensory–motor connection between an action and a situation, what Hitchcock derisively referred to as the 'whodunit'; one needs to understand the relations which determine these actions and situations, the relations which are the condition for explaining the connection between an action and a situation. In *North by Northwest*, to take another example, the Cary Grant character is unwittingly caught within a set of relations, but it is precisely this set of relations (i.e., the undercover plot) which determines the connection between his situation (i.e., his abduction and eventual flight) and his actions (i.e., his efforts to *understand* why he is in this situation, to *understand* the set of relations). It is in doing this that, Deleuze believes, Hitchcock represents the culmination of films that are made within the tradition of the movement-image: that is, as presenting relation-images, Hitchcock's films complete the deductive process which began with the movement-image.

In presenting the relation-image, the films of Hitchcock thus re-create the already-given unity of the movement-image, the prior unity which was the condition for the deductions of affection-, action-, and relation-image. That is, the relation-image mirrors the unity of the movement-image, and as such the deduction comes full circle. Furthermore, we have also seen that this analysis of cinema in terms of the movement-image is, in essence, in accord with Merleau-Ponty's fundamental position. If Deleuze's work on cinema had ended with *Cinema 1*, this would be our conclusion; however, *Cinema 2* discusses a reversal which occurred in cinema: in particular, the position that claims the fundamental difference of the perception-image is conditioned by the movement-image is reversed, wherein it is claimed that it is the fundamental difference of the perception-image which is the condition for the movement-image. This reversal also reflects the reversal Deleuze takes with respect to traditional metaphysics and transcendental philosophy, for example, his reversal of Merleau-Ponty's paradoxes of 'infinite series' and 'identity and difference.'

3. The Poststructuralist Turn

This reversal, in short, consists in extracting from the model–copy relationship a fundamental difference which is the condition and motivation for this relationship; consequently, rather than difference being derivatively related to Identity (i.e., a model), Identity is understood in terms of a fundamental difference or paradox (e.g., Plato's simulacrum). In cinema, for example, it appeared that the movement-image did have at bottom a fundamental difference: that is, the difference between an objective and a subjective movement. This difference, however, was ultimately interpreted to be conditioned by the identity of the movement-image itself, and this reflected the tendency to emphasize the continuous unity of movement that we perceive on the screen while overlooking the fact that it is the difference between frames which is the condition for this movement-image. As a result, the deductions the perception-image began (i.e., perception-image as 'zero degree') are, in the end, completed when the relation-image copies the unity of the movement-image which was its model. In other words, the fundamental difference of the perception-image is derivative of the unity and identity of the movement-image. Similarly, Merleau-Ponty's paradoxical relation between perceiver and perceived – paradox of 'infinite series' – is ultimately derivative of the fundamental unity and identity of a world and body that are always already there. This difference, this paradox of perceiver–perceived, is thus rooted in Being (i.e., his metaphysics, and, later, his ontology, his 'paradox of Being'). In so far as cinema also roots difference, or paradox, in the unity and identity of the movement-image, cinema can be rightly claimed to fall in line with traditional metaphysics and transcendental philosophy. Thus the reversal in cinema entails a reversal of traditional metaphysics and transcendental philosophy.

This reversal, however, is not to be understood as a negation of the tradition, as the replacement of one tradition by its 'photographic negative.' If taken in this way, reversal implies the *identity* of that which it is the negative, the original that is reversed, and thus Deleuze's project would continue to be within the milieu of traditional metaphysics.[80] What the reversal entails, as we have been showing, is an immanent critique of the tradition, a critique which is 'rigorously Freudian' in that it brings to the surface the conditions and motivations of the tradition itself. In doing this, Deleuze is, in a certain sense, solidly within the tradition (after all, an immanent critique is nothing new). He even admits that he is simply carrying forward Nietzsche's task of completing Kant's critique (and, in *Anti-Oedipus*, Deleuze and Guattari believe they are continuing Marx's immanent critique of capitalism, accompanied by an immanent critique of Freud); however, this task does not result in the deduction of the identifiable conditions for thought (e.g., the transcendental deduction of the *a priori* categories), but, rather, reveals an indeducible instance which refuses to be identified, which is never where it is, and which is nevertheless the genetic condition for differentiating between two identifiable, and contradictory, identities. In other words, Deleuze's critique reveals paradox as the fundamental condition, the unthinkable, indeducible condition which is prior to the deductions of thought, to thought's either/or. As Deleuze argues, 'the force of paradoxes is that they are not contradictory; they rather allow us to be present at the genesis of contradiction.'[81] In the end, therefore, the reversal entails confronting the fundamental difference which cannot be thought, the fundamental paradox which is the condition of thought; and this reverses the tradition which claims that it is a fundamental identity which is the condition for thought, an identity which is not only the condition for thought, but the only thing which ever is, or can be, thought.

When this reversal occurs, thought confronts and reveals its own conditions; in other words, thought comes up against that which cannot be thought, the fundamental difference that cannot be identified. This confrontation with thought's own impotence is what I will call the 'crisis of thought.' That is, what becomes unthinkable is the identity which is the only thing that ever is or can be thought, and thus thought comes up against what is radically different (i.e., the conditioned – thought – is not modelled on or similar to the conditions), against what puts its identity into crisis, and which is nevertheless its necessary condition.

As a result of the crisis of thought, the fundamental identity that had been the legitimation of thought, thought's condition and end, suddenly fails to apply, and this failure emerges as a crisis (analogous to crisis, in

Kuhn's sense of the term). Thought is no longer legitimated by a fundamental identity; rather, thought discovers that it is conditioned by what cannot be legitimated, by what fails to be thought in terms of identity. In short, the crisis occurs when thought finds that there are things which are necessarily unthinkable, things which cannot be justified, a story that cannot be told. Furthermore, since the crisis is the result of thought's coming up against the paradox which is its own condition, the crisis emerges as something essential to thought, as 'the passion and pathos' of thought.

This understanding of the crisis of thought as interpreted within the work of Deleuze, expresses a position common to much recent work in current Continental thought.[82] For example, in *The Postmodern Condition*, Jean-François Lyotard argues that Postmodernism is to be understood as resulting from a crisis in modernism. By 'modernism,' Lyotard means the thought which legitimates itself on the basis of what he calls a 'grand narrative.' A grand narrative is a fundamental unity or identity, an identity which is the condition for all that can be known, told, or thought. As examples of grand narratives, Lyotard lists 'the dialectics of Spirit, the hermeneutics of meaning, the emancipation of the rational or working subject, or the creation of wealth.'[83] These narratives function as the discourse which legitimates actual discourses: that is, it is a meta-narrative or meta-discourse which is the condition for an actual and *legitimate* discourse. In other words, all that can possibly be explained and presented is determined in advance by the conditions set forth in the grand narrative. The grand narrative of the Enlightenment, for example, claims that all knowledge claims are legitimate only if they are presented in terms of the unanimity of rational minds; that is, something is legitimated as true only if presented in a manner that all rational minds would recognize as such (e.g., scientific method). The crisis of modernism, for Lyotard, is therefore a crisis of these grand narratives; or, as with Deleuze, thought and discourse come up against that which cannot be legitimated, that which cannot be told or presented in terms of the grand narrative. As Lyotard argues, 'the postmodern would be that which, in the modern, puts forward the unpresentable in presentation itself.'[84]

In describing this unpresentable in presentation, Lyotard, as does Deleuze, claims that it is a fundamental paradox at the heart of modernism, a paradox which leads to the crisis of modernism and, consequently, to postmodernism. Lyotard thus concludes that 'Post modern would have to be understood according to the paradox of the future (post) anterior (modo).'[85] In other words, this fundamental paradox is something that cannot be presented and is itself fundamentally different from the present; that is, the paradox is the fundamental difference at the heart of the present, or that which subverts the identity of the present and divides it into a simultaneous future (*post*) and past (*modo*).

This is precisely how Deleuze understands paradox. Deleuze, as discussed above, claims that the paradox is 'endlessly displaced and absent from its own place' (i.e., never present), and is 'at once past and future.' Deleuze also refers to this paradox, following the Stoics, as *Aion*: 'a future and past divide the present at every instant [i.e., paradoxical instance] and subdivide it *ad infinitum* into past and future.' The crisis of modernism, or the crisis of thought, thus leads to a presentation of the unpresentable, to the presentation of that which is 'absent from its own place,' and it reveals a fundamental difference which cannot be reduced to identity. And it is precisely this crisis which leads to the reversal of traditional metaphysics and transcendental philosophy. Furthermore, this crisis and the resulting reversal reveal the paradox of time, or that fundamental difference which infinitely divides and subverts the present into past (*post*) and future (*modo*). It is for this reason that Deleuze formulates the paradoxes of 'infinite series' and 'identity and difference' in terms of time. This formulation reflects the reversal of traditional metaphysics and transcendental philosophy; or, to put it another way, it exemplifies Deleuze's 'postmodernism.'

This reversal, Deleuze claims, also occurred in cinema. A crisis in the cinema of the movement-image resulted in cinema's turning to a presentation of the unpresentable, or what Deleuze calls the 'time-image.' In other words, cinema runs up against that which is not conditioned by the unity and identity of the movement-image, but rather that which is its condition. That which was conditioned by the prior unity of the movement-image was, as we saw, the sensori-motor link, the link that connected the differentiated sides of the perception-image. Thus the fundamental difference within the perception-image between an objective and subjective movement is a difference bridged by the sensori-motor links, a link which is itself conditioned by the unity and identity of the movement-image. It was then this identity that led to the deduction of the relation-image, the image that mirrors the unity of the movement-image, and is the law or gestalt of the sensori-motor links. Therefore, what is fundamental to the movement-image is not a difference and separation, but an identity and link, an identity and link which leads to the deduction of a whole, or to the whole which can be thought (i.e., thirdness, gestalt).[86]

With the crisis of cinema, however, as with the crisis of modernism and the crisis of thought, there results the presentation of that which is absent from its own place. Consequently, this sensori-motor link is broken, and what is revealed is a paradoxical instance which cannot be thought or presented, a fundamental difference that cannot be bridged, but a difference which is nevertheless the condition for thought. It is for this reason that Deleuze claims in cinema 'what forces us to think is "the impower of thought," the figure of nothingness, the inexistence of a whole which could be thought.' In other words, with the loss of the sensori-motor link, one also loses the possibility of deducing the whole which could be thought, but it is precisely this loss which reveals the paradoxical condition of thought, the unpresentable in presentation, the unthinkable in thought.

The crisis in cinema, therefore, or what Deleuze calls the 'crisis of the action-image,' occurs when the sensori-motor link is broken. Thus the link between an action and a situation, a narrative as seen and a narrative as heard, is broken. The images can no longer be tied to the *present* of sensori-motor functioning. As a result, the visual and sound situations are not tied to a present, but hover as that which is both past and future (i.e., the paradox of future anterior, or the paradoxical instance – *Aion*), the already happened that is yet to come. These images hover like a memory that one cannot place. For example, if I recognize someone but cannot place her, I cannot relate the image (her face) to a sensori-motor situation (i.e., to how she relates or is *connected* to me), and this image is therefore something that has already happened in that it is someone I once knew, but it is also an image that is yet to be placed, is yet to come. The crisis of the action-image thus leads to the presentation of an image that is not present, but is at once past and future. Emerging from this crisis we find, for example, in the realist films of the Italians, a cinema that 'achieve[s] a before and an after as they coexist with the image, as they are inseparable from the image.'[87] That is, this cinema presents an un-*present*-able image, an image that is at once future (*post*) and past (*modo*); or, rather than a cinema of the movement-image, we now have what Deleuze calls the 'cinema of the time-image,' a cinema that reveals the un-present-able nature of time (i.e., *Aion* as the 'paradoxical instance').

The presentation of this paradoxical time-image marks, for Deleuze, the reversal of Merleau-Ponty's formulation of paradox and time. Merleau-Ponty, as we saw, argued that the film is a 'temporal gestalt'; in other words, the film is not only a whole, a relational unity, but also a temporal unity. Time is thus subordinated to the unity of the movement-image, and this unity and whole is the condition for time which is the measure and form of this movement. This subordination of time results in what Deleuze calls the 'conception of time as Chronos,' or chronological time, and even in Merleau-Ponty's last writings this continues to be his position. Time, he claims, is the flesh as 'the measurant (*mesurant*) of all'; that which, in the present, is 'an "ever new" and "always the same" ... the existential eternity.' That is, time is understood in terms of the identity of the flesh, the flesh that is always the same, and it is on the basis of this identity that the past and future are measured. For Deleuze, on the other hand, the paradoxical time-image is that which subverts the identity of the present by presenting the fundamental difference at the heart of the present: that is, the difference between past and future. Time thus appears, not as the measure of movement, but as the fundamental difference that cannot be measured – that is, non-identifiable, un-present-able.

To clarify further this reversal, and to complete this study, we need to tie many loose ends together. In particular, we have argued that the seeds of this reversal, this emphasis upon a paradoxical condition of difference rather than a transcendental condition of identity, were planted by Husserl and Frege, further developed by Merleau-Ponty, and brought to fruition in the work of Deleuze. Consequently, we need to review the problems and issues which were our starting-point, and summarize how they continued to play an important role throughout our investigations. Furthermore, this review will be greatly facilitated by our discussion of cinema, for it was in Deleuze's writings on cinema that one could see most clearly the relationship between Deleuze's project and that of Husserl and Merleau-Ponty. Therefore, in concluding this work we will continue to utilize many of the themes our analysis of cinema brought forth. In fact, to elaborate upon Deleuze's understanding of time and paradox, and to compare Deleuze's theory of sense with Husserl and Merleau-Ponty's, our discussion will focus upon the film Deleuze believes is 'the first great film of a cinema of time, Welles' *Citizen Kane.*'[88]

Conclusion:
The Search for 'Rosebud'

1. The Question

What is 'rosebud'? What does 'rosebud' mean? With Kane's dying word 'rosebud,' these two questions surface. The first question implies that there is some thing, person, or state of affairs in the world which the word 'rosebud' denotes. To answer this question, therefore, one needs simply to determine that which is being referred to or denoted. This is what the reporters proceed to do; however, even though 'rosebud' is sought as an objective fact, it is also thought to be a special fact, one that will give meaning to the whole of Kane's life, or tell us what Kane's life *meant* to Kane. Thus, in answering the first question, the reporters hope to answer the second: what does 'rosebud' *mean*? If they can find *that* which 'rosebud' refers to, then they can determine *what* 'rosebud' meant to Kane, or what Kane 'had in mind' when he died. In determining what Kane meant by 'rosebud,' the reporters thus hope to discover that meaning through which Kane's last act becomes a referring or denoting act (i.e., a meaningful act), and therefore answering the second question implies answering the first: what is 'rosebud'? The two questions imply each other, or resonate off each other, and it is this resonance which conditions the unfolding of the narrative of *Citizen Kane*.

The narrative of *Citizen Kane* thus has two sides, each reflecting one of the two questions. On the one hand, the narrative is turned towards the facts and events; it describes what happened. On the other hand, the narrative is turned towards what Kane's life means, to the whole which these facts and events express. In other words, as the narrative unfolds, it attempts to account both for the facts and for the meaning behind these facts. 'Rosebud' therefore appears in the film both as a fact (i.e., the sled) and as a meaning or concept (i.e., the meaning or concept of Kane's life). The difference between these two, between 'rosebud' as object and 'rosebud' as concept, is irreducible. One cannot reduce the meaning of Kane's life to a single object – a sled – nor can a single concept adequately account for the meaning of his life. But isn't it precisely this reduction that we just claimed to be the motivating condition of the film's narrative? Since Kane is dead, aren't the reporters forced to determine the meaning of his life by deducing it from the object referred to by the name 'rosebud'? And how is it possible that two things which are irreducibly different (concept and object) are nevertheless related? Has not our discussion simply and quickly run up against a major problem (i.e., the problem of difference)? Yes, it has, but it is precisely this problem which *Citizen Kane* describes; furthermore, this has been the problem this essay has continued to explore – beginning with Husserl.

2. Husserl

The problem for Husserl, as we saw, was to account for the relationship between ideal timeless truths and the subjects who intuit these truths in time. Husserl thus recognizes, following Plato, a fundamental and irreducible difference between knowledge and opinion, or between the direct *intuition* of an ideal truth and the indirect *induction* of a natural-scientific truth. However, Husserl claims, unlike Plato, that these ideal timeless truths do not pre-exist their being directly intuited by a subject in time – that is, despite the irreducible difference, there is nevertheless a fundamental relationship between them. Therefore, although irreducibly different from the subjects who intuit these truths, they are none the less dependent upon these subjects – there is an essential connection or link which relates the subject to the object, a link which, in the end, establishes a correlation between them. And it is precisely the effort to account for this link, and to explicate this correlation, which is the problem that dominated Husserl's entire philosophic career.[1]

In explicating this correlation in *Logical Investigations*, Husserl's discussion centres upon an analysis of the 'interpretative sense' of an act. By 'act,' he means an act of consciousness, and by 'consciousness,' he means an 'intentional' act – that is, consciousness is consciousness of something. Therefore, the 'interpretative sense' of an act is that which *links* an intentional consciousness to that intentional object it is a *consciousness of*. In other words, and Husserl is clear on this point, the 'interpretative sense' determines both the directedness of an act and the object that this act is directed towards: 'the matter [i.e., interpretative sense] ... is that peculiar side of an act's phenomenological content that not only determines *that* it grasps the object but also as *what* it grasps it, the properties, relations, categorial forms, that it itself attributes to it.'[2] Within this context, therefore, the problem of accounting for the relationship between ideal truths and the intuition of subjects becomes one of explicating the correlation between an 'intuitive act' and the ideal object towards which this act is directed. In other words, the problem is to explain how a subject comes to have intuitively fulfilled and objective knowledge, and it is exactly the interpretative sense of an act which accounts for this fulfilment – that is, the sense as intended, with its 'properties, relations,' and so on, comes into coincidence with, or is fulfilled by, the self-givenness of an object, by the object that has these 'properties, relations,' and so on.

To further clarify this notion of fulfilment, Husserl uses what we have called the 'linguistic model.' For example, in written or verbal expression, a certain 'matter'[3] is the vehicle through which an expressed 'meaning' is given. This meaning, however, is ideal, and thus independent of the actual characters or sounds used to give it. One could have expressed this same meaning in a variety of different ways; however, this meaning is nevertheless dependent upon its being given in some manner. To understand what someone means, this person must have expressed or intended this meaning. It is therefore this meaning which links the speaker to the hearer, and if I understand what another has said to me, and if I have understood precisely what he has intended me to, or that what he says is true, then we have an example of meaning 'fulfilment.' And this fulfilment, as discussed above, is determined precisely by the sense (i.e., interpretative sense) of an act: 'the essence of meaning-fulfillment is the fulfilling sense of the expression, or, as one may also call it, the sense expressed by the expression.'[4] In other words, the interpretative sense of a linguistic act determines both that this is a meaningful act (as opposed to meaningless vocalizing) and what is meant by this act; and fulfilment, furthermore, is the coincidence of this sense as intended (e.g., by a speaker), with its 'properties, relations,'[5] and so on, with this sense as given (i.e., as understood).

A problem emerges with this account, and it follows from Husserl's claim that there is an irreducible difference between the sense of an act and the intuitive self-givenness of the object that fulfils this sense.[6] The sense is thus never to be confused with an object. It is through the sense that an act becomes directed towards objects, but this sense itself is not an object. To say that it is would result in an epistemological infinite regress, a regress Husserl claimed infected Hume's system. For this reason, Husserl claims the sense of every act determines both *what* an object is given as and *that* an object is given – that is, the sense is never an object, but is the means through which objects are given. However, if direct intuition is the fulfilling act for Husserl, as it is, then the object of an intuitive act will itself be determined by the sense of this act. The problem is thus to account for how we can ever get beyond sense to the independent object which fulfils this sense. In other words, there emerges for Husserl the regress of sense infinitely coinciding with sense; and since it is the self-givenness of an object that is to account for how a subject comes to have intuitively fulfilled and objective knowledge, then unless we can get beyond sense to the actual givenness of this object, this account will remain forever inadequate. Husserl was therefore unable to circumvent the epistemological infinite regress.

It was precisely to resolve this problem that was, we argued, the implicit motivation for Husserl's work in *The Phenomenology of Internal Time-Consciousness*. In short, the irreducible difference between sense and object, intuition and induction, is a difference made possible by an absolute, self-constituting transcendental consciousness. This absolute consciousness is the transcendental differentiating condition, or what we have called 'paradoxa,' which makes possible the irreducible difference between sense and object. This consciousness, however, is to be identified neither with a posited subject (i.e., a psychological ego) nor with a posited object (i.e., a transcendent object), but is, rather, the fundamental transcendental unity within which these posited differences emerge. Consequently, the regress of sense infinitely coinciding with sense, which is a result of the irreducible difference between an intending, positing sense and a posited, given object; this regress is made possible by the unity of an absolute consciousness, by a self-constituting consciousness wherein the positing sense and posited object do, paradoxically, coincide. That is, the *difference* between constituting and constituted, positing and posited, sense and object, is a difference grounded in the *identity* and unity of absolute consciousness. The fundamental differentiating condition is, therefore, a fundamental identity.

This did not, however, solve our problem. Although this absolute consciousness may be the non-regressive condition for the possibility of the regress, it still has not shown how a subject can, in fact, attain intuitively fulfilled and objective knowledge. The problem still remains to show how there can be the coincidence of sense and object, or how a subject comes to intuit ideal objects that are independent of this subject. In short, the problem is to account for that which transcends the subject, for that which is other; and Husserl's inability to give an adequate account is most evident in his account of the other. The other, as we saw, was reduced to the identity of an absolute constituting consciousness; consequently, the other could be seen only as an analogue or mirror of this consciousness, and not as other – that is, as different. And this difficulty remains intractable as long as difference – for example, the other – is understood in terms of a fundamental identity. Therefore, even though Husserl argues for a fundamental differentiating condition, this condition is nevertheless understood to be the fundamental identity and unity of absolute consciousness, and thus the other will always be reduced to this identity – that is, difference will be reduced to identity. Merleau-Ponty, however, recognized this inherent difficulty and attempted to resolve it.

3. Merleau-Ponty

Husserl's quest for the link which establishes the correlation between real subjects and ideal truths ended with the discovery of the pure transcendental ego, or with the absolute consciousness. As a fundamental identity itself, however, there remained the problem of accounting for a *different* transcendental ego – that is, the Other. Merleau-Ponty, in recognition of this difficulty, argues that this fundamental identity and link is not to be understood as an absolute constituting consciousness; rather, it is the already-constituted and -given world that is the condition for differentiating between self and other, consciousness (i.e., sense) and object. In short, it is the always-already-given world that is the 'horizon of horizons' for all our experiences, or the fundamental differentiating condition. Furthermore, this already-given unity not only makes the distinction between self and world possible, but also makes the distinction between self and other possible. Our primordial inherence in the world is thus an experience prior to the irreducible differences of self and object, self and other; in other words, this fundamental paradoxical experience, or what Merleau-Ponty also refers to as the paradoxical coincidence of 'man and the world,' is the condition which allows for these differences to emerge. It is, in the end, the primordial condition whereby 'transcendental subjectivity is intersubjectivity.'

Merleau-Ponty thus grapples with Husserl's problem of accounting for the other, and does so from the other side. The other is not to be explained in terms of an absolute *constituting* consciousness, but in terms of the already-*constituted* world. Consequently, Merleau-Ponty claims that 'the problem of the world, and, to begin with, that of one's own body, consists in the fact that it is all there.'[7] Analogously, the problem of the other is not a problem if we recognize that the self is always and already in the world, and that the self is the exterior (i.e., body) presented to others; similarly, the other is the exterior presented to us. And it is with the recognition of this coincidence of self and world, self and body, which Merleau-Ponty believes is the proper task of the phenomenological reduction (i.e., 'it reveals that world as strange and paradoxical'   the other, and that transcendental subjectivity really is intersubjectivity.

There is a problem with this, however, and it stems from Merleau-Ponty's claim that it is the same lived body which experiences itself as the paradoxical coincidence of self and world, self and other, interior and exterior. In other words, it is the identity of the body-subject which is the condition for differentiating between self and other, 'man and the world,' and thus the fundamental paradoxical experience is an experience of the same body-subject. Recall, for example, Merleau-Ponty's claim that the infinite synthesis which characterizes the paradox of perception – that is, an object is perceived as the infinite synthesis of possible perspectives, but is seen from only one perspective – is a synthesis effected by a subject.[9] Therefore, the fundamental differentiating condition is, as it was for Husserl, a fundamental identity – the identity of the body-subject.

It is precisely this last claim which results in difficulties for Merleau-Ponty's philosophy, and they are the same problems we saw in Husserl's. That is, if the fundamental differentiating condition is a fundamental identity, then the problem becomes one of accounting for difference without reducing it to identity; in particular, the problem is to account for the other as Other. In Merleau-Ponty's early work, this problem is unresolved; the other is indeed reduced to the identity of the body-subject: 'The other's body is a kind of replica of myself, a wandering double which haunts my surroundings more than it appears in them.'[10] But these difficulties were recognized by Merleau-Ponty, and, by the time of his work in *The Visible and the Invisible*, he claims that 'the problems that remain after this first description [i.e., *The Phenomenology of Perception*]: they are due to the fact that in part I retained the philosophy of "consciousness".'[11] In other words, because Merleau-Ponty understood, at the time of *The Phenomenology of Percep-*

tion, the fundamental differentiating condition to be the *identity* of the body-subject – that is, the identity of the self – he was subsequently unable to account for *difference*, for the Other. It is for this reason that Merleau-Ponty will stress, in his last writings, a fundamental difference that is the condition for identity. In short, Merleau-Ponty's notion of *écart* (French for separation, gap, difference) is an effort to understand identity in terms of a fundamental difference, an understanding that breaks with the tradition of accounting for difference on the basis of a fundamental identity.

Despite Merleau-Ponty's break with tradition, however, we argued that he, in the end, claims that difference is ultimately derivative of identity. For example, Merleau-Ponty does say, along Saussurean lines, that difference – for example, language as a system of differences, as diacritic – is the condition which makes identity possible – for example, identifiable significations and meanings. In the language of *The Visible and the Invisible*, Merleau-Ponty claims that 'wild' or 'vertical' Being harbours a fundamental difference and separation (i.e., *écart*), and that it is this difference which makes possible the distinctions of 'domesticated,' 'horizontal' Being – that is, perceiver–perceived, consciousness–object. However, Merleau-Ponty then claims that this is a fundamental difference of the 'same Being,' of the 'one sole Being.' There is thus a fundamental identity and unity within which difference is imprisoned, and subsequently the play of differences (e.g., language as diacritic; wild Being) which makes identification and identity possible is itself grounded in a more fundamental identity (e.g., language as a system or *structure*

a fundamental difference, it is a difference between two types of identity. In short, Merleau-Ponty confronts the ontological difference, the difference between Being and being. As a result, Merleau-Ponty claims there is *Being*, the 'one sole Being,' there are the *beings* of everyday perception (i.e., horizontal Being), and *between* the two there is a fundamental separation, a fundamental gap, or the 'third term' Merleau-Ponty calls 'écart.' But to understand difference as the difference *between* two identities, as the difference between Being and being, is nevertheless to understand difference as something derivative of identity. Difference, in the end, is reduced to identity. Consequently, if, as we are arguing, difference has been traditionally reduced to a fundamental identity, then Merleau-Ponty (as well as Heidegger) must be seen to be part of this tradition. Merleau-Ponty's break with tradition was not a clean break, nor did it last. There was a reconciliation.

It is precisely the clean break with this tradition, however, which is the self-acknowledged characterization of much of the work currently being done in Continental philosophy. This break is more commonly referred to as the 'critique of metaphysics,' and we find the writings of Foucault, Deleuze, Derrida, Kristeva, to name only a few, concerned largely with the critique, or 'deconstruction,' of traditional metaphysics. In particular, Deleuze has argued for a 'philosophy of difference,' for a philosophy that does not reduce difference to identity, but attempts to understand difference in itself. This, however, returns us to our initial question: How, on the one hand, are we to understand difference while, on the other, accounting for that which makes this difference possible? That is, what accounts for the correlation of differences, for the correlation wherein an irreducible difference nevertheless entails a fundamental relationship? In other words, how do we resolve the problem of difference? Husserl and Merleau-Ponty argued for a fundamental identity which accounted for this difference and correlation – that is, absolute consciousness, body-subject, or Being as the unity within which differences between consciousness and object, self and other, emerge. There was thus, as they saw it, a fundamental identity and link between consciousness and object (e.g., self-constituted nature of time-consciousness for Husserl), perceiver and perceived (e.g., paradox of body-subject in *The Phenomenology of Perception*, and paradox of Being in *The Visible and the Invisible*); and this is a link that could never be broken. What might appear to be a rupture of this link is simply, as Husserl and Merleau-Ponty would argue, a failure to understand the more fundamental identity and link which made the apparent rupture possible. The apparent inability to account for the other, for example, reflects the failure to see the fundamental unity and link between self and other (e.g., the failure to see that 'transcendental

the fundamental and primordial link brought in turn the need to account for that fundamental identity and unity which accounts for this link. The link implies this identity; and it was here that we began to see problems; that is, the problem of accounting for difference without reducing it to identity. With this in mind, therefore, our question now becomes: How can we account for the correlation of differences without basing this correlation on a fundamental identity? And another way of asking this question, and the way in which it is asked in *Citizen Kane*, is: How can we correlate differences without linking them, or, more specifically, how can we correlate the object 'rosebud' with what 'rosebud' means to Kane, when that which links the two, Kane, is dead?

4. *Citizen Kane*

The death of Charles Foster Kane is the event around which the rest of the film is to be understood. It is Kane's death, and, in particular, his dying word, 'rosebud,' which motivates the unfolding of the film's narrative. Furthermore, the death of Kane also entails, as did his dying word, two sides. On the one hand, Kane's death is a fundamentally private and personal event. This death is singularly related to Kane, and to Kane's body; therefore, not only is this death something we cannot have access to, but it is also, after the first scene of the film, something irretrievably past, something that has always already happened. Similarly, what Kane 'had in mind,' or what he meant by 'rosebud,' is also irretrievably lost. On the other hand, Kane's death is a very public event, a *newsworthy* event. As such, this event is impersonal, something unrelated to, and independent of, Kane himself – an event impartial to its public access. It is also an event that is always yet to come; that is, and as the impersonal 'voice of God' pronounces in the 'News on the March' clip, 'Death came to Kane, *as it must to all men.*'[12] Likewise, the sense of what Kane meant by 'rosebud' is also independent of Kane, and it is precisely this independence which leads the reporters to believe that they can, at some point in the future, discover this sense. In summary, then, Kane's dying word is an event with two incommensurable yet related sides – that is, death is both related and unrelated to Kane – and it is this incommensurability which best characterizes Deleuze's formulation of the notions 'event' and 'paradox.' In particular, Deleuze understands an 'event' as paradoxa, and thus it is to be identified neither with the private bodily event nor with the impersonal public event; rather, an event, as well as the sense of the word 'rosebud,' is to be understood in terms of the paradox which makes these identifications possible.

This paradox is precisely the paradoxical instance we discussed in chapter VIII. This paradoxical instance is for ever absent from its own place – that is, it is not present – and it infinitely divides the present into a past and a future. The event, in so far as it is always past and always yet to come, is thus an example of this instance, or an example of what the Stoics referred to as *Aion*. An event, however, is also something that occurs with respect to bodies, individuals, and states of affairs. Consequently, an event is something that is dated, given a 'present,' and the greater the event the more likely this 'present' will be both remembered and anticipated in holidays, anniversaries, and so on. That is, the past and present are understood with respect to a 'present,' and thus the event is also an example of what the Stoics referred to as 'Chronos.' The event is therefore something that is both 'present' and 'not present,' related and unrelated to individuals, bodies, and states of affairs; or, as Deleuze claims, there is a 'double structure of every event.'[13] The event is, in short, paradoxically both *Aion* and *Chronos*:

> With every event, there is indeed the present moment of its actualization, the moment in which the event is embodied in a state of affairs, an individual, or a person, the moment we designate by saying '*here*, the moment has come'. The future and the past of the event are only evaluated with respect to this definitive present [i.e., *Chronos*]. On the other hand, there is the future and the past of the event considered in itself, sidestepping each present, being free of the limitations of a state of affairs, impersonal and pre-individual, neutral [i.e., *Aion*].[14]

This paradox of the event is most especially true of death, which Deleuze calls a 'pure event.'[15] On the one hand, as an event, death is independent of its actualizations; it is impersonal, neutral, and awaits its actualizations – that is, it is always past, or prior to its actualizations – and we in turn wait for this event – that is, it is always yet to come. Death thus waits for us, is always already there, 'always to our left';[16] and we wait for its imminent arrival, for that event which is 'not-yet.'[17] On the other hand, and this is Deleuze's central point, death does not exist outside its actualization, does not pre-exist its occurrence. In other words, although death is an impersonal event which is independent of, and neutral to the individuals and bodies that 'die,' it is nevertheless the case that death exists only within this actualization; it 'inheres' or 'subsists' in this actualization. The paradox of death, therefore, is that it is both independent of, and dependent upon, the bodies that die.

This paradox, furthermore, brings us back to the problem with which this essay began: how can that which is independent of real subjects in time and space (i.e., ideal timeless truths or forms) nevertheless be dependent upon these subjects? Or, to put it another way, how can we accept the claim that ideal truths are timeless, independent, and objective, without accepting Platonic Realism – that is, Plato's claim, of which Husserl was critical, that these truths pre-exist their being known? In short, Deleuze is confronted with the problem of difference. We now see that Deleuze responds to this problem: the paradox of the event, for example, death, is such that death is independent, neutral, and timeless – that is, it is timeless if time is understood as *Chronos*, as the flow of 'present' moments; and yet death is nevertheless dependent upon its actualization in the 'present' of some body or individual. Death does not pre-exist this actualization. Deleuze thus brings in paradox, just as Husserl and Merleau-Ponty did, to confront the same problems we have continued to encounter. In fact, Deleuze claims that the problem of accounting for that which transcends our actual, real lives – that is, the transcendence of ideal timeless truths, such as the independence of death from its actualization – and how it is in turn necessarily related to this life, has been the characteristic trait of philosophy since Plato. As Deleuze puts it: 'The philosopher has returned from the dead and goes back there. This has been the living formulation of philosophy since Plato.'[18] In other words, the philosopher attempts to actualize a knowledge and insight into timeless, eternal truths, truths that are independent of one's actual life. If successful, the philosopher thus returns from the dead, from the realm of independent timeless truths (i.e., returns from death as *independent* of actual bodies), and brings these truths to life; however, an actual living philosopher eventually returns to the dead when the event that is always yet to come does come, when it is actualized in the body of the ageing thinker (i.e., death as *dependent* upon actual bodies).

This characterization of philosophy also aptly describes the reporters' search for 'rosebud' in *Citizen Kane*. On the one hand, the reporters hope to understand Kane's dying word; that is, they seek to determine what Kane had in mind when he died, or what he meant. Since Kane is dead, however, they are ultimately attempting to retrieve that which is beyond life, or that which is independent of the actual lives of bodies (i.e., death). In other words, they are trying to 'return from the dead' the meaning of Kane's dying act. On the other hand, since Kane is dead, the reporters are forced to discover the sense of 'rosebud' by asking those who are actually alive what they might know about it. The reporters are thus confronted with the problem of relating that which is independent of life (i.e., the meaning of Kane's dying act) to that which is dependent on life (i.e., the recollections of Kane's surviving acquaintances). In essence, the reporters encounter the same problem which Deleuze claims has characterized philosophy since Plato – namely, what we have called the 'problem of difference.'

At the core of this relationship which philosophy attempts to account for is a fundamental paradox. As a result, this relationship is not, as it was for Husserl and Merleau-Ponty, grounded upon a fundamental coincidence and identity; rather, it is a fundamental difference and disjunction which lies behind this relation. As Deleuze puts it, the paradox, and thus the event, is 'a relation of very precise incommensurability, not an absence of relation.'[19] In other words, there is not a primordial link or identity which makes of the relation between consciousness and object, self and other, *Aion* and *Chronos*, a relationship of harmony which precedes the disruptions and disharmony that results with difference – for example, Merleau-Ponty's 'peaceful coexistence in the world of childhood' prior to the 'struggle between consciousnesses' that begins with the *differentiation* of cogitos.[20] Deleuze claims, to the contrary, that there is, from the start, difference and incommensurability, and that the differentiation *between* self and other, consciousness and object, *Chronos* and *Aion* is in turn made possible by a difference that is not derivative of identity – that is, not a difference *between* or of an already-identified entity. There is, rather, a difference that for ever eludes this identity and continually subverts it, and yet it is this fundamental difference or paradox which makes the identifications and differentiations of thought possible; that is, it makes possible the distinction between consciousness and the objects this consciousness is always a *consciousness of*. It is thus the fundamental difference presupposed in the phenomenological theory of intentionality. Consequently, Deleuze claims that the fundamental condition of consciousness and thought – that is, difference and paradox – is not the same as that which is conditioned – that is, the identity of the objects of consciousness. In short, Deleuze does not accept the claim that the transcendental condition is the same as that which is conditioned – that is, the same in that they are both *identifiable*. He disagrees with the claim, for example, that the transcendental pure ego, or the body-subject, is the identifiable condition for the conditioned experience of identifiable objects in the natural standpoint. Now to further clarify Deleuze's position on this matter, we turn to the example of language, and to Deleuze's claim that 'pure events [i.e., paradoxes] ground language.'[21]

Husserl used, as we saw, the linguistic model to show how an ideal object could nevertheless be dependent upon real actual sounds; hence, the linguistic model was brought in to avoid Platonic Realism. However, Husserl ultimately claimed that the 'sense' (i.e., interpretative sense) is the identifiable link between an expressing act and the meaning being expressed, a meaning that is independent (i.e., transcendent) and could be understood by others. Deleuze, on the other hand, although he recognizes both that the sense of an expression 'does not merge at all with the proposition, for it has an object-ivity (*objectité*) which is quite distinct,' and that this sense nevertheless 'does not exist outside the proposition,'[22] does not claim that sense is the identifiable link *between* these propositions and ideal objects. He claims, rather, that the sense itself has a double structure, that it harbours a fundamental difference which makes possible the distinction *between* propositions and things. In other words, Deleuze understands sense as paradoxa, or as what Foucault has called a 'meaning-event.'[23] As Deleuze puts it: 'The most general operation of sense is this: it brings that which expresses it into existence; and from that point on, as pure inherence, it brings itself to exist within that which expresses it. It rests therefore with the *Aion*, as the milieu of surface effects or events, to trace a frontier between things and propositions.'[24]

The sense is always already past, or is what is prior to and makes possible expression – it makes of an act a meaningful act; and the sense is always yet to come, is that which an expression intends or hopes to convey. The sense is thus always past and future, or, as Deleuze puts it, 'it rests therefore with the *Aion*.' At the same time, the sense, as Deleuze also makes clear, does not exist prior to or outside of its expression, and thus he claims that 'we cannot say that sense exists, but rather that it inheres or subsists.'[25] In short, sense is to be understood as an event and, as with death, is independent of its actualization, and yet dependent upon this actualization. As meaning-event, therefore, sense is to be identified neither with a pure and independent object, with an ideal object that transcends its actualization; nor solely with the expression, with its actualization. As meaning-event, sense is to be understood as paradoxa, or as the 'frontier' and differentiating condition which makes these identifications possible.

Sense has not been widely recognized as a meaning-event, or as paradoxa, and, as Foucault has argued in his essay on Deleuze, this failure has led to two contrasting interpretations. On the one hand, Sartre places 'the event before or to the side of meaning.' There is the rock of facticity, the mute inertia of occurrences, and the experience of nausea; and it is this event which is 'then submitted to the active process of meaning, to its digging and elaboration.'[26] On the other hand, Merleau-Ponty places meaning before the event, 'a domain of primal significations where the event might occur and its possible form.'[27] Either the event is before memory or memory is before the event – either Sartre or Merleau-Ponty. Similarly, the failure to understand the perceptual noema as paradoxa led to two contrasting interpretations: either the perceptual noema is on the side of the subject as a concept, or it is on the side of the object as a percept – either Føllesdal or Gurwitsch. And the failure to understand the flesh as paradoxa also led to this dichotomy: either the flesh is on the side of subjectivity as immanence, or the flesh is on the side of the world as transcendence – either Lefort or Dillon. But as meaning-event, as paradoxa, sense is not to be placed within this dichotomy; rather, Deleuze claims that 'sense is both the expressible or the expressed of the proposition [i.e., concept, subjective], and the attribute of the state of affairs [i.e., percept, objective].'[28] But this is not to be understood in terms of being identifiably both, for the very dichotomy between percept and concept, subject and object, things and propositions, is made possible by sense as paradoxa, as differentiating condition; or, finally, as meaning-event. In other words, sense is to be understood as the boundary which makes these contrasting *identifications* possible, and hence the either/or. Deleuze is straightforward on this point: 'Things and propositions are less in a situation of radical duality' and more on the two sides of a frontier represented by sense.'[29]

A consequence of this double structure of sense, of sense understood as meaning-event, is that there is generated an infinite regress. As the boundary or frontier between things and propositions, the sense is not to be identified with either side; consequently, the sense neither is the expression or proposition itself, nor is the object or state of affairs referred to by this proposition. As a result, to refer to the sense of a proposition, one will need a new name or proposition, but the sense of this proposition will itself be neither the proposition nor the object (i.e., the original sense that is the reference of this new name); and thus to refer to this sense will require another proposition, and so on *ad infinitum*. In other words, Deleuze accepts the regress that is generated because sense coincides neither with propositions nor with objects. This regress results, in addition, in an infinite proliferation of sense, or, as Deleuze puts it, there is 'the name which denotes something and the name which denotes the sense of this name. The two-term regress is the minimal condition of indefinite proliferation.'[30] And this indefinite proliferation, or sense being infinitely referred to, is itself made possible, as we have been arguing, by the paradoxical nature of sense – that is, by sense understood as paradoxa. It is as a consequence of sense as paradoxa, as meaning-event, that there emerges the possibility for the sense of a proposition to be the object (referent) of another proposition – that is, it allows for the possibility of relating propositions to objects, and it is here that we see the reason for Deleuze's claim that sense establishes 'a relation of very precise incommensurability.' That is, as paradoxa, sense makes possible the relation between propositions and things, but sense itself is *incommensurable* with both propositions and things. Sense never coincides with propositions or things, and it is this incommensurability which is the reason for the regress, for the regress of sense being indefinitely named or referred to by that which also has a sense, a sense that can also be referred to; and so on. Ronald Bogue is therefore correct to conclude that, for Deleuze, 'meaning is a simulacrum, a paradoxical, contradictory entity that defies common sense. It is always expressed in language, but it can only be designated by initiating a process of infinite regression.'[31]

A further consequence of this theory, of stating that there is a fundamental incommensurability, paradox, and non-coincidence which is the condition for language and thought, is that Deleuze will no longer be concerned with the problem of transcendence. In particular, Deleuze will no longer attempt to account for that which is immanent being coincident with that which is transcendent, or, as was Husserl's project, of accounting for the coincidence of meaning-giving acts with self-given objects. This fundamental incommensurability for ever subverts such attempts, and ultimately these efforts fail to account for difference. But by arguing for a fundamental difference and paradox, for example, *Aion*, Deleuze claims that it is this which makes the relationship *between* two different identities possible; however, it also entails the impossibility of bringing them into coincidence. It is therefore impossible to reduce difference to identity. Consequently, Deleuze recognizes and accepts the impossibility of perfect coincidence, of totalized knowledge, and argues that all knowledge is only and necessarily partial. We can only have a partial coincidence, a perspectival bias, not because we are intrinsically unable to recognize the complete and total picture (i.e., some pure model, identity, or form), but because our thoughts, knowledge, and words are for ever conditioned by that which is fundamentally different, by that which cannot be reduced to identity. In the end, therefore, we see Deleuze wholeheartedly endorsing Nietzsche's perspectivism: there is not a fundamental identity (i.e., model) of which there are different perspectives (i.e., copies); there are only different perspectives, and a fundamental difference and paradox which continually subverts attempts to totalize these perspectives – that is, to 'herd' these perspectives.

We find these same consequences paralleled in *Citizen Kane*. After the very first scene of the film, Kane is dead; consequently, the reporters will never be able to ask Kane what he meant by 'rosebud.' They will not be able to bring what Kane subjectively meant at the time of his death into coincidence with an object or state of affairs in the world. This link is for-ever broken. However, Deleuze would claim, as we have seen, that there never is such an identifiable link. There is an incommensurable relation-ship between sense and propositions/things, a relationship that pre-vents such an identifiable link and results, instead, in an infinite regress. Similarly, Kane's break with his childhood, for example, the sled, moti-vates Kane's indefinite accumulation of artefacts: 'a collection too vast to count.' There is a fundamental difference and incommensurability, a broken link, which cannot be overcome. Note, for example, that Kane's attempt to go to a warehouse where some of his things are kept – that is, the sled – is diverted when he meets Susan Alexander. She subverts his 'sentimental journey.' This difference and broken link also prevents the reporters from attaining a complete and total knowledge of Kane. The reason is that one object, a sled, cannot tell us about the whole of Kane's life, nor can the events of Kane's life be reduced to a single concept, 'rosebud.' There is a fundamental difference and incommensurable rela-tionship between sense and propositions (e.g., 'rosebud') and things (e.g., the sled); and it is the effort to name or denote this sense, as is the reporters' quest, that results in an infinite regress, a regress which pre-vents a totalized and complete knowledge. Each interview leads the reporter to interview another, and this interviewee directs him to yet another, and so on *ad infinitum*. The same is also true of Kane himself. Kane is firmly installed in *Aion* in that he is for ever trying to bring back what is already past (his 'sentimental journey'), and he is attempting to do this by continually expanding his collection of art, wives, newspaper chains, and so on. The incommensurability of this relationship – that is, the paradox of *Aion* – results in an infinite and non-totalizable regress. Each artwork leads Kane to buy another, and then another, and so on *ad infinitum*. Near the end of the film, for example, when the ageing Kane walks through a hallway with mirrors on both sides, there results an infinite proliferation of Kanes. We are therefore left with only a partial knowledge of the events and objects that were part of Kane's life, and we are left with only a partial knowledge of Kane himself.

The style and structure of the film itself further elaborates these conse-quences. We are given only partial perspectives of objects – note the use of extreme high- and low-angle shots as a means of making the perspec-tive of the camera felt – and, through the memories of Kane's surviving acquaintances, we are given only a partial perspective upon Kane's life. Even the camera's privileged perspective – note the camera's close-up, in the final scene, of the sled; a shot to which only the camera, and hence the viewers of the film, had access to – is only a partial, non-totalizable perspective. The reason is that the camera is always presenting events that have already happened, and it is presenting them within the context of anticipating the future, of anticipating a more complete knowledge of Kane's life, a knowledge that finding what 'rosebud' means will facilitate. The only event of the film which does show Kane in the present is Kane's death, yet it is, as we have seen, the event which is the paradoxical condition of the film. It is also the condition, because it is paradoxical, which prevents our attaining complete knowledge about Kane; that is, it prevents our reducing Kane to either an identifiable object (thus the final close-up of the sled still does not complete the picture, or puzzle, of Kane's life) or an identifiable concept. In other words, the film, even in the case of Kane's death, is continually showing that which cannot be 'present'-ed, that which is already past and always yet to come. Put another way, *Citizen Kane* exemplifies what Deleuze means by the term *Aion*, and it is for this reason, finally, that Deleuze calls *Citizen Kane* 'the first great film of a cinema of time.'[32]

We could continue, naturally. We have just touched the surface of Deleuze's work. We have not discussed his political theory, his critique of Freud and resulting theory of schizoanalysis, or many other crucial aspects of his thought. The same could be said of our work on Merleau-Ponty. We left much of his political theory untouched; we did not go into great detail about his theories of time, space, and freedom; and we did not fully explicate the detailed and involved relationship of his thought to structuralism. And the same is most especially true of our work on Husserl. We focused almost exclusively on his early works, from *Logical Investigations* up to *Ideas*, and left virtually undiscussed Husserl's last great work, *The Crisis of European Sciences and Transcendental Phenomenology*. All this could have been brought in to further clarify the central arguments of this essay. This work is therefore an admittedly partial work, and presents only a partial perspective upon the themes that were our concern. However, as should be clear, we do not consider it a fault that this is only a partial perspective – it is necessarily so. My hope is that this work, despite its partial status and perspective (i.e., its partiality), will nevertheless help others to see the work of Husserl and Merleau-Ponty in a different light. It is also my hope that this work has demonstrated the possibility of many dialogues, dialogues that will be a source of much future work. In particular, we have begun a dialogue between phenomenology and poststructuralism, Frege and Husserl,

Merleau-Ponty and Husserl, philosophy and cinema; yet we could continue with dialogues between Merleau-Ponty and Heidegger, Deleuze and Derrida, Deleuze and Foucault, poststructuralism and Rorty; and so on *ad infinitum*.

Notes

Introduction: The Problem of Difference

1 In particular, Heidegger's late essay 'The End of Philosophy and the Task of Thinking,' in *Basic Writings*, 369–92.
2 Michel Foucault, *The Archaeology of Knowledge*, 203.
3 Ibid.
4 Jacques Derrida, '*Différance*,' in *Speech and Phenomena*, 159.
5 This plays off the two senses of the French word *différer* – to differ and to defer – and makes note of this difference by replacing the second 'e' of the French word for difference – *différence* – with an 'a.'
6 Jürgen Habermas, in *The Philosophical Discourse of Modernity*, trans. Frederick G. Lawrence (Cambridge, MA: MIT Press 1990), 182, claims that 'Derrida stands closer to the anarchist wish to explode the continuum of history than to the authoritarian admonition to bend before destiny.'
7 Ibid., 166. A citation from Derrida's *Of Grammatology*, 19.
8 Habermas, *The Philosophical Discourse of Modernity*, 260.
9 Ibid., 261.
10 Ibid., 256.
11 Ibid., 274.
12 Ibid., 166.
13 Maurice Merleau-Ponty, 'Dialogue and the Perception of Others,' in *Sense and Non-Sense*, 134.
14 Gilles Deleuze, *Différence et répétition*, 293. Deleuze is speaking here of paradox, but, as will be brought out in this work, we take paradox as the fundamental differentiating condition, or as that which supplies the distinctions with which philosophy works, and thus paradox in this sense is another way of referring to the problem of difference.

Chapter I: The Linguistic and Perceptual Models

1 Edmund Husserl, *Logical Investigations*, 149.
2 Ibid., 151. Husserl argues that 'truth and being are "categories" in the same sense, and plainly correlative: truth cannot be relativized, while the objectivity of being is maintained. The relativization of truth presupposes the objective being of the point to which things are relative: this is the contradiction in relativism.'
3 I introduce scare quotes here as a precursor to my discussion of Husserl's use of them in the next chapter; however, it should be clear from what has been said so far that the use of scare quotes is to indicate a modification of meaning; that is, it sets apart the 'reality' which is the ideal condition for what is ordinarily understood by reality (i.e., the real natural world).
4 Husserl, *Logical Investigations*, 61.
5 Ibid., 98.
6 Ibid., 864.
7 Husserl refers here to logical laws; it will become clear why below.
8 Husserl, *Logical Investigations*, 99.
9 Ibid., 864: regarding the presenting contents, Husserl claims that 'we do not perceive these contents.'
10 Ibid., 104.
11 See Edmund Husserl, *Ideas*, § 22, 'The Reproach of Platonic Realism. Essence and Concept.'
12 In other words, Husserl encounters the problem of difference. Furthermore, this is a problem which analytic philosophy has dealt with during the early part of this century. Russell, the early Wittgenstein, and Carnap claimed an independence of logic from psychological and physical objects. See Carnap's *The Logical Structure of the World*, 177, where he argues for the 'independence of logical objects from psychological and physical objects.' This allows for a methodological advantage in terms of analysing psychological and physical objects; however, the problem is to relate the rules of this independent logic to the actions of actual subjects (cf. chapter VI of this volume on the paradox of rule-following, where we discuss this problem in more detail). This is not, however, a problem that went unnoticed either in Husserl's case or in the analytic tradition. In fact, Husserl and Carnap confront this problem by posing a theory of constitution (for Carnap: 'construction'); and the later Wittgenstein, as Kripke has argued, can also be seen as responding to this problem. These issues are discussed in more detail below, but let it be noted now that this is not a difficulty found only in Husserl's phenomenology.

13 Husserl, *Logical Investigations*, 250.

14 Ibid., 584.

15 Ibid., 280.

16 For Husserl our thoughts are 'inauthentic' until their sense is adequately fulfilled; consequently, there is an important sense in which thinking to oneself
entails meaning-intentions which require fulfilment, and thus one's own
thoughts are not always, nor even usually, as Husserl would probably say,
adequately thought.

17 There is on this point a similarity with Grice. Grice, too, claims that meaning
is dependent upon a correlation between an intention to be understood
through a given utterance (i.e., speaker's intention) and the hearer's recognizing this intention on the basis of the utterance and thus coming to understand the meaning (i.e., in Husserlian terminology: a meaning-fulfilment of a
meaning-intention). See Grice's essay 'Meaning.' However, unlike Grice, for
Husserl meaning is neither (1) limited to the physical manifestations of an
intention (i.e., meaning extends beyond linguistic expression to entail all
acts) nor (2) limited to cases of successful fulfilment of an intention; for
example, I can see a person approaching from afar and take it to be a friend,
but when the person gets closer I see that it is not my friend; however, my
original perception of the person as my friend is not without meaning, it is
simply that the intention of this meaning was not fulfilled. The essence of
perception for Husserl is that it is by its nature inadequately fulfilled; an
object is always open to further inspection, but it is not, for all that, meaningless. More on this below, in the next section.

18 Husserl, *Logical Investigations*, 257.

19 Husserl makes this distinction in ibid., 577, n. 2.

20 Ibid., 290.

21 There emerges here an ambiguity in the use of the term 'matter' that is worth
pointing out. There is a temptation to understand 'matter' to be the physical
matter which is animated by a meaning-intention. This temptation follows
from the linguistic model, where the physical sound is the matter which is
animated by a meaning-intention. Husserl even adopts this model with
respect to perception when he claims that sensations (e.g., perceptual sensations of colour, pain, feelings) are not acts but the matter which is taken up
by an act and given an objectifying interpretation through it (*Logical Investigations*, 572–3). To avoid confusion here, Husserl calls this matter 'stuff'
(*Stoff*) and distinguishes it from matter as that which determines the directedness of an act.

22 Ibid., 589.

23 This quote, and the two preceding, are found in ibid., 589.

24 Ibid.
25 Ibid. Husserl goes on to say, on this same page, that 'the matter ... is that peculiar side of an act's phenomenological content that not only determines *that* it grasps an object but also as *what* it grasps it.'
26 Ibid.
27 Izchak Miller develops this theme along Fregean lines in his book *Husserl, Perception, and Temporal Awareness*. He claims that the fulfilment of conditions as set down by the matter of an act can be understood as 'semantic entailment.'
28 Husserl, *Logistical Investigations*, 330.
29 Ibid., 788–9.
30 Ibid., 789.
31 Ibid., 714.
32 Ibid.
33 Although this theme is not stated explicitly in *Logical Investigations*, it is a theme which runs implicitly throughout Husserl's theory of perception. It is only after Husserl has developed his understanding of the transcendental ego as undergoing a universal genesis in time-consciousness (a theme discussed in chapter II) that this theme becomes explicit. For example, in *Cartesian Meditations*, 79, Husserl claims: 'It is owing to an essentially necessary genesis that I, the ego, can experience a physical thing and do so even at first glance. This is true, moreover, not only as regards phenomenological genesis but also as regards genesis in the usual sense, psychological genesis. With good reason it is said that in infancy *we had to learn to see physical things*, and that such modes of consciousness of them had to precede all others genetically.' We will see that this theme is also of central importance to Merleau-Ponty.
34 Husserl, *Logical Investigations*, 309.
35 Ibid., 559.
36 Ibid., 310.
37 Ibid.
38 Robert Sokolowski, in his book *The Formation of Husserl's Concept of Constitution*, and John Brough, in his article 'The Emergence of an Absolute Consciousness in Husserl's Early Writings on Time-Consciousness,' show Husserl moving away from the schematic interpretation of conscious activity as he developed his theory of temporal self-constitution. In the next chapter we hope to show that this latter theory remains true to the linguistic model.
39 Husserl, *Logical Investigations*, 559.
40 Ibid., 776.
41 Ibid., 310.

42 Ibid., 290. This is also a further example of Husserl's emphasizing the matter or content of perception as the immanent form and content of this act.

43 Ibid., 594.

44 Ibid., 853.

45 Aron Gurwitsch's interpretation/criticism of Husserl was in large part motivated by what he felt to be Husserl's failure to recognize this structured aspect of sensations (cf. chapter II).

46 Husserl, *Logical Investigations*, 683.

47 Ibid., 684.

48 Ibid., 685.

49 Ibid., pp. 717–18.

50 Ibid., pp. 658–9.

51 Ibid., pp. 553–6. In particular, Husserl quotes Brentano's *Psychologie*, 111.

52 Brough, 'The Emergence of an Absolute Consciousness in Husserl's Early Writings on Time-Consciousness,' 93.

53 Husserl, *Ideas*, 321, n. 27.

54 Husserl, *Logical Investigations*, 717–18, and 563.

55 Ibid., 501; emphasis added.

56 Ibid. Husserl adds that 'if the verbal resources of language are to be a faithful mirror of all meanings possible *a priori*, then language must have grammatical forms at its disposal which give distinct expression, i.e., sensibly distinct symbolization.'

57 Ibid., 304.

58 Hubert Dreyfus, ed., *Husserl, Intentionality, and Cognitive Science*, 105.

59 In the next chapter we will examine the work of Gurwitsch more closely. We want first to discuss the possible motivations for Husserl's move to noematic analysis. It is our hope to show that ambiguities arise in interpreting Husserl, especially his view of the 'perceptual noema,' largely because the noema is interpreted as a continuation of the perspective Husserl maintained in *Logical Investigations* (i.e., the linguistic model), and do not clarify Husserl's own attempts to resolve difficulties he himself saw in his earlier work, an attempt which motivated the turn to noematic analysis.

60 For example, Dagfinn Føllesdal, Izchak Miller, David Smith, and Ronald McIntyre all interpret Husserl along these lines.

61 Gottlob Frege, *The Collected Writings of Gottlob Frege*, 60.

62 Ibid., 61. Although we are comparing Husserl's and Frege's theory of sense, we need to point out an important difference to avoid confusion. On the one hand, Frege focuses his attention upon sense as it is expressed within linguistic, expressive, or designating acts, and he does not generalize his analysis of sense in this regard to extend beyond these acts. On the other hand, Husserl

does understand sense as the sense of acts generally, as the sense of all acts, including linguistic acts; however, despite this difference, their theory of sense is, in the end, fundamentally the same.

63 Saul Kripke, *Naming and Necessity*, 59.

64 Izchak Miller, in *Husserl, Perception, and Temporal Awareness*, interprets Husserl along classically Fregean lines, where it is through a set of attributes (i.e., set of descriptions) that a sense determines its reference: 'The classical, Fregean sense in which a singular meaning is said to determine a reference for a singular term is this: the reference of a singular term is the unique object, if any, which satisfies the attributive content of the singular meaning expressed by that term ... I now extend the notion of "attributive determination" (after Keith Donnellan) to mental acts and their meanings': 65.

65 In referring to Hume, Husserl claims that the meaning of a certain property cannot be made through an association of ideas, as in a resemblance of impressions, for the resulting ideas would in turn be meaningful only if they, too, had been interpreted on the basis of an association of ideas, and so on. For example, Husserl claims: 'if ever we perceive something as white, and if we only present to ourselves a "resemblance" between the apparent object and other objects, then such a man has involved himself in an *infinite regress*, since talk of this presented resemblance calls for a corresponding reinterpretation': *Logical Investigations*, 398.

66 Ibid., 782–4.

67 We can clarify even further the Kripkean line of criticism in light of our discussion of the infinite proliferation which follows upon the regress inherent in the theory of sense that Frege and Husserl are setting forth. This infinite proliferation of sense makes fixing the reference an insurmountable task which, claims Kripke, has resulted in a false dilemma: either there is an object behind the bundle of qualities which fixes the reference, or the object is nothing but the bundle. Kripke also goes on to be critical of attempts to surmount the infinite proliferation of sense (i.e., descriptions) on the basis of arguing for certain essential descriptive features which can fix the reference despite the infinite proliferation of non-essential descriptive features: *Naming and Necessity, passim*.

68 Rudolph Carnap, *Meaning and Necessity*, 129–30.

69 In *Logique du sens*, Gilles Deleuze argues that this theory of sense, as well as the regress (what he calls the 'paradox of regress'), can be traced back to the Stoics, and that the paradoxical consequences of this theory had been recognized since then as well (he notes Nicolas D'Autrecourt as an example). For a discussion of the Stoic theory of sense, see Benson Mates's *Stoic Logic*, in particular, ch. 2, 'Signs, Sense, and Denotation.' Mates claims, for example, that

the Greek term 'lekton' (λεκτον) coincides with that which is revealed by the sound yet is independent of this sound, and it is the object that is meant while not being the actual object. Mates claims 'lekton' 'may be translated literally as "that which is meant"' (p. 11). Mates's use of scare quotes is analogous to Husserl's use of them, and he uses them for the same reasons as well. More on this in the next chapter.

70 Deleuze, *Logic of Sense*, 28.

71 Derrida's interpretation of Husserl develops this notion of return-questioning (*Rückfrage*). Derrida claims, in *Edmund Husserl's 'Origin of Geometry': An Introduction*, analogous to our claim that the paradox of sense results in an infinite proliferation of sense, that the origins towards which the investigations are returning are indefinitely deferred. This follows, as we have shown above, from the fact that sense always differs from the object. Both these notions of deferring and differing eventually take shape in Derrida's neologism – *Différance*.

72 Husserl, *Logical Investigations*, 700.

73 Ibid., 776.

74 Jacques Taminiaux, 'Heidegger and Husserl's *Logical Investigations*: In Remembrance of Heidegger's Last Seminar,' in *Dialectic and Difference*, 102.

75 Ibid., 103.

76 Husserl, *Logical Investigations*, 717–19.

77 Ibid., 670.

78 Ibid., 781.

79 Ibid., 783.

80 Ibid., 780.

81 Taminiaux, 'Heidegger and Husserl's *Logical Investigations*,' 108.

82 Husserl, *Logical Investigations*, 695. Even in cases where we might not recall the name of an object, this object is nevertheless immediately recognized. For example, one might perceive an object as a certain type of object (Husserl gives an example of a tool [ibid.]) but not recall the name of this object; however, it is, Husserl argues, on the basis of this recognition that one is able to recall the name. In other words, naming presupposes recognition, whereas recognition does not presuppose naming. This also alludes to the theme mentioned earlier of having to learn to see, or recognize, an object.

83 Ibid., 685.

84 Ibid., 695.

85 Ibid.

86 Ibid., 696.

87 Paul Ricoeur, *Husserl: An Analysis of His Phenomenology*, 41.

88 Husserl, *Logical Investigations*, 696.

89 Ibid.
90 As mentioned earlier, rather than a relational identification presupposing the experienced unity of naming, the naming presupposes the *a priori* possibility of a relational identification of any object in general.
91 Husserl, *Logical Investigations*, 697.
92 Ibid., 765.
93 It is to be pointed out here that the perceptual model was initially used to explain how an object could fulfil a number of different acts; thus the perceptual model's whole approach is one that presupposes the identity of an object.
94 Husserl, *Logical Investigations*, 785 (emphasis added).
95 I bring in the term 'constitutes' here to foreshadow Husserl's important theme of constitution, which will become central in his work following *Logical Investigations*. Yet at this stage the 'structuring' role of categorial intuition is analogous to the 'constituting' role of consciousness as Husserl later develops it.
96 Edmund Husserl, *The Phenomenology of Internal Time-Consciousness*, 106.
97 Ibid., 15.

Chapter II: The Perceptual Noema

1 Husserl will expand this distinction, which we discuss below, to entail a difference between thinking and seeing; that is, between thinking about something, or thinking that something is the case (i.e., signitively intending that a certain state of affairs is the case), and actually seeing that something is the case (i.e., being intuitively presented with a certain state of affairs). In both cases, the same matter, the same state of affairs, can be taken up by these acts, but there is a fundamental difference in these acts themselves. In other words, Husserl is maintaining the distinction between the intention of something and the fulfilment of this intention, a relation which we discussed in detail in chapter I. We can also see a further similarity between Husserl and Frege. Frege also maintains a distinction between merely thinking or intending a certain state of affairs, and the fulfilment of this intention, that is, whether or not this state of affairs obtains (what Frege calls its 'truth-value'). In 'Sense and Reference,' Frege claims that thought is not enough, that he is concerned with the truth-value; however, the same state of affairs can be directed to in the sense of seeing its truth-value, or be merely thought of. This is the case in artworks where Frege claims 'we are interested only in the sense of the sentences and the images and feelings thereby aroused. The question of truth would cause us to abandon aesthetic delight for an attitude

of scientific investigation ... It is the striving for truth that drives us always from the sense to the reference': 63.

2 Edmund Hasserl, *Logical Investigations*, 742.

3 For example, Husserl claims that Kant failed to recognize this difference. He argues that Kant 'fails to appreciate the deep difference between intuition and signification, their possible separation and their usual commixture': ibid., 833. In other words, Husserl believes that Kant failed to treat the pre-logical objectivation, the *object-ivation* of intuition which signification merely intends and expresses within language and concepts (i.e., Logos). As a result, Kant 'fails to distinguish between concepts, as the universal meaning of words, and concepts as a species of authentic universal presentation': ibid.

4 On this see especially sections 19 and 20 of the First Investigation. Husserl argues that a symbol emerges through intuition, that a symbol is originally meaningful and expressive of this intuition; however, he claims that the symbol becomes part of a system of rules, much as chessmen (an analogy Husserl uses here) are part of a system of rules and acquire a 'games-meaning' in addition to their original intuitive sense (e.g., intuitive presentation of chessmen as pieces of ivory with a certain shape). In arithmetic, for example, the 'arithmetical signs have, besides their original meaning, their so-to-say *games-meaning*, a meaning oriented towards the game of calculation and its well-known rules' (*Logical Investigations*, 305). It is in this sense that symbols are mixtures of signitive and intuitive acts: on the one hand, the symbol is originally intuitive and is expressive of an intuitive presentation; on the other hand, the symbol becomes part of a larger signitive intention, the intention to calculate, or, by analogy, to checkmate the opponent, and so on.

5 This is perhaps the clearest thread which runs throughout Husserl's entire work. For example, in the introduction to *Logical Investigations*, Husserl states that 'we shall proceed as follows: we shall start from the almost universally accepted contemporary treatment of logic as a technology, and shall pin down its sense and its justification ... The outcome of our investigation of this point will be the delineation of a new, purely theoretical science, the all-important foundation for any technology of scientific knowledge, and its having the character of an a priori, purely demonstrative [i.e., intuitive] science' (pp. 56–7). And, in Husserl's 'Origin of Geometry,' written near the end of his life, he continues to distinguish between intuitive givenness and signitive reference or intention, and claims that, 'in every individual life from childhood up to maturity, the originally intuitive life which creates its originally self-evident structures through activities on the basis of sense-experience very quickly and in increasing measure falls victim to the seduc-

tion of language ... [that is] ... life lapses into a kind of talking and reading that is dominated purely by association' (p. 362).

6 Quoted by Føllesdal in his article 'Husserl's Notion of Noema,' 79. Husserl's manuscript 'Sinn und Noema,' from which the quote was taken, may be found in *Analysen Zur Passiven Synthesis* (The Hague: Martinus Nijhoff 1966), 304–35, and was written in 1920. This particular quote is from page 330.

7 Husserl, 'Sinn und Noema,' 332.

8 There are important differences, however, which Husserl clarifies in *Ideas I*, section 111. Husserl states that fancy is a neutrality-modification of 'remembering in the widest conceivable sense of the term' (p. 285). That is, although recollection posits an object 'as if' it were a present existent, imagination posits an object 'as if' it were present, but does not posit it as existent. Imagination is therefore neutral with respect to the existence of that which is before an imaginative consciousness of something presentified, and this is the sense in which it is a neutralization of recollective presentification.

9 Edmund Husserl, *The Phenomenology of Internal Time-Consciousness*, 50.

10 Ibid.

11 Ibid., 62 (emphasis added).

12 Ibid.

13 Ibid., 101.

14 In Appendix VI, Husserl claims that these immanent objects (i.e., appearances) can be phenomenologically reduced to this absolute consciousness, and that 'the consciousness in which all this is reduced, I cannot myself again perceive, however. For this new perceived entity would again be something temporal which referred back to a constitutive consciousness of just such a kind, and so on, *ad infinitum*': ibid., 150).

15 Ibid.

16 John Brough, 'The Emergence of an Absolute Consciousness in Husserl's Early Writings on Time-Consciousness,' 93.

17 Husserl, *The Phenomenology of Internal Time-Consciousness*, 98.

18 Ibid., 100.

19 Ibid., 152.

20 Ibid., pp. 146–7.

21 Ibid., 147.

22 Ibid., 147.

23 Ibid., 163.

24 For Husserl's discussion of this, see section 39. In this section, Churchill translates the terms as 'tranverse-intentionality' and 'longitudinal-intentionality.' I discuss these in terms of vertical and horizontal intentionality in order to later relate these notions to Merleau-Ponty's use of these terms, in

particular, his use of the term 'vertical Being.' John Brough, however, also
discusses these types of intentionality in the same way, and he goes on to say
that horizontal intentionality is such 'insofar as this intentionality extends
throughout or along the flow itself ... in distinction from the flows vertical
intentionality directed towards the immanent temporal object': 'The Emergence of an Absolute Consciousness in Husserl's Early Writings on Time-
Consciousness,' 96.

25 Husserl, *The Phenomenology of Internal Time-Consciousness*, 106.

26 Ibid. We also quoted this passage at the end of chapter I, when we argued
that this would ultimately be Husserl's solution to the regress we found in
Logical Investigations.

27 Ibid., 159–60.

28 Ibid., 109.

29 Ibid., 154. Husserl continues to recognize this paradoxical consequence in
Cartesian Meditations. There, too, he claims that immanent temporality is a
correlate of the consciousness of internal time; however, this consciousness
itself is a 'fundamental form' which can in turn be taken for an object (i.e., the
implicit self-consciousness) of a new conscious act. As Husserl states: 'These
modes [i.e., forms] of appearance, which make up the consciousness of internal time, are themselves "intentive components of conscious life" and must
in turn be given in reflection as temporalities [i.e., immanent temporal
objects], we encounter here a paradoxical fundamental property of conscious
life, which seems thus to be infected with an infinite regress' (p. 43). This paradoxical consequence is not problematic for Husserl in that he believes this
'fundamental property of conscious life' opens up a horizon, a not-yet perceived, within consciousness itself. The syntheses of consciousness are therefore always opened to further explication, to further determinations, and this
is precisely how Husserl defines a horizon: 'This leaving open, prior to further determinings ... is precisely what makes up the horizon': ibid., 45).

30 Edmund Husserl, *The Crisis of European Sciences and Transcendental Phenomenology*, 293. And, in another passage of this same work, Husserl again recognizes an essential infinite regress: 'Indeed, every 'ground' that is reached
points to further grounds, every horizon opened up awakens new horizons'
(p. 170).

31 Edmund Husserl, *Ideas*, 190.

32 Ibid.

33 Ibid.

34 There is a similarity here with the Wittgensteinian notion of language games.
For example, Wittgenstein claims that, within a language game, we use a
word unhesitatingly, without any sense of ambiguity; however, when we

attempt to define the exact sense of this word, we find only a vague or general family resemblance. See *Philosophical Investigations*.

35 Husserl, *Ideas*, 190.

36 Ibid., 191.

37 Ibid., 190.

38 Ibid., 191.

39 Ibid.

40 Ibid., 220.

41 We can see here how the notion of the pure transcendental ego develops out of this position. It is the invariant pole, or the phenomenological residuum, which is the ideal limit that remains at the end of phenomenological reflection. It needs to be pointed out here, however, that phenomenology itself is for Husserl a descriptive enterprise, and descriptive of the data of the reduced sphere of consciousness (i.e., the immanent data or objectivities of consciousness itself). Consequently, although Husserl recognizes the possibility of apprehending 'in a certain way ... the flux of consciousness as an Idea in the Kantian sense,' the question remains open whether or not the phenomenological descriptions will ultimately take the form of the exact sciences. Husserl claims: 'The pressing question whether within the eidetic domain of the reduced phenomena ... an idealizing procedure may be adopted side by side with the descriptive, substituting for the intuitable data pure and rigorously conceived ideals ... which might then indeed serve as the fundamental nexus for a mathesis of experiences and as a counterpart to descriptive phenomenology, is indeed not settled by the foregoing considerations' (ibid., 183). We will elaborate upon this in the next section as we discuss the relation between the noema and the phenomenological reduction; however, we hope to show that Husserl has indeed presupposed the possibility of such an idealizing procedure, and that it is on the basis of an Ideal Object in general that Husserl accounts for the correlation of meaning-intentions and meaning-fulfilments.

42 Jacques Derrida, *Edmund Husserl's 'Origin of Geometry': An Introduction*, 146–7. The regress being, as in the ones discussed earlier, that the founding of geometry, its origin, would entail an explanation of its founding, and so on, as long as there is not a coincidence within this founding of sense (constitutive) and object (constituted). This is, however, only an explicitly presupposed coincidence, whereas implicitly, as we have shown, the coincidence is not explained.

43 Husserl, *Ideas*, 227.

44 Ibid.

45 Ibid., 228.

46 Ibid., 237.

47 Ibid., 231.

48 Ibid., 232.

49 Ibid.

50 Ibid., 238.

51 In defining the noema as the immanent objective correlate of consciousness, Husserl defines it first in terms of perception, as perception's base meaning, the perceived as such, and in a footnote here Husserl claims that this meaning is to be understood in the sense of the 'meaning that fulfils,' as discussed in *Logical Investigations* (First Investigation, section 14), a meaning that can fulfil even if there is no actual or existing object (i.e., meaning or noema considered as a reduced and immanent objectivity). We discuss this further below, but it appears the reason perception is brought in here continues to be that he understands the objective fulfilment of an intention in terms of the perceptual model.

52 Husserl, *Logical Investigations*, 502.

53 Andre de Murault, *The Idea of Phenomenology: Husserlian Exemplarism*, 128.

54 Husserl, *Ideas*, 160. The entire section 59 discusses this theme.

55 Edmund Husserl, *Ideas III: Phenomenology and the Foundations of the Sciences*, 72.

56 Husserl, *Ideas*, 239.

57 Ibid., 238.

58 Ibid., 283. In *Logical Investigations*, Husserl discusses this neutral consciousness as merely one of a number of acts, in this case a 'merely presentative act.' By this he means: 'Mere presentation ... is passive: it leaves matters "*in suspense*",' and he claims further that 'mere presentation is of a different act-quality, such as surmising, wishing, etc., and one which *differs totally from the assertion of belief*'(p 619; emphases mine). In *Ideas*, however, in order to validate phenomenology as the study of immanent objects (i.e., noetic–noematic correlations), Husserl needs to show the possibility of the phenomenological reduction, and thus the neutral consciousness emerges as one which is 'of highest importance and occupies a position all by itself.'

59 Husserl, *Ideas*, 286–7.

60 Ibid.

61 Ibid., 287.

62 Ibid., 321.

63 The regress here, as discussed above, in section 1, was that the apprehension of an object required a matter to be animated by the apprehending act, but this matter which is animated is itself a content which can be apprehended, an apprehension which requires its own matter, and so on; consequently, we

saw Husserl posit a content, a matter, that is not apprehended in this way: thus, it is 'unconscious.'

64 Ibid., 293.
65 Ibid., 294.
66 Ibid.
67 Ibid.
68 Ibid., 295.
69 Edmund Husserl, *Ideen I, Husserliana*, 406; my translation.
70 Husserl, *Ideas*, 332, n. 1.
71 Ibid., 382.
72 Ibid., 366.
73 Paul Ricoeur, *Husserl: An Analysis of His Phenomenology*, 105.
74 Husserl, *Ideas*, 220.
75 Ibid., 366.
76 Izchak Miller, *Husserl, Perception, and Temporal Awareness*, 29.
77 Dagfinn Føllesdal, 'Husserl's Notion of Noema,' 74. This is Føllesdal's main thesis, number 1, from which he develops a dozen others.
78 Aron Gurwitsch, *Studies in Phenomenology and Psychology*, 339.
79 Ibid., 341.
80 Husserl, *Ideas*, section 1.
81 In our discussion of *Logical Investigations*, this perception of truth took the form of categorial intuition, whereby Being is adequately presented to this intuition: that is, complete self-evidence. In *Ideas*, similarly, truth is understood as the complete self-givenness of Being, a self-givenness for an immanent or eidetic intuition. In section 144, Husserl ties primordial dator intuition together with this notion of Being as complete self-givenness.
82 Edmund Husserl, *Ideen Zu Einer Reinen Phänomenologie und Phänomenologischen Philosophie, Erstes Buch* (The Hague: Martinus Nijhoff 1950), 222.
83 Husserl, *Ideas*, 240.
84 Edmund Husserl, *Ideas Pertaining to a Pure Phenomenology and to a Phenomenological Philosophy, First Book* (The Hague: Martinus Nijhoff 1982), 216.
85 Gibson's translation is intended, I believe, to stress the important distinction Husserl makes between something as a correlate of consciousness ('of something') and something as transcendent to consciousness. Gibson remarks in a 1925 article that, 'according to Husserl the most radical of all distinctions in the nature of Being is that between Being as Consciousness, and Being as that which declares itself in Consciousness, namely transcendent Being': 'The Problem of real and ideal in the phenomenology of Husserl,' 330. Boyce thus discusses the perceptual noema in terms of the *perceiving* act itself rather than in terms of the *perceived* (i.e., perceived as perceived).

86 Husserl, *Ideas*, 320.
87 Husserl, *Ideas III*, 76.
88 Kersten explicitly states this view of the perceptual noema in his article 'Husserl's Doctrine of Noesis-Noema' (in *Phenomenology: Continuation and Criticism*, 114–44]). Kersten's position develops an understanding of the noema as 'suggested by Aron Gurwitsch and Dorion Cairns ... [which concerns] ... the dimension of "passivity" peculiar to intentionality' (p. 114). That is, as we will discuss further below, the noema is understood in terms of that which is given to a passive consciousness, and thus the focus turns to the '*perceived as perceived*.'
89 Husserl, *Ideas*, 240.
90 Husserl, *Ideas II*, 38. And again, in *Ideas*, Husserl claims: 'we say that a spatial configuration, every quality that clothes it, and so the whole "*appearing thing as such*," changes perspectively in manifold ways, whether the presentation is clear or obscure' (pp. 127–8; emphasis added).
91 I am indebted to Hubert Dreyfus for enabling me to see more clearly the rift in interpreting Husserl's notion of the perceptual noema. The distinction he makes in his article 'Husserl's Perceptual Noema' between 'Dagfinn Føllesdal [who] interprets the perceptual noema as a concept [and] Aron Gurwitsch [who] takes it to be a percept' (p. 98) has been very beneficial in aiding my own understanding of Husserl. There are, however, some important differences. Dreyfus claims that the concept theory is the most faithful with respect to Husserl's philosophic intentions; percept theory, he claims, ultimately abandons Husserl's fundamental project. I claim, however, that both tendencies can and should be read into Husserl's work. This is the case because the noema arose out of an effort within *The Phenomenology of Internal Time-Consciousness* to avoid the regress that followed upon the difference between sense (i.e., concept) and object (i.e., percept). Dreyfus recognizes the regress (he speaks of the regress of sense infinitely coinciding with sense in this very same essay), but he acknowledges neither Husserl's recognition of this regress nor his efforts to resolve it; consequently, I believe Dreyfus ultimately affirms only one side of the noema (i.e., concept theory), and unjustifiably disfranchises the other from Husserl's thought (i.e., percept theory).
92 Husserl, *Ideas*, 320.
93 Dagfinn Føllesdal, 'Noema and Meaning in Husserl,' 268.
94 Føllesdal, 'Husserl's Notion of Noema,' 74.
95 Ibid., thesis 3, 75.
96 I use here an example from Ronald McIntyre and David Woodruff Smith, 'Husserl's Identification of Meaning and *Noema*,' 85.

97 In chapter I, this distinction was made between the quality of an act and the content of an act. Føllesdal actually points out the similarity: 'Husserl's Notion of Noema,' 75.

98 McIntyre and Woodruff, 'Husserl's Identification of Meaning and *Noema*,' 86.

99 Føllesdal, 'Husserl's Notion of Noema,' 79. This is the quote: 'The Sinn corresponding to an object is in its turn an object ... it can be made the object of a judgment ... As such it has a Sinn of the second level: the Sinn of a Sinn ... hence we come to an infinite regress, insofar as the Sinn of the Sinn may in its turn be made an object and then again has a Sinn and so on.'

100 Ibid.

101 Referring to Gibson's translation, quoted at the beginning of this section.

102 Miller, *Husserl, Perception, and Temporal Awareness*, 19.

103 Ibid., 57.

104 Aron Gurwitsch, *The Field of Consciousness*, 267.

105 In *Logical Investigations*, Husserl claims that 'signs in the sense of expressions ... appear before us as physical objects ... On this, however, a second [act] is built which goes entirely beyond the experienced sense-material ... [and this] ... Meaning, the characteristic of the expressive sign, *presupposes the sign whose function it is*' (310; emphasis added).

106 The self-constituted consciousness is a self-constituted unity, the unity of immanent time, and it is this unity which allows for the constitution of objective temporal unities, such as the data of perception. In *The Phenomenology of Internal Time-Consciousness*, 106, Husserl recognizes the paradoxical or contradictory nature of this solution: 'As startling (if not at first sight even contradictory) as it may appear to assert that the flux of consciousness constitutes its own unity, it is still true, nevertheless.'

107 Gurwitsch, *Studies in Phenomenology and Psychology*, 291.

108 Ibid., 293.

109 Ibid.

110 Gurwitsch, *The Field of Consciousness*, 261ff. This discussion occurs in the context of a critique of Stout's theory of perception; however, Gurwitsch later claims (p. 269) that this ambiguity affects Husserl's theory as well. The general difficulty is one of explaining how sense (and sensations) are both *what* an object is intended as (e.g., sense-datum as attribute) and *that* which fixes an object for this act (e.g., in perception *that* a sense-datum is there as the matter taken up).

111 Ibid., 271.

112 Gurwitsch, *Studies in Phenomenology and Psychology*, 257.

113 Gurwitsch, *The Field of Consciousness*, 272.

114 Ibid., 274. Here Gurwitsch discusses the perceptual noema and percept interchangeably: for example, 'the percept as a whole or the perceptual noema.'
115 Ibid., 228.
116 Ibid., 224.
117 Ibid., 278.
118 Ibid., 296. To do this would entail an act, a coordinating act, which works upon some given, non-unified, non-structured material (e.g., *hyle*), and this would simply repeat the problematic distinction Gurwitsch wants to avoid. Furthermore, by not making this distinction, Gurwitsch avoids the need for a self-constituting consciousness which would be the condition for this distinction.
119 Ibid., 296.
120 Gurwitsch, *Studies in Phenomenology and Psychology*, 341.
121 Ibid., 173.
122 A reference to Kersten's translation, discussed earlier.
123 Maurice Merleau-Ponty, *The Phenomenology of Perception*, xiv.
124 Maurice Merleau-Ponty, 'The Indirect Language,' in *The Prose of the World* 103–4.

Chapter III: The Middle Path

1 Edmund Husserl, *Crisis of European Sciences and Transcendental Phenomenology*, 166.
2 Edmund Husserl, *Logical Investigations*, 833. We discussed this in chapter II, p. 50.
3 Ibid., 398. This argument emerges as a critique of Hume. For example, if an object is known to be white only on the basis of an impression, Husserl claims that, for Hume, this impression is taken for what it is only in relation to other impressions. That is, the impression we have of an object is interpreted to be white because of the association of ideas – that is, resemblance – but this resemblance entails an interpretation of the resemblance between the impression itself and other impressions. In other words, if we know an object is white only on the basis of an impression, the impression itself is interpreted or known to be white only as it, too, is related to other impressions, and we know these others only in so far as they are associated with others, and so on *ad infinitum*. The reason for this regress, Husserl claims, is that Hume based the knowledge of one object on the knowledge of another (i.e., an impression). Thus he claims, 'if we ever perceive something as white, and if we only present to ourselves a resemblance between the apparent object

(i.e., the given impression) and other objects (i.e., associated impressions), then such a man has involved himself in an infinite regress, since talk of this presented resemblance calls for a corresponding reinterpretation' (p. 398).

4 Edmund Husserl, *The Phenomenology of Internal Time-Consciousness*, 106.
5 Ibid., 154.
6 Paul Ricoeur, *Husserl: An Analysis of His Phenomenology*, 105.
7 Ibid.
8 Edmund Husserl, *Cartesian Meditations*, 64 (emphasis added).
9 Ricoeur, *Husserl: An Analysis of His Phenomenology*, 105.
10 This refers to the title of the Fifth Cartesian Meditation, 'Uncovering of the Sphere of Transcendental Being as Monadological Intersubjectivity,' and also refers to Merleau-Ponty's summation of the problem in *Consciousness and the Acquisition of Language*, which we will refer to below.
11 Merleau-Ponty, *Consciousness and the Acquisition of Language*, 45.
12 Maurice Merleau-Ponty, *The Phenomenology of Perception*, 198.
13 In 'The Philosopher and His Shadow,' in *The Primacy of Perception*, Merleau-Ponty claims that the reduction preserves the whole world of the natural attitude (i.e., the world as transcendent) because 'the very transcendence of this world must retain a meaning in the eyes of "reduced" consciousness, and transcendental immanence cannot be simply its antithesis ... It is, Husserl says in another connection, the mystery of a primordial faith and a fundamental and original opinion (i.e., Urdoxa)' (pp. 162–3).
14 Merleau-Ponty, *The Phenomenology of Perception*, xiv.
15 Ibid., x.
16 Ibid., xii.
17 Ricoeur, *Husserl: An Analysis of His Phenomenology*, 119.
18 Husserl, *Cartesian Meditations*, 94.
19 Ibid.
20 Ibid., 110–11.
21 Ricoeur, *Husserl: An Analysis of His Phenomenology*, 129.
22 Along these lines, in *Cartesian Meditations*, 119, Husserl claims: 'since the other body there enters into a pairing association with my body here and, being given perceptually, becomes the core of an appresentation, the core of my experience of a coexisting ego, that ego, according to the whole sense-giving course of the association, must be appresented as an ego now existing in the mode There, "such as I should be if I were there".'
23 Husserl, *The Phenomenology of Internal Time-Consciousness*, 31.
24 Ibid., 36.
25 Ibid., 39.
26 Ricoeur, *Husserl: An Analysis of His Phenomenology*, 130.

27 Maurice Merleau-Ponty, 'On the Phenomenology of Language,' in *Signs*, 93–4.

28 Merleau-Ponty, *Consciousness and the Acquisition of Language*, 45.

29 Merleau-Ponty, 'On the Phenomenology of Language,' 94.

30 Merleau-Ponty, *The Phenomenology of Perception*, x.

31 As quoted earlier, Merleau-Ponty claims that 'the problem of the world, and, to begin with, that of one's own body, consists in the fact that it is all there': ibid., 198. Furthermore, there are hints, especially in *Ideas II*, that Husserl considered the body as the condition for differentiating between self and other. For example, in a footnote, Husserl claims that 'in the child the self-produced voice, and then, analogously, the heard voice, serves as the first bridge for the objectivation of the Ego or for the formation of the "alter"' (p. 101 fn). That is, Husserl is claiming that it is the self-presence of the body to itself, or the body as constituting and constituted, that is the condition for the distinction between self and other; however, this is only taken to be an analogy, and Husserl clearly takes consciousness, and not the body, to be the more primary level of constitution.

32 Merleau-Ponty, *The Phenomenology of Perception*, xiii.

33 In *The Primacy of Perception*, for example, Merleau-Ponty claims: 'What prohibits me from treating my perception as an intellectual act is that an intellectual act would grasp the object either as possible or as necessary. But in perception it is "real"; it is given as the infinite sum of an indefinite series of perspectival views in each of which the object is given but in none of which is it given exhaustively' (p. 15).

34 Ricoeur, *Husserl: An Analysis of His Phenomenology*, 209.

35 Ibid., 33.

36 Ibid., 210.

37 Merleau-Ponty, *The Phenomenology of Perception*, 49.

38 Merleau-Ponty, *The Structure of Behavior*, 4.

39 Ibid., 5.

Chapter IV: From Psychology to Phenomenology

1 John D. Glenn, Jr, in his article 'The Behaviorism of a Phenomenologist – *Structure of Behavior* and *The Concept of Mind*,' points out a regress in Ryle's philosophy that is analogous to Husserl's: 'Surely it is not behavior *per se*, but behavior observed in some fashion which is the basis for the ascription of mental predicates. But what is the status of this observer – or, more precisely, this observation? Is the latter nothing but another bit of behavior which must itself be observed if it is to provide the basis of any assertion? If so, an episte-

mological infinite regress would follow' (p. 254). Glenn claims that, in order
to avoid the regress, Ryle presupposes the subject that must be somewhere in
order to end it. Husserl, as we have seen, argues for an absolute consciousness to resolve the regress, and it is this move which entailed paradox. Thus
we see the affinity between Husserl and Merleau-Ponty (i.e., Merleau-
Ponty's move to the 'paradox of perception').

2 Maurice Merleau-Ponty, *The Phenomenology of Perception*, 363.
3 Maurice Merleau-Ponty, *The Structure of Behavior*, 127.
4 Ibid.
5 Aron Gurwitsch, 'Contribution to the Phenomenological Theory of Perception,' in *Studies in Phenomenology and Psychology*, 338.
6 Ibid., 341: 'the perceptual noema ... turns out to be the perceived thing, just as
   it presents itself through a concrete act of perception – namely, as appearing
   from a certain side, in a certain perspective, orientation, etc.'
7 Aron Gurwitsch, 'A Non-Egological Conception of Consciousness,' in *Studies
   in Phenomenology and Psychology*, 298: 'The ego is then a synthetic unity of
   these psychic objects, chiefly of the dispositions and actions it supports, and
   it may be found nowhere outside these psychic unities.'
8 Ibid., 346.
9 Maurice Merleau-Ponty, *The Primacy of Perception*, 15.
10 Edmund Husserl, 'The Vienna Lecture,' in *The Crisis of European Sciences and
   Transcendental Phenomenology*, 297.
11 Merleau-Ponty, *The Structure of Behavior*, 11–12.
12 Ibid., 40.
13 Ibid., 55. This comment occurs in the context of a criticism of Pavlov's famous
   salivation experiments. Merleau-Ponty shows that the sound alone was not
   adequate stimulus, but the bell in a certain ensemble. For example, if the
   sound of a bell were followed by another sound, the dog would not respond;
   therefore, the sound cannot be abstracted from the dog's milieu, and thus
   Merleau-Ponty says the stimulus is the ensemble, or milieu, as such.
14 Recent work in cognitive science, in particular connectionism, would claim
   that this is not a problem. Paul Churchland, for example, in his book *A Neuro-
   computational Perspective* (Cambridge, MA: MIT Press 1989), claims that 'a
   typical human brain contains something close to 100 billion neurons. A typical neuron receives synaptic connections from roughly 3000 other neurons.'
   This, in addition to the weighting that each neuron receives, results, Churchland claims, in a total number of possible configurations that far outnumber
   'the total number of elementary particles in the universe' (pp. 131–2). For all
   intents and purposes, therefore, there is an infinite number of neural connections, and thus what Merleau-Ponty took to be a problem is not one. Despite

this, however, some connectionists argue, for example, Andy Clark in *Microcognition* (Cambridge, MA: MIT Press 1989), that thought, perception, and behaviour are nevertheless dependent upon 'emergent structures' of these connections. Clark, in particular, claims that the purely computational approach of strict connectionism (i.e., Churchland) needs to be balanced with an understanding of structure. Thus the concept of structure, although placed in a different context, continues to be seen as important.

15 Merleau-Ponty, *The Structure of Behavior*, 88.

16 Ibid., 32–3.

17 Ibid., 145.

18 Ibid., 159.

19 Ibid., 151.

20 Ibid., 159.

21 Ibid., 187.

22 Ibid., 199.

23 Ibid., 88, quoted earlier.

24 Ibid., 122.

25 Merleau-Ponty, *The Phenomenology of Perception*, xii.

26 Ibid.

27 Maurice Merleau-Ponty, 'The Experience of Others,' trans. Hugh Silverman, *Review of Existential Psychology and Psychiatry* 18 (Fall 1973), 52.

28 Maurice Merleau-Ponty, 'On the Phenomenology of Language,' in *Signs*, 94.

29 Maurice Merleau-Ponty, 'The Child's Relations with Others,' in *The Primacy of Perception*, 119.

30 Ibid., 147. Merleau-Ponty gives an example of a three-year-old girl who tells her father of the cookies she stole from her brother and ate. The child is admonished, cries, and, after the usual reconciliation, promises not to do it again. Then, when the mother comes home, the child repeats the same process.

31 Ibid., 140.

32 Ibid., 119: 'by the objectification of one's own body and the constitution of the other in his difference, there occurs a segregation, a distinction of individuals – a process which ... is never completely finished.' Some of the setbacks that occur will be discussed below, when we look at examples of psychopathology.

33 Ibid., 126–7: 'the chimpanzee was about to reach consciousness of the image or treat what is in the mirror as a simple reflection or symbol of his real body, [but] he recoils from the object and treats it as foreign.' Recent work, however, contests this view and claims that chimps do recognize themselves in a mirror.

34 Merleau-Ponty, *The Primacy of Perception*, 7.

35 Maurice Merleau-Ponty, 'Dialogue and the Perception of the Other,' in *Prose of the World*, 134.
36 Maurice Merleau-Ponty, 'The Philosopher and His Shadow,' in *Signs*, 168 (emphasis added).
37 Ibid., 170.
38 Émile Benveniste makes this same claim. He argues that only humans are capable of indirect discourse, or indirect communication. He cites, for example, bees that are able to communicate the location of only a flower that they have come into sensory contact with, whereas a bee that has not had such contact cannot communicate it to another bee. See *Problems in General Linguistics* (Coral Gables: University of Miami Press 1971), 53ff.
39 Merleau-Ponty, *The Primacy of Perception*, 16.
40 Ibid., 26.
41 Ibid., 27. There are many parallels here with Kierkegaard. In particular, Kierkegaard's discussion of the Absolute paradox of God become man, of the infinite become finite, or of the fundamental truth that is subjectivity; these claims are echoed here in Merleau-Ponty's discussion of the paradox that is our experience of others. See Søren Kierkegaard, *Philosophical Fragments*, trans. D.F. Swenson and Walter Lowrie (Princeton, NJ: Princeton University Press 1985).
42 Merleau-Ponty, *The Structure of Behavior*, 167. As an aside, we can see here another example of the human ability to recognize and use symbols; that is, the human rituals that surround the burial of the dead. In these rituals, there is the preparation of the body for the life beyond death, for the life that transcends their actual life on earth. There is thus a recognition of others as something that transcends their actual finite existence, a recognition of their infinite and absolute nature, and it is this recognition that Merleau-Ponty calls the 'experience of the other.' This is an experience not found in animals, and thus we don't find in animals rituals surrounding death. Anthropological research is currently of the opinion that these burial rituals began during the time of Neanderthal man. Interestingly, and not coincidentally, I would argue, there also appeared around this time the famous cave paintings, paintings that Merleau-Ponty referred to as the first to open the horizon for all future paintings. See 'Eye and Mind,' in *The Primacy of Perception*. See also Robert Wenke, *Patterns in Prehistory* (Oxford: Oxford University Press 1980), 184–6.
43 Edmund Husserl, *Logical Investigations*, 91.
44 Ibid., 99.
45 Husserl, *The Crisis of European Sciences and Transcendental Phenomenology*, 362.
46 Merleau-Ponty, 'The Philosopher and His Shadow,' 162–3.
47 Merleau-Ponty, *The Phenomenology of Perception*, xiv.

48 Ibid., xiii.
49 Merleau-Ponty, 'The Philosopher and His Shadow,' 180.
50 Saul Kripke, *Naming and Necessity*, 53.
51 Ibid., 49.
52 Earlier we discussed this difficulty within the context of the regress of sense infinitely coinciding with sense. Then we claimed that Husserl's difficulty was to account for the coincidence of sense and its object; similarly, the problem for Kripke is to account for the coincidence of a designator with the designated, and Kripke's solution, analogous to the one we will see Merleau-Ponty take, is that it is the already-given object that is this coincidence (i.e., rigid designator).
53 Merleau-Ponty, *The Phenomenology of Perception*, 330.
54 Ibid., 361.
55 Ibid., 297.
56 Merleau-Ponty, *The Primacy of Perception*, 16. We can see here another parallel with Kierkegaard. The relationship between faith and paradox is an important theme in Kierkegaard. Reason, Kierkegaard claims, cannot justify faith, and the leap of faith is a leap made with a recognition of the paradox, a leap made despite the offence to reason that this paradox entails.
57 Ibid., 16.
58 Ibid., 19.
59 Ibid.
60 Ibid., 242.
61 Merleau-Ponty, *The Phenomenology of Perception*, 96–7: 'To concern oneself with psychology is necessarily to encounter, beneath objective thought which moves among ready-made things, a first opening upon things without which there would be no objective knowledge. The psychologist could not fail to rediscover himself as experience, which means as an immediate presence to the past, to the world, to the body, and to others at the very moment when he was trying to see himself as an object among objects.'

Chapter V: Merleau-Ponty and the Transcendental Tradition

1 Maurice Merleau-Ponty, *The Phenomenology of Perception*, 61.
2 Ibid., 63.
3 Immanuel Kant, *Prolegomena to Any Future Metaphysics* (New York: Bobbs Merrill 1950), 59.
4 Edmund Husserl, *Logical Investigations*, 833. We also discussed this early in chapter II.
5 Ibid.

6 The transition from Husserl's work in *Logical Investigations* to a transcendental phenomenology, a move begun in *The Phenomenology of Internal Time-
Consciousness*, was the theme of the first part of this work.

7 At this point there is an interesting convergence of Husserl, Kant, and
Heidegger. On the one hand, Husserl's criticism of Kant is, in many ways,
similar to Heidegger's critique. For example, Heidegger claims that Kant
presupposes a notion of being as, to use Heidegger's language, being-
present-at-hand. As a result, the difficulty is to show how a subjective being,
a being '"in me",' is related to an objective being, or to that being '"outside of
me".' In other words, the difficulty is to account for the relationship between
a subject and the world. For Heidegger, however, it is this relationship, a relationship that is conditioned for Kant, that emerges as the fundamental condition; that is, it is a subject *already in the world* (*Being and Time* [New York:
Harper and Row 1962], 206) that is the condition which makes possible being
as being-present-at-hand, and it is therefore the condition for differentiating
between a being 'inside me' and a being 'outside of me': see *Being and Time*,
203–6. Therefore, what Kant takes to be conditioned (i.e., our being-in-the-
world or *Dasein* as conditioned by the *a priori* categories) is, according to
Heidegger, presupposed and unwittingly used as the model to explain the
conditions (i.e., being as being-present-at-hand).

   On the other hand, in Heidegger's later work, he begins to interpret Kant
in a more Husserlian manner. In particular, Heidegger argues that it is
through self-affection, self-affection as the presencing of self to self in time,
that the objectifications and representations of knowledge and thought are
made possible. Daniel Dahlstrom, in 'Heidegger's Kantian Turn,' explores
this theme, but in the end he argues that, although Heidegger interprets Kant
to be arguing for self-affection as the fundamental condition, Heidegger
would have been more accurate in saying that this is what Kant should have
said, not what he did say. Dahlstrom also recognizes that the relationship
between time and self-affection was also a path Husserl himself took, but
argues that Heidegger did not adequately recognize this. Dahlstrom thus
claims that 'the Husserlian backdrop is more essential in a positive sense
than Heidegger seems to have been able or ready to acknowledge' (p. 344).
That Heidegger did not explicitly acknowledge Husserl in his interpretation
of Kant becomes particularly striking when one reads in Heidegger's edito-
rial foreword to *The Phenomenology of Internal Time-Consciousness* that 'the
pervading theme of the present study is the temporal constitution of a pure
datum and the self-constitution of 'phenomenological time' which underlies
such a constitution' (p. 15). In other words, there is already in Husserl's
work, as Heidegger attempts to show in Kant, the claim that it is the self-

constituting time-consciousness (i.e., self-affection) which is the condition that makes possible objectivity, even the objectivity of perception.

8 I refer again to Heidegger, as noted above; furthermore, in recognition of the moves Heidegger made in this direction of placing consciousness in the world (i.e., *Dasein*), a move that avoids the Husserlian claim of positing an absolute consciousness, Merleau-Ponty asks: 'What, in fact do we mean when we say that there is no world without being in the world? Not indeed that the world is constituted by consciousness, but on the contrary that consciousness always finds itself at work in the world ... [or] ... as Heidegger says ... [consciousness is] ... *lumen naturale*, given to itself': *The Phenomenology of Perception*, 432.

9 Merleau-Ponty, *The Phenomenology of Perception*, 198.

10 Maurice Merleau-Ponty, 'Metaphysics and the Novel,' in *Sense and Non-Sense*, 28.

11 On this point, Merleau-Ponty is in agreement with Husserl, and in disagreement with Kant, that 'Hume went, in intention, further than anyone in radical reflection, since he generally tried to take us back to those phenomena of which we have experience, on the hither side of any formation of ideas – even though he went on to dissect and emasculate this experience': *The Phenomenology of Perception*, 220.

12 Ibid., 407.

13 Ibid., 365.

14 Ibid., 405.

15 Aron Gurwitsch, *Studies in Phenomenology and Psychology*, 257.

16 Ibid., 293.

17 Ibid., 298.

18 Maurice Merleau-Ponty, 'Phenomenology and the Sciences of Man,' in *The Primacy of Perception*, 57.

19 Maurice Merleau-Ponty, 'The Philosopher and His Shadow,' in *Signs*, 166.

20 Merleau-Ponty, *The Phenomenology of Perception*, 313. This sentence has been mistranslated. The French reads 'conscience primordiale,' and has been translated to read 'primordial constancy.' I have quoted it here with its correct translation: 'primordial consciousness.'

21 Ibid., 303 n. 1. Merleau-Ponty refers to Kurt Koffka's *Principles of Gestalt Psychology* (New York: Harcourt Brace 1935), 94ff.

22 Merleau-Ponty, *The Phenomenology of Perception*, 111–12.

23 Ibid., 131: 'in the normal person the subject's intentions are immediately reflected in the perceptual field, polarizing it, or placing their seal upon it, or setting up in it, effortlessly, a wave of significance (i.e., virtual as virtual). In the patient the perceptual field has lost this plasticity.'

24 Ibid., 291.

25 Ibid., 184.

26 It is precisely this coincidence of words and things, whether it be a paradoxical coincidence or not, that poststructuralists, and, in particular, Foucault,
criticize. In *Les Mots et les choses* ('Words and Things,' though translated in
English as 'The Order of Things'), Foucault claims that words and things are
irreducibly different, and that neither can be reduced to the other: 'It is not
that words are imperfect, or that, when confronted by the visible, they prove
insuperably inadequate. Neither can be reduced to the other's terms: it is in
vain that we say what we see; what we see never resides in what we say': *The
Order of Things*, 9. Merleau-Ponty would agree that neither could be reduced
to the other's terms, yet he claims that, at the level of the 'primordial silence,'
there is the paradoxical coincidence of what is seen and what is said, a coincidence that makes language possible even though language is never able to
recapture it (i.e., the 'philosopher's failure').

We will discuss this further, in the final part of this work; however, there is
an interesting point of agreement between Merleau-Ponty and the poststructuralists, and this surrounds the discussion of words that are taken for things
by schizophrenics. Deleuze, for example, discusses Artaud's claim that
words actually hurt him, that they affected his body; in other words, the
word has a physical effect, like a thing. As Merleau-Ponty would say, the failure of the schizophrenic to act upon the fundamental paradox of experience
(i.e., the coincidence of self and world) results in the failure of the subject to
take up the task of expression; consequently, the schizophrenic is unable to
clearly differentiate between words and things, and often, as Artaud does,
discuss them in the same terms (e.g., inflicting pain). For Merleau-Ponty,
however, this failure is the failure of a subject, of a subject whose unity or
totality is manifest in each of his behaviours; that is, despite the failure, there
is, Merleau-Ponty argues, a structure of the subject (i.e., a vital structure). The
poststructuralists, on the other hand, claim that this failure is symptomatic of
a loss of the subject, or it is a failure that cannot be reduced to the structure of
the subject. They argue that there is an irreducible difference that forever
eludes this net of structure – for example, the irreducible difference between
words and things. On this topic, Deleuze, Foucault, Kristeva, and, to some
degree, Derrida can be seen to take up this line of criticism.

27 Merleau-Ponty claims that to understand psychological disturbances we
need to treat 'the human subject as an irremovable consciousness which is
wholly present in every one of its manifestations': *The Phenomenology of
Perception*, 120.

28 Maurice Merleau-Ponty, 'The Indirect Language,' in *Prose of the World*, 78.

29 Ibid., 112. The paradox of expression = the expression of the inexpressible; being given that which is not given; or, finally, recognizing the virtual as virtual.

30 Ibid.

31 Ibid., 88: 'Man taken as concrete being is not a psyche joined to an organism, but the movement *to and fro of existence* which at one time allows itself to take corporeal form and at others moves toward personal acts ... there is not a single impulse in a living body which is entirely fortuitous in relation to psychic intentions, not a single mental act which has not found at least its germ or its general outline in physiological tendencies' (emphasis added).

32 I refer to the quote with which this section began.

33 Merleau-Ponty, *The Phenomenology of Perception*, 291 (emphasis added).

34 Maurice Merleau-Ponty, *The Consciousness and the Acquisition of Language*, 45.

35 Merleau-Ponty, *The Phenomenology of Perception*, 198.

36 We discussed this regress earlier with respect to Ryle. We quoted Glenn's claim that Ryle's theory does in fact commit this type of regress, a regress that Merleau-Ponty, as we will see, avoids.

37 Merleau-Ponty, *The Phenomenology of Perception*, 91.

38 Ibid., 92.

39 Ibid.

40 Merleau-Ponty, *The Primacy of Perception*, 26. This refers to our earlier discussion wherein this was the definition of the paradox of perception. Now, however, we are bringing it in to show that Merleau-Ponty accepts the Husserlian claim that there is a subject which makes possible this infinite synthesis.

41 Merleau-Ponty, *The Phenomenology of Perception*, p. 212.

42 Merleau-Ponty, 'Dialogue and the Perception of the Other,' in *Prose of the World*, 134.

43 Claude Lefort, 'Flesh and Otherness,' in *Ontology and Alterity in Merleau-Ponty*, ed. Galen Johnson and Michael Smith (Evanston, IL: Northwestern University Press 1990), 3–13.

44 Merleau-Ponty, *The Primacy of Perception*, 19.

45 David Michael Levin, in *The Body's Recollection of Being* (New York: Routledge and Kegan Paul 1985), offers this interpretation of Merleau-Ponty. In fact, he argues that this bodily interpretation of the ontological difference eliminates what Levin believes to be Heidegger's 'exceedingly formal ontology of the analytics of Dasein,' by placing it into the context of 'the body of experience ... the body's own being as pre-reflective, pre-conceptual and pre-ordained relatedness-to-Being' (p. 16).

46 Maurice Merleau-Ponty, 'Phenomenology and the Sciences of Man,' in *The Primacy of Perception*, 94.

47 Ibid.

48 Merleau-Ponty, *The Phenomenology of Perception*, 153.

49 Recall our earlier comparison to Kripke. Kripke claimed it is due to the fact that an object is given that we can speak of possibilities of this object. In Merleau-Ponty's terms, it is due to the fact that the identity of the body image is given that we can stylize upon this body.

50 Merleau-Ponty, 'The Indirect Language,' 61.

51 Ibid., 58.

52 Maurice Merleau-Ponty, *Résumés des cours*, 178 (translation mine).

53 Maurice Merleau-Ponty, *The Structure of Behavior*, 30. This example is still appropriate, although at the time of this book Merleau-Ponty had not formulated his notion of style as a system of equivalences.

54 Merleau-Ponty, *The Phenomenology of Perception*, 355.

55 Maurice Merleau-Ponty, 'Science and the Experience of Expression,' in *Prose of the World*, 43.

56 Merleau-Ponty, 'The Indirect Language,' 39.

57 Merleau-Ponty, 'Dialogue and the Perception of the Other,' 142.

58 Ibid., 139.

59 Merleau-Ponty, 'From Mauss to Lévi-Strauss,' in *Signs*, 120.

60 Merleau-Ponty also analogizes this task to that of an archaeologist: 'We must rediscover the structure of the perceived world through a process similar to that of an archaeologist. For the structure of the perceived world is buried under the sedimentations [i.e., domestications] of later knowledge': *The Primacy of Perception*, 5.

61 Merleau-Ponty, *The Phenomenology of Perception*, 394.

Chapter VI: The Social Self

1 Paul Ricoeur, *Husserl: An Analysis of His Phenomenology*, 209.

2 Ibid.

3 Maurice Merleau-Ponty, 'Phenomenology and the Sciences of Man,' in *The Primacy of Perception*, 82.

4 Ibid.

5 Ibid., 54 (emphasis added).

6 Maurice Merleau-Ponty, *The Phenomenology of Perception*, 363; also quoted earlier.

7 Merleau-Ponty, *The Primacy of Perception*, 16.

8 Maurice Merleau-Ponty, *The Visible and the Invisible*, 136.

9 Maurice Merleau-Ponty, *The Structure of Behavior*, 210.

10 Maurice Merleau-Ponty, 'Cézanne's Doubt,' in *Sense and Non-Sense*, 16.

11 Ibid., 12.

12 Merleau-Ponty, *The Phenomenology of Perception*, 150.

13 Maurice Merleau-Ponty, 'Eye and Mind,' in *The Primacy of Perception*, 162.

14 Ibid., 164.

15 Ibid., 167.

16 Ibid., 187. This is analogous to Merleau-Ponty's discussion of the 'transcendental contradiction' that makes consciousness possible. In this instance, however, the contradiction is one at the heart of Being, not peculiar only to humans.

17 Ibid., 182. Merleau-Ponty refers here to Hermes Trismegistus. This theme will emerge in the next section as well, and we will see a profound similarity with Wittgenstein's claim that philosophy, in the end, attempts to emit an 'inarticulate sound.'

18 Ibid., 190.

19 Merleau-Ponty, *The Phenomenology of Perception*, 403.

20 Ibid., 183.

21 Ludwig Wittgenstein, *Philosophical Investigations*, p. 81 (§ 201).

22 Saul Kripke, *Wittgenstein: On Rules and Private Language*, 60.

23 Ludwig Wittgenstein, *On Certainty*, 17.

24 Wittgenstein, *Philosophical Investigations*, 56 (§ 142).

25 Kripke, *Wittgenstein*, 98. Kripke quotes from *Philosophical Investigations*, 226.

26 Wittgenstein, *Philosophical Investigations*, 172 (§ 693).

27 Wittgenstein, *On Certainty*, 8.

28 Wittgenstein, *Philosophical Investigations*, 93 (§ 261). This ties in both to the 'problem of difference' and to Husserl's critique of Platonic realism; that is, just as Husserl criticized the notion that there are pre-existing truths or forms, so, too, does Wittgenstein criticize the notion that the meaning of a word pre-exists its use. Husserl's problem was, then, to show how this truth, although it doesn't pre-exist its coming to be known, is nevertheless independent of the subject who intuits and knows it – that is, he was confronted with the problem of difference. Wittgenstein, by our reading, goes one step further: he recognizes the intractability of this problem – namely, that the problem has no identifiable (no *articulate*) solution. Consequently, his task is simply to describe each articulate sound or 'expression only as it occurs in a particular language-game' (ibid.).

29 Wittgenstein, *On Certainty*, 47.

30 Ibid., 28.

31 Maurice Merleau-Pont, *Consciousness and the Acquisition of Language*, 77.

32 Merleau-Ponty, *The Phenomenology of Perception*, 197.

33 Ferdinand de Saussure, *Course in General Linguistics*, 76.
34 Ibid., 67.
35 Ibid., 2.
36 Ibid., 113.
37 Ibid., 110: ' The characteristic role of a language in relation to thought is not to supply the material phonetic means by which ideas may be expressed. It is to act as intermediary between thought and sound.'
38 Ibid., 113.
39 Ibid., 118.
40 Merleau-Ponty, *The Phenomenology of Perception*, 196.
41 Maurice Merleau-Ponty, 'The 'Indirect Language,' in *Prose of the World*, 39.
42 Ibid., 42.
43 Merleau-Ponty, *Consciousness and the Acquisition of Language*, 80.
44 Merleau-Ponty, *The Visible and the Invisible*, 171.
45 Ibid.
46 Ibid., 183.
47 Ibid., 201. Merleau-Ponty recognizes, in the working notes, the Saussurean inspiration for this move to Being: 'The Saussurean analysis of the relations between signifiers and the relations from signifier to signified and between the significations (as differences between significations) confirms and rediscovers the idea of perception as a *divergence* (*écart*) by relation to a *level*, that is, the idea of the primordial Being, of the Convention of conventions, of the speech before speech.'
48 Ibid., 200.
49 Ibid.
50 Ibid., 185.
51 Maurice Merleau-Ponty, *Humanism and Terror*, 62.
52 Merleau-Ponty, *The Phenomenology of Perception*, 355.
53 Merleau-Ponty, *Humanism and Terror*, 102.
54 Ibid., pp. 116–17.
55 Maurice Merleau-Ponty, 'From Mauss to Lévi-Strauss,' in *Signs*, 117.
56 Ibid.
57 Ibid., 120.
58 Ibid., 116–17: 'Social facts are neither things or ideas; they are structures.'
59 Maurice Merleau-Ponty, 'Phenomenology and the Sciences of Man,' in *The Primacy of Perception*, 92.
60 Merleau-Ponty, *The Visible and the Invisible*, 136.
61 Ibid., 199.
62 Ibid., 204.
63 Ibid., 229: 'The invisible is there without being an object, it is pure transcen-

dence, without an ontic mask. And the 'visibles themselves, in the last analysis, they too are only centered on a nucleus of absence.'

64 Ibid., 219.

Chapter VII: Untaming the Flesh

1 Maurice Merleau-Ponty, *The Visible and the Invisible*, 272.
2 Ibid., 216.
3 M.C. Dillon, 'Merleau-Ponty and the Reversibility Thesis,' 377.
4 Merleau-Ponty, *The Visible and the Invisible*, 272.
5 Ibid., 135–6. Quoted by Claude Lefort in 'Flesh and Otherness,' in *Ontology and Alterity in Merleau-Ponty*, ed. Galen Johnson and Michael Smith (Evanston, IL: Northwestern University Press 1990), 4–5.
6 Maurice Merleau-Ponty, 'Eye and Mind,' in *The Primacy of Perception*, 167. Quoted in chapter VI.
7 Lefort, 'Flesh and Otherness,' 8.
8 Merleau-Ponty, *The Visible and the Invisible*, 261.
9 Ibid., 87–8.
10 Ibid., 264.
11 Ibid., 266.
12 Lefort, 'Flesh and Otherness,' 5.
13 Merleau-Ponty, *The Visible and the Invisible*, 147.
14 Ibid., 267. Quoted by Lefort in 'Flesh and Otherness,' 12.
15 Ibid., 139. Quoted by Lefort in ibid., 7.
16 Merleau-Ponty uses these terms, and in this context, many times throughout *The Visible and the Invisible*. See 200, 204, 212, 271–2.
17 Ibid., 102.
18 Ibid., 255–6.
19 Maurice Merleau-Ponty, 'The Philosopher and His Shadow,' in *Signs*, 168. Written in 1959, just before his work on *The Visible and the Invisible*.
20 Lefort, 'Flesh and Otherness,' 12.
21 Ibid., 11.
22 Merleau-Ponty, *The Visible and the Invisible*, 191–2. There is a mistranslation in the English version of this text. There is a 'not' placed before the phrase 'an absence from oneself.'
23 Ibid., 197.
24 Ibid., 225.
25 Ibid., 216. Quoted in full above.
26 Ibid., 195.
27 Dillon, 'Merleau-Ponty and the Reversibility Thesis,' 377.

28 Ibid.
29 Ibid.
30 Ibid., 378.
31 Ibid.
32 M.C. Dillon, 'A Reply to Lefort,' in *Ontology and Alterity in Merleau-Ponty*, ed. Johnson and Smith, 17.
33 Merleau-Ponty, *The Visible and the Invisible*, 200.
34 Ibid., 183.
35 Dillon, 'Merleau-Ponty and the Reversibility Thesis,' 381.
36 Merleau-Ponty, *The Visible and the Invisible*, 148.
37 Dillon, 'Merleau-Ponty and the Reversibility Thesis,' 379.
38 This is Gary Brent Madison's criticism of Dillon. Madison claims that 'Dillon seeks to give the impression that Merleau-Ponty abandoned "the thesis of subjectivity," "the transcendental approach," but I do not believe that this was at all the case ... Merleau-Ponty's radically reflective approach – the concept of the flesh – enables him to conceive of otherness as a kind of internal phenomenon, rather than, as Dillon in effect says, an encroachment from the outside': 'Flesh as Otherness,' in *Ontology and Alterity in Merleau-Ponty*, ed. Johnson and Smith, 32–3.
39 Merleau-Ponty, *The Visible and the Invisible*, 139.
40 Madison, 'Flesh and Otherness,' 11.
41 Michel Foucault, *The Archaeology of Knowledge*, 203.

Chapter VIII: Cinema Paradoxa

1 Maurice Merleau-Ponty, *The Primacy of Perception*, 16.
2 Maurice Merleau-Ponty, *The Phenomenology of Perception*, 324.
3 Ibid., 69.
4 Merleau-Ponty, *The Primacy of Perception*, 26.
5 Maurice Merleau-Ponty, 'On the Phenomenology of Language,' in *Signs*, 93–4.
6 Ibid., 94.
7 Maurice Merleau-Ponty, *The Visible and the Invisible*, p. 136.
8 Ibid., 264.
9 For example, when the flesh of the world commingles with the flesh of the body, when I give my flesh and it returns to me as the flesh of the world. Or again, Merleau-Ponty claims that we need to understand that 'the true philosophy = apprehend what makes the leaving of oneself be a retiring into oneself, and vice versa. Grasp this chiasm, this reversal. That is the mind': ibid., 199.

10 Gilles Deleuze, *Logic of Sense*, 228.
11 Ibid., 165.
12 Ibid., 166.
13 Merleau-Ponty, *The Visible and the Invisible*, 248–9; and *The Phenomenology of Perception*, 424: 'No one of time's dimensions can be deduced from the rest. But the present (in the wide sense, along with its horizons of primary past and primary future), nevertheless enjoys a privilege because it is the zone in which being and consciousness coincide ... In the present and in perception, my being and my consciousness are at one.'
14 Merleau-Ponty, *The Visible and the Invisible*, 267.
15 Gilles Deleuze, *Cinema 2*, 261: Deleuze speaks of this as 'a time-image for itself, with its two dissymetric, non-totalizable sides.'
16 Ibid., 155.
17 Ibid., 168.
18 Gilles Deleuze, *Cinema 1*, 2.
19 Maurice Merleau-Ponty, *Consciousness and the Acquisition of Language*, 77. This is also another example of the paradox of identity and difference.
20 Merleau-Ponty, *The Phenomenology of Perception*, 198.
21 Ibid., 88.
22 Ibid., 122, n. 1.
23 Ibid., 144.
24 Ibid., 313.
25 Ibid., 68.
26 See especially Maurice Merleau-Ponty, 'The Film and the New Psychology,' in *Sense and Non-Sense*, 48–59. I refer to this article in detail below.
27 Merleau-Ponty refers to Pudovkin's example of the shot of a woman's face. The face is expressionless; however, when it is followed by a shot of a funeral, and what appears to be her dead son, then the face is interpreted to be expressing sadness; likewise when it is followed by a joyous celebration, she appears to be expressing joy.
28 Many of the early films got audiences roaring with laughter just by showing a man sneeze, or by showing the Keystone Cops hanging on to a speeding paddy wagon. This filming of bodies moving in the world appeals to one's own body as anchored to a world. Since then there have been other methods of leading viewers to more directly associate their own body with the action of the film (e.g., the simulation screens, 3D, Sensurround, etc.).
29 Merleau-Ponty, *The Phenomenology of Perception*, 68.
30 Merleau-Ponty, 'The Film and the New Psychology,' 58.
31 Ibid.
32 Henri Bergson, *Creative Evolution*, 322–3.

33 Henri Bergson, *Matter and Memory*, 38.

34 Ibid., 37.

35 The reason Bergson uses the term 'image' here is to account for the relation-ship between idealism and realism (i.e., the concept 'image' arises as a response to the problem of difference). As Bergson puts it, 'by "image" we mean a certain existence which is more than that which the idealist calls a *representation*, but less than that which the realist calls a *thing* – an existence placed halfway between the "thing" and the "representation"': ibid., 9.

36 Ibid., 36.

37 Ibid., 38.

38 Ibid., 39.

39 Deleuze, *Cinema 1*, 60–1.

40 Deleuze, *Logic of Sense*, 105–6.

41 Ibid., 106.

42 Michel Foucault, 'Theatrum Philosophicum,' in *Language, Counter-Memory, Practice*, 172.

43 Plato, *The Sophist*, translated with commentary by Seth Benardete (Chicago: University of Chicago Press 1986), 167.

44 Deleuze, *Logic of Sense*, 256.

45 Ibid., 74.

46 Merleau-Ponty, *The Phenomenology of Perception*, 61.

47 Ibid., 63.

48 Ibid., 394: 'the founding term, or originator – time, the unreflective, the fact, language, perception – is primary in the sense that the originated is pre-sented as a determinate or explicit form of the originator, which prevents the latter from reabsorbing the former, and yet the originator is not primary in the empiricist sense and the originated is not simply derived from it, since it is thought the originated that the originator is made manifest ... This ambigu-ity (i.e., paradox) cannot be resolved.'

49 Ibid., 198.

50 Deleuze, *Cinema 1*, 83.

51 Ronald Bogue, *Deleuze and Guattari*, 78.

52 Bear in mind our earlier discussion and critique of difference understood as the difference between two already-identified entities, for example, frames in this instance. This will become important as we discuss what Deleuze believes to be a reversal which occurred in cinema.

53 See our earlier discussion, in Chapter II.

54 Bergson, *Matter and Memory*, 36.

55 Recall our earlier discussion and note 35, above, which show that the term 'image' is used in response to the problem of difference.

56 Bergson, *Matter and Memory*, 22.

57 Ibid., 42.

58 Deleuze, *Cinema 1*, 58.

59 Deleuze, *Cinema 2*, 31.

60 Charles Sanders Peirce, *Charles S. Peirce: Selected Writings*, ed. Philip Wiener (New York: Dover 1958), 383.

61 Charles Sanders Peirce, *Philosophical Writings of Peirce*, ed. Justus Buchler (New York: Dover 1955), 76.

62 Ibid.

63 Peirce, *Charles S. Peirce: Selected Writings*, 383.

64 Ibid.

65 Deleuze, *Cinema 2*, 32.

66 Bergson, *Matter and Memory*, 42.

67 Ibid., 56–7.

68 Peirce, *Charles S. Peirce: Selected Writings*, 383.

69 Ibid., 385.

70 Deleuze, *Cinema 1*, 155.

71 Merleau-Ponty, *The Phenomenology of Perception*, 78 n. 2.

72 Sensation is equivalent to affection-image here, for it is the sensation which allows for the possibility of its being taken up in an act that sees an object. Recall our earlier discussion of this with respect to Husserl. We do not see sensations, as Husserl claimed (e.g., 'I do not see color-sensations but colored things,' *Logical Investigations*, 559), but these sensations are the necessary pre-givens that makes the perception of some thing, some *second*, possible.

73 Merleau-Ponty, *The Phenomenology of Perception*, 78 n. 2.

74 Merleau-Ponty, 'The Film and the New Psychology,' 54.

75 Deleuze, *Cinema 2*, 32.

76 Ibid., 39.

77 Deleuze, *Cinema 1*, 65.

78 Ibid., 85.

79 Ibid., 200

80 This is Habermas's criticism of poststructuralism. See the introduction to this essay, where we discuss this criticism in more detail.

81 Deleuze, *Logic of Sense*, 74.

82 Derrida, for example, argues that there is a fundamental difference (*différance*) which for ever defers the possibility of unity, or the possibility of the identity of self-presence. In Levinas, the other is that which is absolutely different, it is the difference which cannot be thought, the difference that is our fundamental condition (or God, as Levinas also refers to it), but a condition that cannot be reduced to identity.

83 Jean-François Lyotard, *The Postmodern Condition*, xxiii.
84 Ibid., 81.
85 Ibid.
86 It is for this reason that Deleuze also refers to the relation-image as the mental-image – that is, as the whole that can be thought.
87 Deleuze, *Cinema 1*, 212.
88 Deleuze, *Cinema 2*, 99.

Conclusion: The Search for 'Rosebud'

1 Husserl recognizes the dominance of this theme in his work, and in *The Crisis of European Sciences and Transcendental Phenomenology*, written near the end of his life, Husserl says in a footnote, quoted earlier, that 'the first breakthrough of this universal correlation between experienced object [e.g., an ideal object] and manners of givenness [e.g., given to 'direct intuition'] (which occurred in my work on my *Logical Investigations* around 1898) affected me so deeply that my whole subsequent life-work has been dominated by this task of systematically elaborating on this *a priori* of correlation' (p. 166).
2 Edmund Husserl, *Logical Investigations*, 589.
3 As discussed earlier in this essay, 'matter,' in this context, is not to be confused with 'matter' as that which determines both that an act is directed and what it is directed towards (as quoted above). This use of the term 'matter' refers to the physical or real sounds, marks, and so on, that are in themselves meaningless, but are in turn taken up and interpreted by an act. Husserl uses the German term *Stoff* late in *Logical Investigations* to avoid this confusion. It is also to avoid confusion that we have used the term 'interpretative sense' rather than 'interpretative matter,' although Husserl uses them interchangeably.
4 Husserl, *Logical Investigations*, 290.
5 We can see here where current Anglo-American interpretations of Husserl can find commonalities with Frege's theory of reference – that is, the referent is that object which is picked out on the basis of the 'properties, relations,' and descriptions that are the sense or *Sinn* of this object.
6 Husserl's criticized Kant for failing to appreciate this 'irreducible difference': *Logical Investigations*, 833.
7 Maurice Merleau-Ponty, *The Phenomenology of Perception*, 198.
8 Ibid., xiii.
9 Ibid., 212.
10 Maurice Merleau-Ponty, 'Dialogue and the Perception of the Other,' in *Sense and Non-Sense*, 134.

11 Maurice Merleau-Ponty, *The Visible and the Invisible*, 183.

12 The 'voice of God' was commonly used to describe the loud, booming, and impersonal voice that narrated many of the newsclips during the war. This theme of the impersonality of news, and of news reporters, runs throughout *Citizen Kane*. Much of this could be explained as a parody of newspaper tycoons such as William Randolph Hearst (note the allusion to the Spanish-American War, and the *independent* and *impersonal* attitude of the newspaper to the actual events); however, in the context of what we are arguing, we offer a supplementary reading. Since Kane is dead, the link to his personal and private life is absent, and thus we are forced to understand Kane indirectly, through the interviews the reporters have with friends of Kane. The impersonality of this is evidenced in the fact that the reporter is always seen only from the back. His character is never developed – he is an impersonal character. We expand on these themes below.

13 Gilles Deleuze, *Logic of Sense*, 151.

14 Ibid.

15 Ibid., 152.

16 Carlos Castaneda, *Journey to Ixtlán* (New York: Pocket Books 1974), 33.

17 Martin Heidegger, *Being and Time*, 287. This is the section in which Heidegger discusses *Dasein* as a Being-towards-death.

18 Gilles Deleuze, *Cinema 2*, 209.

19 Ibid., 256.

20 Merleau-Ponty, *The Phenomenology of Perception*, 355.

21 Deleuze, *Logic of Sense*, 166.

22 Ibid., 21.

23 Michael Foucault, 'Theatrum Philosophicum,' in *Language, Counter-Memory, Practice*, 174.

24 Deleuze, *Logic of Sense*, 166.

25 Ibid., 21.

26 Foucault, 'Theatrum Philosophicum,' 175.

27 Ibid.

28 Deleuze, *Logic of Sense*, 22.

29 Ibid., 24.

30 Ibid., 30.

31 Ronald Bogue, *Deleuze and Guattari*, 73.

32 Deleuze, *Cinema 2*, 99.

Bibliography

Apel, Karl-Otto. 'Linguistic Meaning and Intentionality: The Relationship of the A Priori of Language and the A Priori of Consciousness in Light of a Transcendental Semiotic or a Linguistic Pragmatic.' In *Phenomenology and Beyond: The Self and Its Language*. Dordrecht: Kluwer Academic 1989

Ashbaugh, Anne Freire. 'The Philosophy of the Flesh and the Flesh of Philosophy.' *Man and World* 20 (1987): 217–23

Bachelard, Suzanne. *A Study of Husserl's Formal and Transcendental Logic*. Evanston, IL: Northwestern University Press 1968

Bergson, Henri. *Creative Evolution*. Translated by Arthur Mitchell. Lanham, MD: University Press of America 1983

Biederman, Irving. 'Higher-Level Vision.' In *Visual Cognition and Action*, ed. Daniel N. Osherson, Stephen Michael Kosslyn, and John M. Hollerbach. Cambridge, MA: MIT Press 1990

Bogue, Ronald. *Deleuze and Guattari*. New York: Routledge 1989

Brentano, Franz. *Psychologie vom empirischen Stadpunkt*, in *Philosophische Bibliothek*, vol. II. Hamburg: Meiner 1874

Brough, John B. 'The Emergence of an Absolute Consciousness in Husserl's Early Writings on Time-Consciousness.' In *Husserl: Expositions and Appraisals*, ed. Frederick A. Elliston and Peter McCormick. Notre Dame, IN: University of Notre Dame Press 1977

Cairns, Dorion. *Guide for Translating Husserl*. The Hague: Martinus Nijhoff 1973

Carnap, Rudolf. *The Logical Structure of the World*. Berkeley: University of California Press 1967

– *Meaning and Necessity*. Chicago: University of Chicago Press 1947

Casalis, Mathieu. 'Merleau-Ponty's Philosophical Itinerary: From Phenomenology to Onto-Semiology.' *Review of Existential Psychology and Psychiatry* 18 (1986): 84–97

Casebier, Allan. 'Transcendence, Transparency, and Tranaction: Husserl's Middle Road to Cinematic Representation.' *Husserl Studies* 5 (1988): 127–41

Caws, Peter. *Structuralism: The Art of the Intelligible.* Atlantic Highlands, NJ: Humanities 1988

Cesarz, G.L. 'Meaning, Individuals, and the Problem of Bare Particulars: A Study in Husserl's *Ideas.*' *Husserl Studies* 2 (1985): 157–68

– 'Body, Spirit and Ego in Husserl's Ideas II.' *Analecta Husserliana* 16 (1983): 243–58

Cobb-Stevens, Richard. 'Derrida and Husserl on the Status of Retention.' *Analecta Husserliana* 19 (1985): 367–82

– 'Hermeneutics Without Relativism: Husserl's Theory of Mind.' In *Husserl and Contemporary Thought*, ed. John Sallis. Atlantic Highlands, NJ: Humanities 1983

– *Husserl and Analytic Philosophy.* Boston: Kluwer Academic 1990

Dahlstrom, Daniel. 'Heidegger's Kantian Turn.' *Review of Metaphysics* 45 (December, 1991): 329–61

Dastur, Françoise. 'Consciousness and Body in the Phenomenology of Merleau-Ponty: Some Remarks Concerning Flesh, Vision, and World in the Late Philosophy of Maurice Merleau-Ponty.' *Analecta Husserliana* 18 (1984): 117–26

Deleuze, Gilles. *Bergsonism.* Translated by Hugh Tomlinson and Barbara Habberjam. New York: Zone 1988

– *Cinema 1: The Movement-Image.* Translated by Hugh Tomlinson and Barbara Habberjam. Minneapolis: University of Minnesota Press 1986

– *Cinema 2: The Time-Image.* Translated by Hugh Tomlinson and Barbara Habberjam. Minneapolis: University of Minnesota Press 1989

– *Différence et répétition.* Paris: PUF 1968

– *Expressionism in Philosophy: Spinoza.* Translated by Martin Joughin. New York: Zone 1990

– *Foucault.* Translated by Sean Hand. Minneapolis: University of Minnesota Press 1988

– *Kant's Critical Philosophy.* Translated by Hugh Tomlinson and Barbara Habberjam. Minneapolis: University of Minnesota Press 1984

– *Logic of Sense.* Translated by Mark Lester. New York: Columbia University Press 1990

– *Logique du sens.* Paris: Minuit 1969

– *Masochism: Coldness and Cruelty.* New York: Zone 1989

– *Nietzsche and Philosophy.* Translated by Hugh Tomlinson. New York: Columbia University Press 1983

– *Spinoza: Practical Philosophy.* Translated by Robert Hurley. San Francisco: City Lights 1988

Deleuze, Gilles, and Felix Guattari. *Anti-Oedipus: Capitalism and Schizophrenia*. Preface by Michel Foucault. Translated by Robert Hurley, Mark Seem, and Helen R. Lane. New York: Viking 1977
- *A Thousand Plateaus: Capitalism and Schizophrenia*. Translated by Brian Massumi. Minneapolis: University of Minnesota Press 1987
- *Kafka: Toward a Minor Literature*. Translated by Dana Polan. Minneapolis: University of Minnesota Press 1986
Deleuze, Gilles, and Claire Parnet. *Dialogues*. Translated by Hugh Tomlinson and Barbara Habberjam. New York. Columbia University Press 1987
- *Dissemination*. Translated by Barbara Johnson. Chicago: University of Chicago Press 1981
Derrida, Jacques. *Edmund Husserl's 'Origin of Geometry': An Introduction*. Translated by John P. Leavey, Jr. Lincoln: University of Nebraska Press 1989
- *Of Grammatology*. Translated by Gayatri Chakravorty Spivak. Baltimore: Johns Hopkins University Press 1976
- *Speech and Phenomena*. Translated by David B. Allison and Newton Garver. Evanston, IL: Northwestern University Press 1973
- *Writing and Difference*. Translated by Alan Bass. Chicago: University of Chicago Press 1978
Dillon, M.C. 'Gestalt Theory and Merleau-Ponty's Concept of Intentionality.' *Review of Existential Psychology Psychiatry* 18 (1986): 117–40
- 'Merleau-Ponty and the Reversibility Thesis.' *Man and World* 16 (1987): 365–88
- *Merleau-Ponty's Ontology*. Bloomington: Indiana University Press 1989
Dreyfus, Hubert. 'Husserl's Phenomenology of Perception.' Diss. Harvard University, 1963
- 'Husserl's Perceptual Noema.' In *Husserl, Intentionality, and Cognitive Science*, ed. Hubert Dreyfus. Cambridge, MA: MIT Press 1983
- ed. *Husserl, Intentionality, and Cognitive Science*, Cambridge, MA: MIT Press 1983
- 'Brentano and Husserl on Intentional Objects and Perception.' In *Husserl, Intentionality, and Cognitive Science*, ed. Hubert Dreyfus. Cambridge, MA: MIT Press 1983
Føllesdal, Dagfinn. 'Husserl's Notion of Noema.' In *Husserl, Intentionality, and Cognitive Science*, ed. Hubert Dreyfus.
- 'Husserl's Theory of Perception.' In *Husserl, Intentionality, and Cognitive Science*, ed. Hubert Dreyfus
- 'Noema and Meaning in Husserl.' *Philosophy and Phenomenological Research* 50, Supp. (Fall 1990): 263–70.
- 'Phenomenology.' In *Handbook of Perception*, Vol. 7: *Language and Speech*, ed. Edward Corterette and Morton Friedman. New York, Academic 1976

Foucault, Michel. *The Archaeology of Knowledge*. Translated by A.M. Sheridan Smith. New York: Pantheon 1973
- *Language, Counter-Memory, Practice*. Edited and translated by Donald F. Bouchard. New York: Cornell University Press 1977
- *The Order of Things*. New York: Vintage Books 1970. Alan Sheridan's translation of *Les Mots et les choses*
Frege, Gottlob. *The Collected Writings of Gottlob Frege*. Edited by P. Geach and M. Black. Oxford: Basil Blackwell 1970
Gallagher, Shaun. 'Hyletic Experience and the Lived Body.' *Husserl Studies* 3 (1986): 131–66
Gibson, W.R. Boyce. 'The Problem of Real and Ideal in the Phenomenology of Husserl.' *Mind* 34 (1925): 325–41.
Glenn, Jr, John D. 'The Behaviorism of a Phenomenologist – *Structure of Behavior* and *The Concept of Mind*.' *Philosophical Topics* 13/2 (Spring 1985): 252–61.
Grice, H.P. 'Meaning.' *Philosophical Review* 66 (1957): 377–88
Gurwitsch, Aron. *The Field of Consciousness*. Pittsburgh: Duquesne University Press 1964
- 'Husserl's Theory of the Intentionality of Consciousness.' In *Husserl, Intentionality, and Cognitive Science*, ed. Hubert Dreyfus. Cambridge, MA: MIT Press 1984
- *Studies in Phenomenology and Psychology*. Evanston, IL: Northwestern University Press 1966
Habermas, Jürgen. *The Philosophical Discourse of Modernity*. Translated by Frederick G. Lawrence. Cambridge, MA: MIT Press 1990
Heidegger, Martin. *Basic Writings*. Edited by David Farrell Krell. New York: Harper and Row 1977
- *Being and Time*. Translated by John Macquarrie and Edward Robinson. New York: Harper and Row 1962
Holstein, Michael E. 'The Writer as Shaman.' *Analecta Husserliana* 18 (1984): 309–22
Hopkins, Burt. 'Husserl's Account of Phenomenological Reflection and Four Paradoxes of Reflexivity.' *Research in Phenomenology* 19 (1989): 180–94.
Husserl, Edmund. *Analysen Zur Passiven Synthesis*. The Hague: Martinus Nijhoff 1966.
- *Cartesian Meditations*. Translated by Dorion Cairns. Boston: Martinus Nijhoff 1988
- *The Crisis of European Sciences and Transcendental Phenomenology*. Translated by David Carr. Evanston, IL: Northwestern University Press 1970
- *Experience and Judgment: Investigations in a Genealogy of Logic*. Translated by James S. Churchill and Karl Ameriks. Evanston, IL: Northwestern University Press 1973

- *Formal and Transcendental Logic.* Translated by Dorion Cairns. The Hague: Martinus Nijhoff 1969
- *Ideas.* Translated by W.R. Boyce Gibson. New York: Collier 1962
- *Ideas II: Studies in the Phenomenology of Constitution.* Translated by Richard Rojewicz and Andre Schuwer. Boston: Kluwer Academic 1989
- *Ideas III: Phenomenology and the Foundations of the Sciences.* Translated by Ted E. Klein and William E. Pohl. Boston: Martinus Nijhoff 1980
- *Ideen I, Husserliana.* The Hague: Martinus Nijhoff 1950
- *Logical Investigations.* Translated by J.N. Findlay, 2d ed., 2 vols. Atlantic Highlands, NJ: Humanities 1970
- 'The Origin of Geometry.' In *The Crisis of European Sciences and Transcendental Phenomenology.* Translated by David Carr. Evanston, IL: Northwestern University Press 1970
- *Phenomenology and the Crisis of Philosophy.* Translated by Quentin Lauer. New York: Harper and Row 1965
- *The Phenomenology of Internal Time-Consciousness.* Edited by Martin Heidegger. Translated by James S. Churchill. Bloomingtion: University of Indiana Press 1964
Ingarden, Roman. 'The Letter to Husserl about the VI [Logical] Investigation and "Idealism."' *Analecta Husserliana* 4 (1976) 419–37
Kersten, Frederik. 'Husserl's Doctrine of Noesis-Noema.' In *Phenomenology: Continuation and Criticism*, ed. F. Kersten and R. Zaner. The Hague: Martinus Nijhoff 1973
Kidder, Paul. 'Husserl's Paradox.' *Research in Phenomenology* (1987): 227–42
Kockelmans, Joseph J., ed. *Phenomenology: The Philosophy of Edmund Husserl and Its Interpretation.* Garden City, NY: Anchor 1967
Kolakowski, Lezek. *Husserl and the Search for Certitude.* Chicago: University of Chicago Press 1975
Kripke, Saul. *Naming and Necessity.* Cambridge, MA: Harvard University Press 1980
- *Wittgenstein: On Rules and Private Language.* Cambridge, MA: Harvard University Press 1982
Landgrebe, Ludwig. *The Phenomenology of Edmund Husserl.* Edited by Donn Welton. Ithaca, NY: Cornell University Press 1981
Larrabee, Mary Jeanne. 'The Noema in Husserl's Phenomenology.' *Husserl Studies* 3 (1986): 209–30
Lecercle, Jean-Jacques. *Philosophy through the Looking Glass.* La Salle: Open Court 1985
Lefort, Claude. 'Flesh and Otherness.' In *Ontology and Alterity in Merleau-Ponty*, ed. Galen Johnson and Michael Smith. Evanston, IL: Northwestern University Press 1990

Levinas, Emmanuel. *Existence and Existents*. Translated by Alphonso Lingis. Boston: Martinus Nijhoff 1978
- *The Theory of Intuition in Husserl's Phenomenology*. Translated by Andre Orianne. Evanston, IL: Northwestern University Press 1973
- *Totality and Infinity*. Translated by Alphonso Lingis. Pittsburgh: Duquesne University Press 1969
Lévi-Strauss, Claude. *The Savage Mind*. Chicago: University of Chicago Press 1966
Lingis, Alphonso. 'Hyletic Data.' *Analecta Husserliana* 2 (1972): 96–101
- 'Intentionality and Corporeity.' *Analecta Husserliana* 1 (1971): 75–90
- 'The Sensitive Flesh.' In *The Collegium Phaenomenologicum*. The Netherlands: Kluwo Academic 1988
Lyotard, Jean-François. *The Postmodern Condition*. Translated by Brian Massumi and Geoff Bennington. Minneapolis: University of Minnesota Press 1984
Madison, Gary Brent. *The Phenomenology of Merleau-Ponty*. Athens: Ohio University Press 1973
Mates, Benson. *Stoic Logic*. Los Angeles: University of California Press 1961
McIntyre, Ronald, and David Woodruff Smith. 'Husserl's Identification of Meaning and Noema.' In *Husserl Intentionality and Cognitive Science*, ed. Hubert Dreyfus. Cambridge, MA: MIT Press 1987
Mensch, James R. *The Question of Being in Husserl's 'Logical Investigations'*. Boston: Martinus Nijhoff 1981
Merleau-Ponty, Maurice. *Adventures of the Dialectic*. Translated by Joseph Bien. Evanston, IL: Northwestern University Press 1973
- *Consciousness and the Acquisition of Language*. Translated by Hugh J. Silverman. Evanston, IL: Northwestern University Press 1973
- *Humanism and Terror*. Translated by John O'Neill. Boston: Beacon 1969
- *The Phenomenology of Perception*. Translated by Colin Smith. Atlantic Highlands, NJ: Humanities 1962
- *The Primacy of Perception*. Evanston, IL: Northwestern University Press 1973
- *Prose of the World*. Edited by Claude Lefort. Translated by John O'Neill. Evanston, IL: Northwestern University Press 1973
- *Résumés des courses*. Paris: Gallimard 1984
- *Sense and Non-Sense*. Translated by Hubert Dreyfus and Patricia Allen Dreyfus. Evanston, IL: Northwestern University Press 1964
- *Signs*. Translated by Richard C. McCleary. Evanston, IL: Northwestern University Press 1964
- *The Structure of Behavior*. Translated by Alden L. Fisher. Pittsburgh: Duquesne University Press 1983
- *The Visible and the Invisible*. Translated by Alphonso Lingis. Evanston, IL: Northwestern University Press 1968

Miller, Izchak. *Husserl, Perception, and Temporal Awareness*. Cambridge, MA: MIT
    Press 1984
Mizuno, Kazuhisa. 'The Paradox of the Phenomenological Method.' *Analecta
    Husserliana* 8 (1979): 37–54
Mohanty, J.N. *Husserl and Frege*. Bloomington: Indiana University Press 1982
– 'Husserl's Theory of Meaning.' In *Husserl: Expositions and Appraisals*, ed.
    Frederick A. Elliston and Peter McCormick. Notre Dame, IN: University of
    Notre Dame Press 1977
– 'Life-World and A Priori in Husserl's Later Thought.' *Analecta Husserliana* 3
    (1974): 46–65
– 'A Note on the Doctrine of Noetic-Noematic Correlation.' *Analecta Husserliana*
    2 (1972): 317–21
Murault, Andre de. *The Idea of Phenomenology: Husserlian Exemplarism*. Translated
    by Gary L. Brecken. Evanston, Il.: Northwestern University Press 1974
Natanson, Maurice. *Edmund Husserl: Philosopher of Infinite Tasks*. Evanston, IL:
    Northwestern University Press 1974
– 'The Ghost of Perception.' In *Husserl and Contemporary Thought*, ed. John Sallis.
    Atlantic Highlands, NJ: Humanities 1983
Park, Ynhui. 'Merleau-Ponty's Ontology of the Wild Being.' *Analecta Husserliana*
    16 (1983): 313–26
Ricoeur, Paul. *Husserl: An Analysis of His Phenomenology*. Translated by Edward
    G. Ballard and Lester E. Embree. Evanston, IL: Northwestern University Press
    1967
Riley, Michael D. 'The Truth of the Body: Merleau-Ponty on Perception,
    Language, and Literature.' *Analecta Husserliana* 18 (1984): 479–94
Sainsbury, R.M. *Paradoxes*. New York: Cambridge University Press 1988
Sallis, John. 'The Identities of the Things Themselves.' In *Husserl and Contempo-
    rary Thought*, ed. John Sallis. Atlantic Highlands, NJ: Humanities 1983
Saussure, Ferdinand de. *Course in General Linguistics*. Edited by Charles Bally
    and Albert Sechehaye. Translated by Roy Harris. La Salle: Open Court 1989
Schmidt, James. *Maurice Merleau-Ponty: Between Phenomenology and Structural-
    ism*. New York: St Martin's 1985
Smith, David Woodruff, and Ronald McIntyre. *Husserl and Intentionality: A Study
    of Mind, Meaning, and Language*. Boston: D. Reidel 1982
– 'Husserl's Identification of Meaning and Noema.' In *Husserl, Intentionality, and
    Cognitive Science*, ed. Hubert Dreyfus. Cambridge, MA: MIT Press 1984
Sokolowski, Robert. *The Formation of Husserl's Concept of Constitution*. The
    Hague: Martinus Nijhoff 1970
– *Husserlian Meditations*. Evanston, IL: Northwestern University Press 1974
Solomon, Robert. 'Husserl's Concept of the Noema.' In *Husserl: Expositions and*

Appraisals, ed. Frederick A. Elliston and Peter McCormick. Notre Dame: University of Notre Dame Press 1977

Starobinski, Jean. *Words upon Words: The Anagrams of Ferdinand de Saussure*. Translated by Olivia Emmet. New Haven, CT: Yale University Press 1979

Taminiaux, Jacques. *Dialectic and Difference* Atlantic Highlands, NJ: Humanities 1990

Waldenfels, Bernhard. 'The Despised Doxa: Husserl and the Continuing Crisis of Western Reason.' In *Husserl and Contemporary Thought*, ed. John Sallis. Atlantic Highlands, NJ: Humanities 1983

Welton, Donn. 'Husserl's Genetic Phenomenology of Perception.' In *Husserl and Contemporary Thought*, ed. John Sallis. Atlantic Highlands, NJ: Humanities 1983

– 'Structure and Genesis in Husserl's Phenomenology.' *Husserl: Expositions and Appraisals*, ed. Frederick A. Elliston and Peter McCormick. Notre Dame, IN: University of Notre Dame Press 1977

Willard, Dallas. *Logic and the Objectivity of Knowledge*. Athens: Ohio University Press 1984

– 'The Paradox of Logical Psychologism.' In *Husserl: Expositions and Appraisals*. ed. Frederick A. Elliston and Peter McCormick. Notre Dame, IN: University of Notre Dame Press 1977

– *On Certainty*. Edited by G.E.M. Anscombe and G.H. von Wright. Translated by Denis Paul and G.E.M. Anscombe. New York: Harper and Row 1969

– *Philosophical Investigations*. Translated by G.E.M. Anscombe. Oxford: Basil Blackwell 1983

Wittgenstein, Ludwig. *Tractatus Logico-Philosophicus*. Translated by D.F. Pears and B.F. McGuinness. Intro. Bertrand Russell. London: Routledge and Kegan Paul 1961

Yuille, A.L. and S. Ullman. 'Computational Theories of Low-level Vision.' *Visual Cognition and Action*, ed. Daniel N. Osherson, Stephen Michael Kosslyn, and John M. Hollerbach. Cambridge, MA: MIT Press 1990

Zaner, R.M. 'Special Contribution to the Debate: Passivity and Activity of Consciousness in Husserl.' *Analecta Husserliana* 3 (1974): 199–226

Index